D1084345

THE POETRY OF PATHOS

The Poetry of Pathos

Studies in Virgilian Epic

GIAN BIAGIO CONTE

Edited by
S. J. HARRISON

OXFORD
UNIVERSITY PRESS

OXFORD

UNIVERSITY PRESS

Great Clarendon Street, Oxford OX2 6DP

Oxford University Press is a department of the University of Oxford.
It furthers the University's objective of excellence in research, scholarship,
and education by publishing worldwide in

Oxford New York

Auckland Cape Town Dar es Salaam Hong Kong Karachi
Kuala Lumpur Madrid Melbourne Mexico City Nairobi
New Delhi Shanghai Taipei Toronto

With offices in

Argentina Austria Brazil Chile Czech Republic France Greece
Guatemala Hungary Italy Japan Poland Portugal Singapore
South Korea Switzerland Thailand Turkey Ukraine Vietnam

Oxford is a registered trade mark of Oxford University Press
in the UK and in certain other countries

Published in the United States
by Oxford University Press Inc., New York

British Library Cataloguing in Publication Data

Data available

Library of Congress Cataloging in Publication Data

Data available

Typeset by SPI Publisher Services, Pondicherry, India
Printed in Great Britain
on acid-free paper by
Biddles Ltd., King's Lynn, Norfolk

ISBN 978-0-19-928701-7

1 3 5 7 9 10 8 6 4 2

Editor's Preface

In assisting with the publication in English of an expanded version of Gian Biagio Conte's latest Italian book, it is an especial pleasure for me to present the writings of a scholar whom I particularly admire. His practical help has of course been vital in producing the current volume, and I would like to thank him for that and for his many other kindnesses.

The real work of the English translation was done by Elaine Fantham (Chapters 2 and 5–8) and Glenn Most (Chapters 3, 4, and 9); my interventions have been restricted to editorial tidying, and these distinguished scholars deserve the full credit for these renderings. I am especially grateful to Elaine Fantham for supplying her version of Chapter 7 for the purposes of this book with impressive celerity, and for kindly providing footnotes for that chapter, and to Glenn Most for generous help with checking the final text of the volume. My thanks too to Daniel Johnson for timely help in producing the text of Chapter 9. The anonymous referees for Oxford University Press should also be thanked for some useful and salutary comments.

This volume translates the contents of *Virgilio: L'epica del sentimento* (Turin, 2002), with the addition of Chapters 1 and 5, both published here for the first time, and Chapters 7 and 9, both previously published in Italian in G. B. Conte, *Virgilio: il genere e i suoi confini* (2nd edition; Milan, 1984). An earlier English version of Chapter 2 appeared in *Proceedings of the Cambridge Philological Society*, 45 (1999), 17–42, one of Chapter 4 in S. Spence (ed.), *Poets and Critics Read Virgil* (New Haven, 2001), 44–63, and one of Chapter 9 in *Beginnings in Classical Literature* (Yale Classical Studies, 29; 1992), 147–59.

S.J.H.

Corpus Christi College, Oxford
November 2005

Contents

1

Introduction by Stephen Harrison

GIAN BIAGIO CONTE has been an internationally acknowledged leading scholar of Roman poetry and prose for several decades. He has played a major part in the study of Latin literature in both Italy and the Anglophone world, primarily through his own influential writings, but also through his foundation in 1978 of the important journal *Materiali e discussioni per l'analisi dei testi classici*,[1] through the string of distinguished scholars who have been taught by him at Pisa, and through his extensive personal contacts with other Latinists in Italy, the UK, and the USA. In the introduction to this volume, I will try first to describe this new collection of papers on Virgil, and then to characterize Conte's scholarly output as a whole and its development over the years.[2]

1. VIRGIL: THE EPIC OF PATHOS

In much of the collection which this volume largely translates, first published in Italian in 2002 and containing pieces mostly written in the 1990s, Conte makes a crucial argument: that the exceptional status of the *Aeneid* in Latin literature derives from its remarkably complex and ambiguous poetic texture. He especially emphasizes the

[1] Not forgetting its series of monograph supplements, in which several important works by Conte pupils have been published, e.g. Barchiesi (1984), Labate (1984), Bonfanti (1985), and fourteen further volumes: for details see *http://www.libraweb.net/riviste.php?chiave=17* (accessed 8.6.2004).

[2] Excellent accounts of Conte's work can also be found in the two introductions by Charles Segal to its major English translations (Conte 1986a, Conte 1994b).

way in which the *Aeneid* transforms its Homeric model in the light of Roman ideology and by employing other generic models; we find a consistent injection of emotional sensibility, expressed by the author through his engaged framing of the narrative (*sympatheia*, sympathy) and by his created characters through the focalization of events from their point of view (*empatheia*, empathy). This careful literary presentation of the plot works on the emotions of the reader, creating an 'epic of pathos'. This tackles what has often been seen as the central issue of Virgilian criticism, that of how the *Aeneid* managed to create a new and effective mode of epic in a period when the genre appeared to be debased or exhausted.

Chapter 2, 'The Virgilian Paradox', goes back to the origins of modern debate on Virgil in the Romantic period, where the supposed natural primitivism and fresh *naïveté* of Homer was commonly and unfavourably contrasted with the more artificial and sophisticated Virgilian epic. Conte here argues that Virgil too sensed from the beginning that the naturalness and noble simplicity of Homer was essentially irrecoverable in the cultural context of the first century BC, but that he had the opportunity to create a Homer for his own times: 'to transform Homer by disassembling his narrative structures in order to reassemble them in a new ensemble with a modern significance, contaminating but also continuing the two poems [i.e. the *Iliad* and *Odyssey*] as if the new poet were in fact Homer himself *redivivus*, now bringing to an end his interrupted work: this is Virgil's project' (Chapter 2, p. 37). He charts the quintessential ambiguity of the *Aeneid*, both reflecting the traditionally nationalistic ideology of Roman epic in the steps of Naevius and Ennius, and showing an extraordinary empathy with the focalizations and feelings of individual characters, many of whom represent a point of view at odds with the direction of the nationalistic plot (especially Dido and her characterization through Greek tragedy); the consequent incorporation of multiple perspectives creates a 'polycentric' text which is able to accomplish the quasi-impossible task of renewing and refreshing the tired epic tradition of antiquity.

Crucial in all this is the role of fate, which, by preserving and promoting the teleological plot of the establishment and rise of Rome, prevents the epic collapsing into the conflicting and unresolved passions of drama. This is one of several strategies deployed by the controlling poet-narrator, whose choices and interventions act as a further shaping and unifying force: 'while the empathetic multiplication of point of view generates a dramatic structure in which individual subjectivities fragment the text as they emerge in their various affirmations of truth, the *sympatheia* of the omniscient narrator is able to recall each fragment to the objectivity of a unitary vision' (Chapter 2, p. 56). Aeneas himself is emblematic of the poem's essential doubleness, poised between a ruthless destined protagonist and a humane suffering victim.

Chapter 3, 'Anatomy of a Style', the most substantial in the book, looks to ground these critical perceptions in detailed analysis of the epic language of the *Aeneid*. Conte focuses on the characteristic Virgilian figure of *enallage*, in the most common form of which two nouns exchange their expected epithets, and argues that it demonstrates the truth of Friedrich Klingner's dictum 'maximum freedom, maximum order': Virgilian poetic language deviates from the norm by (for example) the exchange of epithets, but that exchange is carefully managed so that the regular combination can be seen behind the irregular innovation. The reader is thus offered both an unexpected linguistic combination and the traces of an expected one. The obvious element of poetic defamiliarization involved here suggests clear links with Conte's early interest in formalism, but characteristically this linguistic effect is set in the context of ancient as well as modern literary theory. Such a concern with the combination of words, with *iunctura* or *synthesis*, is persuasively placed in the context of the Greek stylistic theories of Dionysius of Halicarnassus, a fascinating demonstration of the affinity of Virgilian poetics with the literary criticism of the time.[3]

Conte shows how the phenomenon of *enallage* was noted in the ancient commentators and associated with Virgil's supposed *cacozelia*, 'lack of taste', but conversely how its defamiliarizing effect actually elicits the feeling of sublimity traditionally seen in epic by critics such as 'Longinus': the fact that it is not much found in either the *Eclogues* or the *Georgics* is (as he suggests) crucial evidence for its purpose in

---

[3] One might add here that other Virgilian stylistic concerns can now be seen to have contact with the rather different literary-critical ideas of another contemporary, Philodemus: see Armstrong *et al.* (2004).

the *Aeneid*, recreating by a different and more complex route some of the effects of the lofty and noble language of Homer. This function of poetic language in arousing appropriate emotion in the reader is thus a crucial part of the 'epic of pathos' in providing the basic building blocks for authorial sympathy and character empathy. This is presented as one of the major demands on the reader made by the *Aeneid*: here as elsewhere the sheer linguistic and emotional density of the poem needs to be faithfully reflected in readerly and analytical vigilance. Conte argues persuasively that though this emotional function aims at replicating a traditional epic effect, its origins lie in the diction of Greek tragedy: even at the linguistic level, the emotional power of Virgil's epic has key connections with ancient drama.

In Chapter 4, 'Aristaeus, Orpheus, and the *Georgics* once again', Conte returns to a topic he treated some twenty years ago (Conte (1984*a*), 43–54, translated in Conte (1986*a*), 130–40). Reacting favourably to Jasper Griffin's justly influential article on *Georgics* 4 (Griffin 1979/1985), he agrees that readers need an interpretation which can encompass the whole of the *Georgics* and show its essential unity. Reinforcing his crucial original perception that Aristaeus is an extrapolation on the mythical level of the farmer of the *Georgics* (a brilliant interpretation of *Georg.* 4.326–32), he here makes the further and equally convincing argument that the Aristaeus story consciously echoes the myths of Platonic dialogues in enacting on the mythical level and in final climactic position the essential message of the didactic work (which he still identifies as a contrast of lifestyles and approaches, objecting to those who want to argue for direct allegory). Centrally important too is his analysis of the Alexandrian narrative technique of the Aristaeus-episode, arguing incontrovertibly that the juxtaposition of two structurally similar but crucially different stories is a key part of interpretation, just as it is in Catullus 64.

Chapter 5, 'The Strategy of Contradiction', first appearing in this volume, uses the insights gathered in the analyses of the remainder of the book to discuss and deconstruct the two most prominent positions in the interpretation of the ideology of the *Aeneid*. Conte argues that we are too keen to remove contradiction and ambiguity in our interpretations of literary discourse, and that the polarity of the period since 1945 between the so-called 'Harvard School' of Virgilian pessimistic critics and their optimistic 'European' opponents has been undesirable and has fortunately broken down in more recent scholarship. Conte himself argues for a more inclusive and balanced approach which fits the doubleness he has consistently identified in the poem's literary texture (Chapter 5, pp. 153–4): 'The reader who accepts the double proposition of the poet cannot be content with superficially harmonizing the contradictions, but must accept the negative without separating it from the positive and seek out a new order of thinking'. This essential doubleness is seen most easily in characterization. Mezentius is both a theomachic monster and a grieving father redeemed by love for his son; Turnus is both a murderous barbarian and a vulnerable and sympathetic youth; Aeneas is both a ruthlessly successful imperial operator and a man who fails to achieve personal or familial fulfilment: these apparent contradictions are presented in the same work as equally valid. Once again the model of Greek tragedy is invoked as a discourse underlying the darker and more complex side of Virgil's Roman epic, counterbalancing its nationalist and imperial teleology: Aeneas' 'sacrifice' of Turnus recalls Greek tragic obsession with human sacrifice in acts of vengeance, while Dido's suicide looks back to that of Sophocles' Ajax in its use of deception and another's sword, and the clash of different kinds of justice in the poem presents a fundamentally tragic dilemma.

Importantly, such ambiguity extends to the political element of the poem: we find individual resistance and suffering juxtaposed with collective victory and achievement, but should not seek to discount one in favour of the other. Conte's provisional but persuasive conclusion, embodying the critical power of his argument, argues that traditionally polarized critical positions can now be honourably abandoned: 'Harvard' and 'European' critics can be 'satisfied, above all, that through their critical opposition they have brought to light some contradictory aspects of the text. I hope to have proved that these contradictions do indeed exist, but that they are internal to the text and form part of an artistic strategy' (Chapter 5, p. 169).

Chapter 6, '*Defensor Vergilii*', provides a fascinating and well-informed analysis of the work of Richard Heinze on the *Aeneid* in his epoch-making *Virgils epische Technik* (1902). This does not merely (as one might expect in this volume on the 'epic of pathos') present Heinze's well-known role as the founder of the modern study of the poem's subjectivity, but most effectively sets his concerns and critical stance in the German intellectual context of his time. Conte here well notes the 'carve-up' of Virgilian topics between Heinze and his friend Norden, simultaneously engaged on his great edition of *Aeneid* 6 (Heinze did drama, characters, and narrative presentation, Norden got religion and poetic diction), but more importantly shows how Heinze was fundamentally concerned to rebut the German Romantic criticism of Virgil as artificial and derivative. Here Wilhelm Dilthey's hermeneutic historicism and the view that the interpretation of literature is 'recreation' is brilliantly shown to be an animating principle of Heinze's view on the *Aeneid*'s recreation of Homer. This is an exemplary piece of reception criticism, setting a scholarly work carefully against its intellectual background and showing how crucial current interpretative ideas were in fact formed over a considerable period of time.

Chapter 7, 'Towards a New Exegesis of Virgil', continues the theme of Virgilian scholarship. In this contribution to the bimillenary celebrations of the anniversary of Virgil's death, Conte points to the importance and diversity of the commentary tradition on Virgil and to the cultural situatedness of its practitioners, with illuminating remarks on such figures as Germanus (16th century), de la Cerda (17th century), Forbiger and Nettleship (19th century), Traina and Putnam (20th century), and (especially) on how a modern commentary might cope with modern literary circumstances, which should be required reading for all intending Virgil commentators. The topic of commentary and the assembly of parallels naturally leads to issues of intertextuality, and here Conte makes again the crucial distinction set out in *Memoria dei poeti e sistema letterario* (see below) between 'copy-model', the simple reproduction of an existing piece of literary language or theme, and 'code-model', the invocation in a new work of the ideology and generic parameters of a previous work, especially important for the business of commentary. Once again Conte's affinity with reader-response theory is clear: readerly competence in the relevant literary traditions (i.e. 'repertory' in reader-response terms) is the key element in interpretation, and cultural context plays a crucial role in any interpretation of a literary text: 'clearly this involves a recodification of a text from the past according to the categories and requirements of a new cultural epoch' (Chapter 7, pp. 203–4).

The brief Chapter 8, 'The Meeting of Stylistics and Textual Criticism', shows how even the most small-scale linguistic phenomena exemplify large and significant literary ideas. The division of the capital manuscripts in the transmitted text of *Aeneid* 10.24 presents us with either *inundant sanguine fossae*, 'the ditches swim with blood', a striking intransitive use of a normally transitive verb but paralleled at 11.382,[4] or the more normal *inundant sanguine fossas*, 'they flood the ditches with blood'. Conte triumphantly shows that *fossae* must be correct, and that this passage not only demonstrates in this intransitivization the typical Virgilian defamiliarizing deviation from normal language discussed in the form of enallage in Chapter 3 above, but also echoes both linguistically and in its closural narrative function the formulaic Homeric phrase ῥέε δ' αἵματι γαῖα (*Iliad* 4.451, 8.65). Thus Virgilian syntactic innovation actually recalls Homeric diction and narrative technique, a brilliant microcosm of the *Aeneid*'s position between tradition and originality.

The volume concludes (as did Conte 1980*a*) with Chapter 9, 'Proems in the Middle', a justly famous piece which has added a notable term to the grammar of classical literary scholarship. Here Conte traces the development of the poetic proem from plot-summary to programme, and famously stresses how programmatic restarts are to be found at the beginning of the second half of many poetic works and books, both in Virgil (*Eclogue* 6, *Georgics* 3, *Aeneid* 7) and elsewhere (Lucretius 4; Horace, *Odes* 4.8). This is a key tool in the analysis of Latin and other poetry (e.g. Milton).[5]

Taken together, these pieces show Conte's characteristic powers of focused analysis and critical exploitation of detailed verbal style in Latin literature, his enviable knowledge of scholarship on Virgil's poetry and its varied intellectual contexts, and his capacity to apply appropriate elements of literary theory with penetrating effect to the task of interpretation. There are also some interesting asides on his own intellectual development, especially on his debt to Friedrich

---

[4] See now the comments of Horsfall (2003), 241 (agreeing with Conte).

[5] Thus the invocation of Urania at the head of *Paradise Lost* 7 divides the epic into two major sections: cf. A. Fowler (1971), 433. Conte's short article and the interest in middles in Latin poetry has led to a whole volume on the subject—see Kyriakidis and De Martino (2004).

Klingner (with whom he studied in Munich in the 1960s), and some intriguing revisitings of his previous work; the formalist/ structuralist tendencies of some of his earlier writings are here tempered and specialist theoretical terms are used much less freely. But above all, these pieces bear witness to a consistent readerly vigilance, a determined concern to tease out the dense and demanding texture of Virgil's poetry at all levels, whether ideological, generic, or lexical, and show why Conte (as he himself says of Klingner) is a 'virgilianista principe' (Conte (2002), 7).

2. GIAN BIAGIO CONTE: A RETROSPECT

In his scholarly work since the 1960s, while focusing especially on Latin epic, Conte has also ranged across Latin literature from Plautus, Lucretius, and Catullus through Ovid to Pliny the Elder and Petronius, and has shown his encyclopaedic interests in his best-selling history of Latin literature (Conte 1987*a*, Eng. tr. Conte 1994*a*). His methodological position has evolved interestingly over that period, from a pronounced structuralist/formalist flavour in his early work to a position which allows more to the intentions of the author as well as to the interpretative role of the reader. In what follows I aim to chart the main landmarks of his development, and to end with a bibliography of his most important work.[6]

Conte's earliest articles as an emerging scholar in the 1960s were on Lucan (plus two interesting pieces on Lucretius (Conte 1965 and 1966*a*), centring on the diatribe element and Lucretian sublimity, anticipating Conte 1990), and he talks some twenty years later of his 'transformation from young interpreter of Lucan into scholar of Augustan poetry' (Conte (1988), 6). Two of these (Conte 1966*b* and 1970*a*) were later gathered together with his 'test commentary' on the Scaeva episode in Lucan 6.118–260 (Conte 1974*b*) and another short piece (Conte 1988) into a useful volume on Lucan (Conte 1988, as yet untranslated); another (Conte 1968) was reprinted in his first

---

[6] The bibliography does not claim to be exhaustive, but hopes to include Conte's most significant books and articles. Unless otherwise noted, translations of quotations from work published only in Italian are my own.

major book (Conte 1974*a*; this paper was omitted in the condensed English translation in Conte 1986*a*, but is summarized briefly there [p. 93]). In these pieces Conte's trademark combination of textual analysis and theoretical engagement is well to the fore, as well as his interest in the characterizing features of the epic genre and its boundaries and in literary intertextuality and allusion: his piece on Lucan's proem (Conte 1966*b*) raises important detailed parallels with the proem of the *Iliad*, and argues persuasively that here Lucan's '*aemulatio* as original poet still moves inside this tradition, but only to break its bonds, to deny it' (Conte (1988), 22), and the briefer pieces on Ennius and Lucan (Conte 1970*a*) and on the theme of 'the day of judgement' in Lucan and Virgil (Conte 1988=Conte 1989) point similarly to the modification and inversion of important epic models. This sense of ideological transformation is one of Conte's most important modifications to the interest in 'arte allusiva' shown by Giorgio Pasquali, who had taught Conte's teacher La Penna in Pisa, showing that fundamental concepts as well as linguistic elements could be ironized and inverted in literary allusion.

The selective 'test commentary' on the Scaeva episode reprinted in this volume (1974*b*) shows that Conte has complete control of all the commentator's skills (identification of literary models, consciousness of epic convention, interest in textual criticism, linguistic register, syntax, morphology, segmentation, word-order and sound-effect) and should be consulted for any detailed reading of the passage. Its brief introduction underlines the close link between linguistic analysis and the ideology of the epic genre, seeing in Lucan 'the sense of denial, the gesture of an opposition which rebels against the traditional model', arguing that 'the form of expression arouses a first consciousness of the crisis with which he has invested the language already sanctified in the epic tradition' (Conte (1988), 3–4), and seeing in Lucan's rhetoric a paradoxical proof of his sincerity: 'It is by his rhetorical conceits, absurdly, that Lucan communicates his authenticity'.

In the same year that the 'test commentary' on Lucan was first published appeared Conte's first major book, *Memoria dei poeti e sistema letterario* (Conte 1974*a*, mostly translated in the section 'Poetic memory and literary system' in Conte 1986*a*; part was previously published as Conte 1971). In his introduction Conte argues that Pasquali's 'arte allusiva' and the idea of learned, playful emulation is too simple a model for literary allusion, and that the search for parallels needs a theory of intertextuality; allusion is like a rhetorical figure, both having immediate linguistic significance and bearing an added level of meaning for the alert reader. Conte codifies this as poetic memory, the way in which poets actively engage with previous texts in more than verbal details, recalling a 'poetic *setting* rather than the individual *lines*' (Conte (1986*a*), 35): the reader is made to recall not only the 'copy-model', 'the single word to be precisely imitated' (31), but also the 'code-model', 'a system of conscious, deliberate rules that the author identifies as indicators of ways in which the text must be interpreted' (31); the 'code-model' is most commonly that of a particular literary genre. Here there are links not only with structuralism in the idea of literary systems, but also with reader-response theory and the idea of an interpretative community: Conte's theory requires an implied reader equipped with a repertory of reading which is equivalent to that of the ancient poet and of his learned modern interpreters: 'the author presupposes the competence of his (or her) own Model Reader' (30).

When Conte turns to detailed analysis in this book, there are also strong traces of formalism and Prague School linguistics. Linking Catullus 101 with the opening of the *Odyssey* and with several passages in *Aeneid* 6, he argues that Catullus' use of Homer is casual, while Virgil's use of Catullus is ideological. Here again he provides a corrective to Pasquali's emulative *arte allusiva*: Virgilian use of Catullus is a sympathetic appropriation of the poetics of tragic loss, not an attempt to outdo a predecessor (32–9). Allusion, intertextuality, or poetic memory (these terms are interchangeable for Conte)[7] is a form of linguistic marking; like other figures of speech, it characterizes poetic discourse as marked and special, presenting a remembered passage from another poetic text as self-consciously reused and participating in a literary system such as another (or the same) literary genre. Allusion, then, must always carry some rhetorical and hermeneutical baggage and can never be simply the evocation of a linguistic parallel.

---

[7] See D. P. Fowler (2000), 111–37, for debates on the definition of these terms.

Literary systems, argues Conte, are not the only systems embedded in texts. Arguing against the 'storm of antihistoricism' (48) of his own time, he points out that each text is necessarily historically situated and that this cannot be ignored in interpretation: the text is no mere horizontal linguistic system but 'a profoundly contextualized network of association, echoes, imitations, allusions—a rich root system reaching down and entwined with the fibres of the culture in its historical dimension' (49), and 'when poetic memory works upon culture, it transforms the fragments of specific factual or historical material into an essential component of a systematically organized poetic discourse' (50).

Poetic memory can be activated in two ways, Conte argues: 'integrative allusion', in which another poet's style is appropriated in a harmonious way, and 'reflective allusion', in which a confrontation and dialogue is conducted with the remembered text in such a way as to stress the autonomy of the remembering text (66). This idea forms one of the basic tenets of Conte's later work on genre, to which we will return, since it underlies the scenes of intergeneric debate which he there identifies, but it also points to an important element in Conte's thinking, the autonomy of the literary or poetic text, its creation of its own literary identity through its unusual, marked manipulation of language in figures of speech such as allusion: 'the gap that the rhetorical function creates in language…aims to disturb its strictly communicative aspect in order to endow it with a "thickness" of meaning and to validate the autonomy of poetic discourse' (68).

Against this background we find Conte's first major statement on the *Aeneid* (70–6). Following a formalist interest in beginnings which will have famous consequences in his later work (Conte 1976/1992*a*), he reminds us how the openings of both the *Iliad* and the *Odyssey* are manipulated in the proem of the *Aeneid*, and argues that the *Aeneid* represented both a rerun of Homeric epic and its transformation in a profoundly different ideological context and literary tradition (76): 'Virgil's ideological decision to write a national poem also conditioned his style. The Homeric genre was to be reappropriated and necessarily reintegrated into the diction used by Naevius and Ennius'. Such reference in Augustan Rome to the epic norm codified by Homer provided liberation rather than restriction: 'reference to the norm obviously does not mean submission to the norm: rather it delimits the common space within which new poetry can both emulate tradition and speak with a fresh voice' (81).

In the late 1970s appeared the essays on Virgil which were collected in Conte's next book, *Il genere ei suoi confini* (Conte 1980*a*, enlarged edition Conte 1984*a*, Eng. tr. (largely) in the 'Genre and its Boundaries' section of Conte 1986*a*), the work which brought him to major international prominence. This contains his well-known essay on the appearance of the love-poet Gallus in Virgil's tenth *Eclogue* (= Conte 1979) in which he argued that the interpretation of the poem depends on a deliberate confrontation between neighbouring literary genres (pastoral and love-elegy—Conte (1986*a*), 126: 'the sense of the tenth *Eclogue* is actually founded on a display of the difference between these two genres'), and that this confrontation achieves generic renewal by 'rescuing both from the conventional static nature of literary institutions' (128). This is followed by an analysis of *Georgics* 4 (first published in the 1984 edition but based on Conte 1980*b*) in which Aristaeus is importantly seen as the mythical instantiation of the farmer of the poem, Orpheus as a neoteric lover, and the clash between their two stories (articulated by a Catullan/Hellenistic embedded structure) as a clash between two models of life, the erotic/indulgent and the dutiful/severe, in which the latter is given predominance as the spirit of the *Georgics*.

The book's major essay on the *Aeneid*, 'Virgil's *Aeneid*: towards an interpretation' (= Conte 1978*a*), carries on the arguments of Conte 1974*a*, presenting the poem as balanced between a literary code (that of Homeric epic) and a societal norm (that of first-century BC Rome). Here we find important reflections on literary genre as the framework which enables this balance to take place (Conte (1986*a*), 147: 'genre is the organizing system that links, in stability, particular ideological and thematic contents with specific expressive structures... in an historically evolving rhetorical relationship'). Conte stresses the impact on the *Aeneid* of 'contamination' of the epic norm with features from other genres (150: 'Virgil inserted into the *Aeneid* other modes of signification alongside those peculiar to the epic norm and thus discovered other literary registers, forms of expression and themes'), leading to a relativization of the ideological values usually presented unproblematically by epic (181: 'he wished to display the ideological bias of the epic norm by showing that the truth, which it claimed entirely for itself, was relative, and he did so by setting other points of view alongside its own perspective'), and a broader, more thoughtful view of the poem (183: 'not a glorification of the Augustan restoration but a meditation (modulated in various tones) on the reasons why one person or one people had emerged victorious in its painful struggle against another'). This is a key, balanced interpretation of the poem which all Virgilian scholars should read.

Two further pieces on the *Aeneid* follow, that on the ekphrasis of the sword-belt of Pallas in book 10 (= Conte 1970*b*) and that on the 'Helen-episode' in book 2 (= Conte 1978*b*). Conte makes notable contributions to both these well-known scholarly problems, arguing persuasively that the scenes of the Danaids' murder of their husbands on their wedding-nights on Pallas' sword-belt refers symbolically to the premature death of its wearer, also killed before his time,[8] and that Homeric imitation in the Helen-episode (Venus' restraint of Aeneas picking up Athena's restraint of Achilles in *Iliad* 1) together with further impressive intertextualities suggests Virgilian authorship of this disputed passage. The last essay in the 1980 edition (= Conte 1976) was not translated in Conte (1986*a*) but was rendered later as Conte (1992*a*) and reprinted in this volume (see above).

The last essay in the 1984 edition (Conte 1982*a*, appearing in English translation for the first time in this volume) is of considerable interest, for here he turns his attention to the long tradition of Virgilian exegesis and reinforces his important ideas on literary genre. Here we find remarks on critics from Germanus in the sixteenth century, Juan Luis de la Cerda in the seventeenth, to Forbiger, Conington, and Nettleship (nicely distinguished) in the nineteenth; we also find the exposition of the difference between different types of Homeric imitation in Virgil, the 'Homeric manner' in which a particular Greek linguistic structure is obviously echoed, and the 'Homeric code', use of the thematic and structural grammar of Homeric epic to create a new version of it (Conte (1984*a*), 148). This clearly picks up Conte's earlier formulation (1974*a*/1986*a*) of the

---

[8] Though Turnus too will die before his time and that too may be prefigured here (see Harrison 1998).

difference between the 'copy-model' ('modello-esemplare') and the 'code-model' ('modello-codice'). Conte also again emphasizes that readerly competence in detecting any intertextuality through access to the literary system of manner and code is more important and more accessible than authorial intentionality (147; there are clear reader-response links here).

Once again he emphasizes the importance of historical context in the modification of literary tradition (152: 'clearly this involves a recodification of a text from the past according to the categories and requirements of a new cultural epoch'), and stresses the 'distortion of epic objectivity' (154) through the use of character focalization as a key element in Virgilian originality. Methodologically, he commends (154) Traina's approach to the contribution of sound to sense in Latin poetry, and expresses some caution (156–7) on Putnam's reliance on verbal resemblance as an interpretative tool. He concludes by stressing the necessary partiality of any literary interpretation, but urging that detailed focus and general ideological grasp in the manner of Klingner make the most desirable combination.

Much of Conte's energies in the early 1980s were directed at his highly successful *Letteratura Latina / Latin Literature: A History* (Conte 1987*a* [various later editions], Eng. tr. Conte 1994*a*), in which he enjoyed the assistance of a group of distinguished Italian (and later Anglophone) Latinists.[9] The scope and depth of Conte's enterprise and its high value has been rightly stressed by its reviewers, and the introduction to the English translation (Conte (1994*a*), 1–10) is one of Conte's most interesting statements on the interpretation of literature. Here there is naturally considerable emphasis on literary history, both on the historical contextualization of literature and on the history of genres as themselves historical sequences, and a clear attack on the anti-historicism which Conte had already identified as a weakness in modern literary studies (cf. Conte (1974*a*), 48, discussed above). The need to reconstruct the original intention of the literary work is seen as the crucial task of the interpreter: 'without the tension that drives us to seek an original intention in the literary work, our very relation to these works loses any real interest. I see no other protection from the arbitrary incursions of many modern interpreters, who may be eager readers but whose views are unconsciously alien to the

---

[9] Full details in Conte (1994*a*), xxxiii.

original historical contexts and cultural codes' (Conte (1994*a*), 3). Conte's notion of the conscious construction of texts to elicit certain responses comes close to restoring the importance of authorial intention, but in the end he maintains the autonomy of texts as literary codes and systems decipherable by model readers (Conte (1994*a*), 3): 'every literary text is constructed in such a way as to determine the intended manner of its reception. To identify by philological means the intended addressee within the text itself means to rediscover the cultural and expressive codes that originally enabled that addressee to understand the text.'

The introduction also gives us more insight into Conte's ideas on literary genre and its crucial role in interpretation. Literary genre is seen as a set of dynamic literary systems with clear identifying features decipherable by readers ('models of discourse, complexes of metaphors, strategies of communication, and techniques of style', 4) which are both open to renewal through modification and mutual dialogue and yet always classifiable under a single heading: '[a genre] can be combined, reduced, amplified, transposed and reversed; it may suffer various types of functional mutations and adaptations: the content and expression of one genre may become associated with another. But it remains true that in the ancient literary system any combination of literary forms and structures, however complex and disparate it may be, always respects a single discursive project (this we would call a "genre")' (5). He insists on the view, developed in his earlier work on *Georgics* 4 and *Eclogue* 10 in *Il genere e i suoi confini* (see above), that particular genres represent particular ways of viewing the world and its values and that this is crucial for interpretation (4): 'the various literary genres are languages that interpret the empirical world: genres select and emphasize certain features of the world in preference to others, thereby offering the representation of various forms of the world, different models of life and culture'.

These themes are naturally foregrounded in Conte's collection *Genere e lettori*, 'Genres and Readers', which gathers pieces from the 1980s (Conte 1991, Eng. tr. Conte 1994*b*). Here Conte ranges over a number of genres, and in an interesting introduction returns once again to the fundamental issues of literary interpretation. He engages with the prominence of the reader in the era of reader-response theory, framing the 'reader-addressee' as crucial in interpretation of any text, but maintains still that the text has its own discoverable intention and shapes its own readership (Conte (1994*b*), xix): 'searching for the text's intentionality—which is not a naïve recourse to the author's intentions—will mean searching for the semantic energy that binds a work's diverse and apparently incongruous elements into a significant whole, that energy which invests, motivates and shapes the reader-audience originally programmed by the form of the text'. This 'form of the text' is usually literary genre with its various codes and structures, to be recognizable by the reader, whose competence to identify them is crucial in interpretation, like the capacity of musicians to read musical notation and play the relevant notes (p. xx): 'this competence is the force that makes sure that a text's score is correctly performed'. This insistence on the autonomy of the text perhaps elides too much the contribution of the author's intentions, which like the interpretation of the reader must occur in a context of literary competence; but these are admittedly problematic to discover.

The central three chapters of the book all began life as introductions to translations and editions of Latin authors for the general public (Conte 1990, 1986*b*, and 1982*b*), and deal with Lucretius, love-elegy, and Pliny the Elder. Conte rightly fits Lucretius into the didactic, Hesiodic division of epic, and argues plausibly that 'Lucretius is inconceivable without the Alexandrians' (Conte (1994*b*), 8). But his key argument is that Lucretius' appropriation of Empedocles restores grandeur and sublimity to the didactic epic after the more etiolated productions of Aratus and Nicander (19: 'the didactic genre recuperates the Empedoclean model by rediscovering the greatness of a lofty and passionate mode of writing'), an interesting anticipation of the similar assertion of the importance of Empedocles for Lucretius by David Sedley (Sedley 1998): the grandeur of the cosmos is fully reflected in high language and lofty argument, and the poem stimulates the reader to become a 'sublime reader', able courageously to accept the austere message of Epicureanism through (paradoxically) renouncing the tranquillity of *ataraxia* and participating in the poet's own missionary fervour.

On love-elegy Conte reasserts the views on genre as systematic codification to be found in the introduction to his *Latin Literature*, and plausibly argues that 'the genre of elegy seems to be the most complete realization of such a systematic codification' (37), with its especially carefully constructed ideology and particularly tight series of conventions (*militia amoris, servitium amoris,* suffering, frustration, enclosed escapism). These pages (35–43) constitute for me the most penetrating analysis of the key generic features of Latin love-elegy, even before they get to the stimulating analyses of the *Remedia Amoris* and the *Ars Amatoria*. Both these poems are seen as witty rationalizing revisions of the established passionate elegiac code, deconstructing the hallowed idea that the lover and the love-poet must be identical, and renewing elegy through mixing in elements of didactic epic and looking outside the remarkably narrow purviews of the elegiac world, using all the variety of activities available in modern Rome, traditionally avoided by the blinkered lover, as realistic props for seduction in the *Ars* and as therapeutic distractions in the *Remedia*. Finally, Conte's account of Pliny the Elder as 'the inventory of the world' notes the match between the order of the Roman Empire and that of the natural universe, argues intriguingly that Pliny's historical position under the *pax Romana* led naturally to a desire to itemize the world in a permanent archive, and suggests that though Pliny himself rejects the label of paradoxography and adopts a consistently rational approach to the world, his work nevertheless reflects 'the capacity to be astonished and the capacity to astonish' (104).

The two final chapters of the English version of the book[10] return to the theory of genre in antiquity. In 'Genre between Empiricism and Theory' Conte argues that the dichotomy of the title is a false one: arguing against both the 'recipe' approach to 'genres of content' in the work of Francis Cairns and 'nebulous and abstract' theoretical ideas, Conte asserts again his view that literary genre is a dynamic and active system which combines specific ideology and specific formal content, a 'strategy of literary composition' (107). In a case study of Virgil's *Eclogues*, Conte shows how Virgil pared down the heterogeneous Theocritean collection and, while including evident

---

[10] The first of these was delivered as a conference paper in Austin, Texas, in 1990 and first appeared in English as Conte (1992*d*); the second, generated as Conte's contribution (in English) to an APA panel on his work in 1992 was also printed in article form in English as Conte (1992*c*), in Italian as Conte (1992*b*).

gestures towards and confrontations with other kinds of writing on the boundaries of pastoral, kept his poetic book firmly in the bucolic tradition; it is in such deliberately staged intergeneric spectacles, he argues, on 'flaunting the difference between...genres' (121), as in the familiar poetic *recusatio*, that texts of the Augustan period most clearly demonstrate their identity within the established system of genres.

In his 'Concluding Remarks: "The Rhetoric of Imitation" as a Rhetoric of Culture', Conte provides an interesting retrospect for an American audience on the ideas of the two books which *The Rhetoric of Imitation* (Conte 1986*a*) condensed for an Anglophone readership. Having characterized himself in the previous chapter as a 'pre-deconstructionist critic' (118), Conte here suggests with some irony that he has been 'cured' of his early structuralist/formalist tendencies, and that his interests have moved from 'how a text functions' to 'how a text communicates' (130). Here we are on the familiar Contean ground of textual autonomy within a dynamic but identifiable literary system in a particular historical/ideological context, and of the need of the text to find an appropriate model reader, who 'reads the literary text in terms of the cultural models it presupposed' and 'sees how it wanted to communicate with the readers it imagined and projected' (133). Texts, in fact, can only be meaningfully read against the background of ancient generic systems (137: 'a work's meaning and structure can only be grasped in relation to models, while the models themselves are derived from a long series of texts of which they are the invariants'), since they were themselves composed against that background (138): 'the importance I would like to attach to codes, genres, institutional and conventional languages, and the like, in the analysis of ancient texts ends up actually bringing us closer to the real conditions in which ancient literature was elaborated. I mean that the ancient poets actually worked in this way; it was with a practical awareness of these languages that they learned to read and write poetry, to judge it according to conventions they themselves recognized'.

In 1995 Conte gave the Sather Lectures at Berkeley, a well-merited accolade, and chose to speak not on Virgil but on a prose author. This was Petronius, who has for some years been a regular subject of his seminars at Pisa and of textual and exegetical notes (Conte 1987*b*,

1992*e*, 1999*b*), and the object of ongoing work by Conte on a joint commentary with Mario Labate. The resulting volume, issued with impressive celerity, was his first book published solely in English, *The Hidden Author* (Conte 1996*a*). Its chief argument is that in the *Satyrica* we are presented with Encolpius as a 'mythomaniac narrator', a naïve young intellectual reading the low-life events of a sordid story in terms of elevated literary models such as epic and tragedy, while placed by the urbane 'hidden author' (the Petronius of the text) in low-life melodramatic situations from novelistic and mimic contexts, with irony resulting from the evident gap between the two. This provides a very fruitful approach to two key issues in Petronian interpretation—the precise status of Encolpius as narrator (how far is he himself satirized?), and the central importance of literary parody. Conte also interestingly inclines to agree with those who have seen a serious purpose in the *Satyrica*; though we are presented with the literary pretensions of the narrator and their deflation by the author, the text as a whole (he argues) reveals nostalgia for an irrecoverable literary and moral greatness, and its deflating irony at least sometimes engenders 'a paradoxical suspicion of a profound seriousness' (Conte (1996*a*), 169).

Conte's views on the highly contested generic issue in the *Satyrica* are naturally of particular interest. Until the publication of the *Iolaus* papyrus in 1971, most scholars were happy to acknowledge that the prosimetric form of the *Satyrica* was owed to the Roman prosimetric tradition of Varro's Menippean satire. But the existence of a low-life prosimetric narrative in Greek which has no apparent Menippean connections has caused some rethinking, and it is now plausible to argue as Conte does (140–70) for a fundamentally novelistic affinity for Petronius' narrative; likewise Conte does not forget (124–5) that the excessive meal of the *Cena Trimalchionis* and other satiric themes derive not from Menippean satire but from Roman hexameter satire, an important formative element for Petronius. In general, this book is a valuable addition to the modern literature on Petronius, and bodes well for future work on this author.

Thirty years after the publication of his first major book, and with such an impressive and important body of work to his name, Gian Biagio Conte remains a powerful and creative force in Latin literary scholarship, as the papers in this volume clearly show.

PRINCIPAL WRITINGS OF GIAN BIAGIO CONTE

(* = translated for the first time in this volume; ** = reprinted in this volume)

(1965), 'Il trionfo della morte e la galleria dei grandi trapassati in Lucrezio III, 1024–1053', *SIFC* 27: 114–32.

(1966*a*), "Yψoς e diatriba nello stile di Lucrezio (*De rer. nat.* II, 1–61)', *Maia*, 18: 338–68.

(1966*b*), 'Il proemio della Pharsalia', *Maia*, 18: 42–53 (reprinted in Conte 1988).

(1968), 'La guerra civile nella rievocazione del popolo: Lucano 2.67–233', *Maia*, 20: 224–53.

(1970*a*), 'Ennio e Lucano', *Maia*, 22: 132–8 (reprinted in Conte 1988).

(1970*b*), 'Il balteo di Pallante', *RFIC* 98: 292–300 (reprinted in Conte 1974*a* and 1985; translated in Conte 1986*a*).

(1971), 'Memoria dei poeti e arte allusiva', *Strumenti critici*, 16: 325–32 (reprinted in Conte 1974*a* and 1985; translated in Conte 1986*a*).

(1974*a*), *Memoria dei poeti e sistema letterario* (Turin) (2nd edn. Turin, 1985; largely translated in Conte 1986*a*).

(1974*b*), *Saggio di commento a Lucano. Pharsalia 6.118–260. L'aristia di Sceva* (Pisa) (revised reprint in Conte 1988).

(1976), 'Proemi al mezzo', *RCCM* 18: 263–73 (reprinted in Conte 1980*a* and 1984*a*; translated in Conte 1992*a*).

(1978*a*), 'Saggio d'interpretazione dell'*Eneide*: ideologia e forma del contenuto', *MD* 1: 11–48 (reprinted in Conte 1980*a* and 1984*a*; translated in Conte 1986*a*).

(1978*b*), 'L'episodio di Elena bel secondo dell'*Eneide*: modelli strutturali e critica dell'autenticità', *RFIC* 106: 53–62 (reprinted in Conte 1980*a* and 1984*a*; translated in Conte 1986*a*).

(1979), 'Il genere e i suoi confini: interpretazione dell'egloga decima di Virgilio', in *Studi di poesia latina in onore di Antonio Traglia* (Rome), 377–404 (reprinted in Conte 1980*a* and 1984*a*; translated in Conte 1986*a*).

(1980*a*), *Virgilio: il genere e i suoi confini* (Turin).

(1980*b*), 'Aristeo, Orfeo e le Georgiche: struttura narrativa e funzione didascalica di un mito'; introduction to A. Barchiesi, *Virgilio: Georgiche* (Milan) (reprinted in Conte 1984*a*; translated in Conte 1986*a*).

Introduction by Stephen Harrison

*(1982a), 'Verso una nuova esegesi virgiliana: revisioni e propositi', in *Virgilio e noi. None giornate filologiche genovesi* (Genoa), 73–98 (reprinted in Conte 1984a).

(1982b), 'L'inventario del mondo: ordine e linguaggio della natura nell'opera di Plinio il Vecchio', in *Plinio: Storia Naturale 1*, ed. A. Barchiesi *et al.* (Turin), xvii–xlvii (reprinted in Conte 1991; translated in Conte 1994b).

*(1983a), 'Fra stilistica e critica del testo: *Eneide* 10, 24', *RIFC* 111: 150–7 (reprinted in Conte 2002).

(1984a), *Virgilio: il genere e i suoi confini* (2nd edn.; Milan).

(1985), *Memoria dei poeti e sistema letterario* (2nd edn.; Turin).

(1986a), *The Rhetoric of Imitation: Genre and Poetic Memory in Virgil and Other Latin Poets* (Ithaca).

(1986b), introduction to *Ovidio: Rimedi contro l'amore*, tr. C. Lazzarini (Venice), 9–53 (reprinted in Conte 1991; translated in Conte 1994b).

(1987a), *La letteratura latina: Manuale storico dalle origini alla fine dell' impero romano* (Florence) (translated in Conte 1994a).

(1987b), 'Una correzione a Petronio (*Sat.* 89 v.31)', *RFIC* 115: 33–4.

(1988), *La 'Guerra Civile' di Lucano* (Urbino).

(1989), 'I giorni del giudizio: Lucano e l'antimodello', in *Mnemosynum. Studi in onore di Alfredo Ghiselli* (Bologna), 95–100 (also in Conte (1988), 33–9).

(1990), introduction to *Lucrezio: La natura delle cose*, tr. L. Canali (Milan), 7–47 (reprinted in Conte 1991; translated in Conte 1994b).

(1991), *Genere e lettori: Lucrezio, l'elegia d'amore, l'enciclopedia di Plinio* (Milan).

**(1992a), 'Proems in the Middle', in F. M. Dunn and T. Cole (eds.), *Beginnings in Classical Literature* (Yale Classical Studies, 29; Cambridge, 1992), 147–59.

(1992b) ' "La retorica dell'imitazione" come retorica della cultura', *Filologia Antica e Moderna* (Calabria), 41–2 (translated in Conte 1992c).

(1992c), ' "Rhetoric of Imitation" as Rhetoric of Culture: Some New Thoughts', *Vergilius*, 38: 45–55 (reprinted in Conte 1994b).

(1992d), 'Empirical and Theoretical Approaches to Literary Genre', in K. Galinsky (ed.), *The Interpretation of Roman Poetry* (Frankfurt), 103–24 (reprinted as 'Genre between Empiricism and Theory', in Conte 1994b; earlier Italian version in Conte 1991).

(1992e), 'Petronio, Sat. 141', *RFIC* 120: 300–12.

(1994a), *Latin Literature: A History* (Baltimore).

(1994b), *Genres and Readers* (Baltimore and London).

(1996*a*), *The Hidden Author: An Interpretation of Petronius' Satyricon* (Berkeley and London).

*(1996*b*), '*Defensor Vergilii*: la tecnica epica dell'*Eneide* secondo Richard Heinze', introduction to R. Heinze (tr. M. Martina), *La tecnica epica di Virgilio* (Bologna), 9–23 (reprinted in Conte 2002).

*(1998*a*), 'Aristeo, Orfeo e le *Georgiche*: una seconda volta', *SCO* 46: 103–36 (reprinted in Conte 2002).

(1998*b*), 'Il paradosso virgiliano: un'epica drammatica e sentimentale', introduction to M. Ramous (tr.), G. Baldo (comm.), *Virgilio: Eneide* (Venice), 9–55 (translated as Conte 1999*a*).

**(1999*a*), 'The Virgilian Paradox', *PCPS* 45: 17–42.

(1999*b*), 'Tre congetture a Petronio', *MD* 43: 203–11.

**(2001), 'Aristaeus, Orpheus and the *Georgics* again', in S. Spence (ed.), *Poets and Critics Read Virgil* (New Haven), 44–63.

*(2002), *Virgilio: L'epica di sentimento* (Turin).

These works (along with the further items referred to in this Introduction and in the remainder of the book) are also listed in the final Bibliography of this volume.

2

The Virgilian Paradox: An Epic of Drama and Pathos

EVERY powerful critical idea is the product of a particular interpretative situation: we could even say, with considerable simplification, that it is the product of a prejudice. Every cultural moment develops its own critical myth (or prejudice), and reasons and interprets within the limits of this horizon. Often it needs only a short time for the myth to wither, for the prejudice to decay; we realize that its claims, born of a particular historical perspective and valid only in part, were too high, and that it was not content to accept this merely partial validity.

But when a critical myth fades away, not everything is doomed to disappear. There are still positive traces, still a residual value which, once appropriately adjusted and corrected, can be recovered. To achieve this, a more powerful interpretative system must arise which absorbs the error within a new perspective. Whatever survives the testing may become a new instrument of interpretation, perhaps one destined to last forever—or at least for a short time longer (this is how progress is made).

This is why one good rule in the practice of criticism is not to forget the history of criticism. The first advantage is that of avoiding the repetition of old errors, since the prejudices that occasioned them have now been definitively tested and pronounced unacceptable. The second is that we can recover for a new critical use some partial 'truth' which, in its absolute form, had falsely shaped a previous frame of judgement. The special and peculiar merit of this method is to salvage elements of judgement already sifted and refined by the filter of history.

In the history of Virgilian studies one highly seductive critical myth operated in early German romanticism and shaped more than a century of classical philology, especially in Germany. This is the impassioned myth of the 'primitive', which understood poetry as the product of spontaneous energy and saw in Homer a veritable force of Nature. This, the myth invented by Winckelmann and preserved by Herder and Wilhelm von Humboldt, preached the *edle Einfalt und stille Grösse* (noble simplicity and calm grandeur) of the Greeks, and simultaneously denied value to Virgil and to all Latin literature, since it was derivative and lacking in originality. The cost was immense, and it took much labour on the part of a few exceptional interpreters before we could reach a new and balanced appraisal which finally allowed us to measure the differences between diverse cultures and ages. First a new conception of poetry had to assert itself: we had to understand that the right kind of originality is not one that resembles nothing else, but one that cannot be reduced to these resemblances. Only then would resemblances and borrowings appear as constitutive elements of literary language itself, as necessary manifestations of culture. Then poetry would reveal itself inside and coexistent with its culture, no longer outside or prior to it.[1]

If these judgements were mistaken, their motives were not. At that time an effort was being made to understand the nature of the antique, and Homer came before all the others. And not only before them; he was the quintessence of the antique, the paradigm of an origin; in a sense, he was not part of history, since history came after him. Homer was nature: he was spontaneous poetry; he was like a state of innocence, but he was also the touchstone for all the poetry that followed him. The mistake of the early Romantics was an error of history rather than of psychology: they were arguing in terms of natural substance, not of cultural product.

But the mistake, however costly, was also fertile. Schiller and Friedrich Schlegel developed a theory of poetic modes which gave a new meaning and direction to the hoary 'quarrel of the Ancients and Moderns'. With some differences between themselves they constructed an opposition between 'naïve' and 'sentimental' poetry; the former is purely natural, a spontaneous imitation of nature—it

---

[1] See my discussion in Ch. 6 below.

is objective, impersonal, composed of things; the latter is reflective, personal, and self-conscious.

There can, of course, never have been a purely 'naïve' poet or an age that was totally 'naïve'. Schiller's mistake was to think too much in terms of opposites, of pure types, and of completely distinct ages. But even with these reservations, the theory offers a profound intuition into the process of literature, and above all it grasps rather well the real situation of a literature that is viewed as modern in relation to an ancient one, an ancient literature that is cherished as primeval and virginal, and understood as nature pure and simple, unaffected by external factors.

We know that Homer was not pure nature, not spontaneity without art (according to the Romantics, art was an extraneous intrusion composed of reflection and acquired technique, a secondary form of wisdom) but Schiller liked to believe that he was.[2] However, Schiller's critical illusion is not doomed to disappear completely; if the critical myth is adjusted and its false perspectives are corrected, it is still of value. For we can still make use of the historical dialectic between the 'naïve' and objective poet Homer, on one side, and 'sentimental' and reflective, artfully conditioned poetry, on the other.

I call Schiller's illusion fertile because Virgil too had a similar feeling, or at least found himself in the cultural situation of a modern who looked from a vast distance at the great poetic model who had told his tale with calm detachment, had spoken in contact with nature, intimate with the cosmic forces which he was able to transform into glorious gods. For Virgil, as for Schiller, Homer stood for the calm life of creativity, the inner necessity of events and of human existence, the grandiose impersonality of one who looks with an objective eye and knows no alternative to the universe that he is representing.

---

[2] The idea is now increasingly widespread among interpreters of Homer that 'despite the lack of direct intervention by the primary narrator-focalizer, the *Iliad* is far from objective or impersonal: it is full of implicit colouring or focalizers' (Taplin (1992), 52). Among the many analyses of the problems of the point of view and of narrative focalization in Homer, see e.g. Delrieu, Hilt, and Letoublon (1984), Scully (1986), de Jong (1987), Bremer *et al.* (1987), Martin (1994), Segal (1994), and Felson-Rubin (1994). On the objectivity of Homer's narrative style see Bassett (1938), chs. 2 and 3, Griffin (1980), ch. 4, and Effe (1983).

Homer was distant for Virgil. Virgil saw in him what he himself lacked, he saw a goal to aim at even if he knew from the start that it was unreachable. The *naïveté* of the poet of the *Iliad* and *Odyssey* was essentially the simplicity that defined itself against art, and art was nothing but the subsequent consciousnes of the modern poet, a consciousness divided within itself and which had long since lost the original unity of sensibility and thought. The awareness of this dissociation allowed Virgil freedom and variety, while for him Homer was marked by inevitability and immutability. Virgil felt irrevocably doomed to the reflective, the self-critical, to the divorce between head and heart.

In this respect I find Schiller's intuition productive, recoverable on condition that it is seen in its historical context and made concrete. We should realize that the modernity of Virgil is precisely that of much of Augustan culture, which paradoxically sought a direct and immediate contact with those remote and glorious Greek poets who seemed to have been the first creators of poetry itself: Homer, Hesiod, Alcaeus, Archilochus, Pindar. This was a perfectly anachronistic ambition, an ambition in which the modern quest for the *original* of the Augustans became a quest for the *originary*, that is, a return to the very origins of poetry—an ostensibly impossible challenge, an outrageous challenge, destined to create not only a new originality, but some of the absolute masterpieces of an unrepeatable epoch such as the Augustan era.

To write an epic-heroic poem which made of Virgil the modern Homer, was, as I have said, an anachronistic ambition—which I would now redefine in the Nietzschean sense of 'untimely', 'unzeitgemäss'. By this I mean not just unexpected and 'against the grain', non-conformist, but above all pushing forward beyond the present time, ready to act upon the future. From awareness of modernity was born the greatest challenge, the effort to reach an inaccessible objective by following the path which seemed to depart furthest from the modern, the longest and most unforeseen path. The modern poet, wanting to find a new synthesis between his 'sentimental' nature and his lost *naïveté*, had to triumph over himself as well; he had somehow to return to being a new kind of naïve poet.

Virgil knows he is the poet of modern imperfection. He is split in two by his own art, and by art I mean the awareness that poetry is not a natural gift, but the laborious product of poets who meditate on the world and on life. Virgil knows that, since Homer, philosophical thought has characterized itself through the renunciation of simplicity: he knows above all that experience of tragedy has robbed the modern poet of his *naïveté*. But tragedy is also the strongest feature of modernity, if not tragedy as a literary genre, at least tragedy as the spirit of crisis, as the form of doubt and questioning. From Homer's feast the great tragic poets had drawn the material to represent a world that had since known the impulses of liberty and of critical reasoning, a world no longer characterized by an inner sense of life's necessity. But paradoxically (as we shall see) it is just the divided language of tragedy that Virgil used to reconquer a sense of the universal.

The loss of Homeric *naïveté* impoverished Virgil: in return his modern conquest of critical reasoning and feeling made him richer. The naïve presented itself to him as a past now become the object of nostalgia: being past, it had long since been superseded, but as object of nostalgia it was an ideal to strive for, as at one and the same time he looked back at a lost perfection and strained towards it. Homer lacked the contradictory complexity of moral thinking, the divided consciousness and the reflectiveness of the tragic: Virgil lacked the simple harmony of nature and necessity. It was as if the *Aeneid* sought to attain, through reason, the harmony which the emergence of reason itself had disrupted.

In Homer, myth and history simply coincided: the absolute and the relative, the sacred and the profane, made up a single universe, inasmuch as human life was lived by heroes and determined by gods. For Virgil, human history had long since been detached from myth. As a new epic poet he felt obliged to represent precisely what could not be represented by a traditional epic poet, that is the tension of the contradictions operating in history. The 'sentimental' poet had to maintain a double attitude, deploying a double language to represent the contrast between the real world and the idea(l)s which did not find realization in this world. As a sign of these contradictions he had many desires to express, many anxieties to reconcile, if he wanted to embody a new order.

There is one line above all of the *Aeneid* which I believe demonstrates in exemplary fashion the Virgilian manner, that most original synthesis through which Latin epic looks back nostalgically at the great 'naïve' model of Homer and at the same time allows us to recognize the modern 'sentimental' resonance of a divided sensibility. Elsewhere I have cited this verse to show how Homeric imitation is inscribed in the very matrix which generates the Virgilian text; now I would like to use it to show how the constant return to Homer is not only a sign of nostalgia and awareness of distance, but also a gesture that reveals the whole Virgilian ambition to transform the great Greek model in a modern way, by impressing upon it the essential characteristics of a new artistic sensibility.

The verse occurs in the most 'tragic' book of the epic, in the narrative of Troy's last night, at the centre of the furious slaughter by Pyrrhus (Neoptolemus) and just before the murder of Priam: *quinquaginta illi thalami spes tanta nepotum* (*Aeneid* 2.503).[3] The memory of *Iliad* 6.244 inevitably imposes itself on the reader: πεντήκοντ᾽ ἔνεσαν θάλαμοι ξεστοῖο λίθοιο. The effort of recovering Homer's voice drives Virgil to reproduce the first hemistich of the model as if he were simply making a transliteration; the individual letters of the Greek are almost repeated in Latin, and the rhythmic and verbal movement of the two isometric cola is virtually interchangeable: πεντήκοντ᾽ ἔνεσαν θάλαμοι ∼ *quinquaginta illi thalami*, where *illi* is the mark of memory, 'those fifty bedchambers' of Priam's sons described by Homer when they were a safe refuge and Hector used to visit them. But Homer had ended the verse with the clausula ξεστοῖο λίθοιο ('of well-polished stone'). Over the descriptive objectivity and materiality of Homer's model is superimposed, in strong contrast, the sympathetic and reflective—'sentimental' that is—intrusion of Virgil's *spes tanta nepotum*, 'such great hope of grandchildren'.

The extreme closeness to the model (in the first part of the verse up to the penthemimeral caesura the sounds and rhythms are the same, as if it was the same language that produced them) clearly reveals the very difficult and original balance attempted by Virgil. The challenge he makes is as follows: the more the new text, suffused by a pathetic subjectivity, cleaves to the old model, impersonal,

---

[3] The variant *spes ampla* (Cod. Gudianus; *spes am... P*) might find support from Prop. 3. 22, 41–2 *hic ampla nepotum | spes et venturae coniugis aptus amor* (see Austin ad loc.).

objective, composed of things, the more the new voice makes itself felt, modern, sentimental, and reflective. The closeness is extraordinary, the distance vast. The difference between the two literary modes generates a new arrangement of epic language. The variation *spes tanta nepotum* contains, condensed by connotations, many of the peculiar motifs upon which the tight framework of the Virgilian text is constructed: hope disappointed by death, life as a succession of generations, death marked by the bitterness of an injustice suffered without reason.

As I said, they are condensed through connotation so that their meaning emerges—rising and fermenting—from within a phrase in which there is implicitly hidden a marginal, reflective idea which adds a shadowing thought to the previous words. Often it is appositions which complete the utterance with an intense note of pathos, just as in *spes tanta nepotum*. So for example at 1.29–30 (=3.87) *iactatos ... | Troas reliquias Danaum atque immitis Achilli* ('remains from [the slaughter by] the Danaans and the ruthless Achilles'), spoken bitterly by the Trojans who have outlived the end of their city; or at 2.448–9 *aurataque trabes, veterum decora alta parentum | devolvunt* ('those lofty ornaments of our ancient fathers'), referring to the gilded ceilings of the fine Trojan houses at the moment when the Greeks demolish them, a sentimental addition by the poet who recalls sorrowfully the vain illusion of past generations, so proud then to construct what is now mercilessly destroyed; or at 2.797–8 *matresque virosque, | collectam exsilio pubem, miserabile vulgus* ('women and men, a people gathered for exile, a pitiful crowd'), a note of compassion for the defeated compelled to flee; or again at 3.305 *et geminas, causam lacrimis, sacraverat aras* ('she had consecrated two altars, cause for tears'), Andromache celebrating funeral rites before Hector's cenotaph; or at 4.646–7 [Dido] *furibunda ... ensem ... recludit | Dardanium, non hos quaesitum munus in usus* ('in her fury she unsheathed the Trojan sword, a gift requested not for this purpose'), where the apposition has an extraordinary dramatic effect: Aeneas himself had given the sword to Dido with which she now kills herself through a tragic turn of destiny; or again like 6.377 *sed cape dicta memor, duri solacia casus* ('but listen and remember my words, consolation for your hard fate'), in the heartfelt words addressed by Aeneas to the unburied Palinurus.

Elsewhere it is the structure called *dicolon abundans* or 'theme and variation' that lends itself to a gesture of reflection. This redundant and typically epic structure is a recurring trait of Virgilian style, in which the same conception is repeated, almost tautologically but with lexical and syntactical variation, in coordinated half-lines or successive lines.[4] The first part of the line gives the theme, and the second is a variation upon it, but sometimes the second part, while apparently expressing an idea similar in content to the first, can add a note of pathos and focus an intensification of feeling, as in 2.12 *quanquam animus meminisse horret, luctuque refugit* ('although my mind is loath to remember and shrinks in grief'); or at 2.361–2 ... *quis funera fando | explicet aut possit lacrimis aequare labores?* ('who could unfold the deaths in words or shed tears equal to the sufferings?'); or at 3.707–8 *hinc Drepani me portus et inlaetabilis ora | accipit* ('next I was received in the harbour of Drepanum and that joyless shore'); or again in 4.281 *ardet abire fuga dulcisque relinquere terras* ('he burned to depart in flight and to leave the sweet land'), where the adjective *dulcis* is empathetic, referring indirectly to the emotions of Aeneas; the poet's narrative voice lets itself be saturated by the subjectivity of the person within the narrative.[5] Even the famous passage at 1.461–2 *sunt hic etiam sua praemia laudi, | sunt lacrimae rerum et mentem mortalia tangunt* ('Here too there are due rewards for glorious achievement, there are tears for what has passed and human fate touches the heart') can be analysed as a *dicolon abundans* in which *et mentem mortalia tangunt* varies and gives pathos to the first colon (*mortalia* is a variation on *rerum*).[6]

Virgil, as a 'pathetic' poet of feeling, *reflects* on the impression which things make upon him: this gesture of reflection is the focus of

---

[4] See the extensive treatment in Ch. 3 of this volume.

[5] On this and other examples of 'deviant focalization' see D. P. Fowler (1990).

[6] Sometimes the pathetic amplification can occur even in a supplementary relative clause, like 2.248–9 *nos delubra deum miseri quibus ultimus esset | ille dies, festa velamus fronde per urbem* or at 2.426–8 *cadit et Rhipeus, iustissimus unus | qui fuit in Teucris et servantissimus aequi | (dis aliter visum)*: the added thought integrates the utterance and intrudes as a bitter reflection on events. At other times it is the similes—like expanded narrative epithets—which become the source of pathetic intensification; they illustrate the narrative by glossing it with subjective and sentimental notations. On this aspect of Virgilian similes, see e.g. West (1969), G. Williams (1983), 60–7, Lyne (1987), 119–26 and (1989), 63–99.

the emotion that he himself experiences and conveys to the reader. Things, that is objects, events, speeches and words, are associated with an idea, and their poetic force depends entirely on this association. Homer is a 'naïve' poet, and his acts of representation, even when they are objects of extreme pathos, create a plain impression (those German Romantics would have called it 'calm'), whereas the impression given by the 'pathetic' poetry of Virgil is always disturbed by thought, provoking a certain tension; a Virgilian representation of something invites the reader to associate an affective idea with it, and keeps him suspended between two diverse perceptions.

From a Schillerian perspective one might say that the Homeric image is finite, whereas the Virgilian image seems intended to grow through the power of continuous reflection. It is an open, unbounded representation. The truth is that Virgil transforms the work into his own nature. There is nothing in his work except himself, because the object is completely absorbed into the subject, and to discover the object we must seek it out in the subject. Before representing things the poet expresses the freedom of his own thoughts; things exist but also signify, and they signify more than their own simple nature. Virgilian representation submerges itself in the power of ideas, and contains something extra, since it contains the longing for what should have been, not the calming of that longing.

In Homeric narrative there is a single point of view: there is a fixed 'focus' which transcends the limits of the authorial persona to identify itself with a seemingly objective reality. The text is maintained on a single plane, imperceptible because it is flat and uniform, without contrasts or depth; its single point of view is just the 'relation of truth' which it maintains with the represented world. There is one single centre which controls all the values unfolded by the text:[7] an immmutable and 'calm' image of things, persons, and events, whether gods

---

[7] In this respect the book by Irene de Jong (1987) is highly debatable and essentially inexact. The author, perhaps with the simple intention of provoking debate (which nonetheless stands in contrast to the attitude of cautious moderation that she maintains in other parts of the book), actually claims that the presentation of the narrative in the *Iliad* should be considered 'subjective, engaged and emotional' (227). Behind her claims lie a misunderstanding and a distortion; she confuses the narrative features of the contents (sorrowful events and feelings) with the narrative features of the form (the way of representing this sorrow). The fact that the external narrator (Homer) inclines to a narrative largely composed of dialogues should not be

are on stage intervening in the action or heroes acting, hating, and dying. This is the hidden source of Homer's famous epic objectivity. The narratorial perspective in pre-Virgilian Roman epic (Naevius, Ennius, and others) is similar at least in this respect. Here too, as far as we can reconstruct it, there was a single point of view, unmoving and external, which kept its sights on the national history of Rome, and celebrated its rise to greatness. The archaic Latin epic poets felt responsible for a truth which they guaranteed as absolute and incontrovertible; on one side the imperial destiny of Rome, on the other side her enemies (but we will see this more clearly below). Narration was an ideologically stable continuity. The reader confronted a fixed model of the history of mankind within which the text of the action unfolded. The single point of view was ensured when the poet identified himself with truth, that is the tradition and morality of the community. Here too, as an effect of the fixed perspective, a sort of objectivity came into being that did not acknowledge contradictions.

When the point of view is single, and the focal centre is fixed, the image of truth is not tied to the perspective assumed by the discourse; in fact the perspective is univocal because reality itself appears as univocal. But when the world reveals itself as irreducibly complex, and truth no longer seems unique and single, and 'wrong' is perversely mixed with 'right', and one's awareness of things is no longer simple and spontaneous, but marked by reflexivity and tension, then a single point of view is no longer possible. The form of reporting which binds the text to the reality represented can no longer be single, there is no longer one predominant naive truth, but many different truths that oppose each other. Now there emerges a many-sided language, a structure of multiple associations, a truth

confused with a 'subjective style', which is quite another matter. I suspect the author is confusing the 'primitivism' of Homer as narrator (an illusion of late-Romantic criticism, now rightly rejected) with the detachment of the narrator from the reported events (a quite different thing, and the foundation of Homeric objective narrative). Even the emotions aroused in the reader by the narrative cannot be invoked as proof of an affective narrative; indeed it is possible that the poet narrates in order to arouse emotions, without indicating his own emotional participation and his own presence in the form of the text. That is just what Homer does. Nevertheless, one should not underestimate the closeness of narrator and audience: see M. W. Edwards (1991), 2–7.

disassembled according to relative points of view. The text becomes polycentric.[8]

The polycentrism of the *Aeneid* is above all a triumph of complexity against a simple and single way of seeing, overcoming the false objectivity which flattens out the world in a monistic vision. It is the poetic technique that Virgil, thrusting beyond the veil of appearances, uses to reconstruct the historic depth and thickness of individual truths that had been suppressed. In the traditional ideology of the Roman epic, the established image of reality and of national history covered over every other perspective of truth like a top layer. Beneath this triumphalist surface lay hidden moments of stifled crisis and guilt denied, above all the suppressed consciousness of all the ruthless cost of *imperium* and the anguished memory of civil strife. Virgil lets this deep dimension of denied events emerge to animate his text; and from this comes a complex and contradictory narrative structure, dramatically articulated in a plurality of personal points of view. In this way the ideological vision of the traditional historical epic loses its absolute power. Alongside the dominant truth other partial truths push themselves forward, individual urgings that now find a voice and a hearing in the text.

In the traditional Roman epic a grand political and historical design had claimed and blended into itself every personal and subjective element: a totalizing, overarching truth cancelled out all personal truths and submerged every opposition between individuals. The only opposition that could be significant was that which set an entire nation against another. As a result, within the epic plot of human and divine action, the opposition between nations projects itself into a cosmic and divine opposition: thus the polarity of 'Carthage against Rome' becomes that of 'Juno against Jupiter'. In the *Annals* of Ennius a reconciliation of Juno with Rome corresponded to the resolution of the rivalry with Carthage through victory in the second Punic War.[9]

---

[8] Here I recapitulate some of the ideas and arguments expounded in Conte (1986*a*), 152–61.

[9] Cf. Enn. *Ann.* 291 Vahlen *Romanis Iuno coepit placata favere* (the reconstruction of the hexameter proposed by Hug, based on Serv. *ad Aen.* 1.281): compare also Vahlen's discussion pp. cxix ff.; Buchheit (1963), 54 f., 144 f. The hostility of Juno to Rome had its first beginnings in the goddess's hostility towards Troy. It is likely that

Virgil takes over this traditional opposition and the obligatory pairings of Jupiter with Rome and Juno with Carthage, but at the same time he complicates this fixed scheme: Dido (that is, her love and her personal story, her motivation and her feelings) does violence to what was too simple and blinkered an opposition. Her personal point of view brings into view a truth that would otherwise have remained suppressed. The antagonistic function represented by Juno and the hostile Carthaginian people is fragmented in a series of personal events: the goddess's hostility to Rome had the unforeseen consequence that her human representative Dido had first to become a victim of the divine intrigue. When the model is reformulated in the dramatic code, the language of feelings doubles and transforms the language of narration. It is probable that Virgil derived the role of the Carthaginian queen from Naevius, but in Naevius she did not have to represent much more than a means of retrojecting into the mythic past the historic struggle between the two peoples: certainly not everything we find in the fourth book of the *Aeneid* could have occurred in the *Bellum Punicum*.

For Virgil, Dido is not just the figure that sanctions eternal enmity between the two nations: the poet recognizes her right to suffer to the last degree from the overthrow and destruction of her own personal world. The tragic characters and language of the Euripidean *Medea* and *Hippolytus* (the passion of Phaedra) have entered into the text and contaminated it with different registers. As is well known, in the language of drama the individual's point of view pervades the very structure of discourse: the dramatic text, through its constitutive form, is designed to expound competing rights, interpersonal conflict, and the opposition of individual truths. The great dramatic poets had invented the art of setting free the voices of other men and women; Virgil, the epic poet of pathos, learned from them how to grant space to those individual voices, making himself their witness and their champion. The readers of the *Aeneid*, modern readers long since cut off from the naive world of Homeric epic, were called upon

the motif of the goddess's appeasement did not have the same prominence in the *Annals* as in the *Aeneid*; but it is difficult to say how relevant it was to Naevius: cf. Skutsch (1985), 46. An important contribution is Feeney (1984), where the abundant specific bibliography is discussed. See also the useful observations of Johnson (1976), 124–7.

to assume for themselves the new rights of critical thinking and moral freedom: just like the new epic poet, they were led to attempt a synthesis of *naïveté* and sentimentality, and to become reflective thinkers.

Once given a hearing, the different voices dispute the truth of the text, constantly relativizing it and saturating it with subjectivity; the ideological frame of reference of the *Aeneid* is formed by a plurality of partial truths in competition with each other. They attack and so compromise the univocal and fixed point of view of traditional Roman epic. The impersonal oppositions (Carthage/Rome or Italians/Trojans) become personal (Dido/Aeneas, Turnus/Aeneas) and are reduced to the confrontation of single points of view, each one not entirely false, perhaps even relatively true within its own horizon. Every character is as it were 'positioned' with regard to his or her own point of view, and so finds the power to impose meanings on the surrounding world, to observe it and take a view of it.[10] Now what matters is not so much what each character stands for in the world as what the world means to the character, and even what he means for him/herself.

If we leave aside Callimachus, whose poetic choices were the exception and not the rule in the literary world of his time, Hellenistic epic chose either material that was partly mythological and partly mythologized history, or material from contemporary history. Over three centuries countless poems were dedicated to the heroizing exaltation of the deeds of kings and princes, countless *epe* celebrated the history of different regions and the mythical (or legendary) foundation of cities such as Rhodes and Alexandria. Alongside this courtly mythological poetry (local and encomiastic history), a more traditional type of mythological epic must have enjoyed a wide diffusion. There are enough traces of these two types of epic for us to assert with some probability that Callimacheanism was a relatively isolated

---

[10] Twenty years ago, with somewhat different critical interests, I defined the point of view as 'the form of relationship that passes between the semantic system of the text and the represented universe' and spoke about a 'relationship of truth which binds the manner of representing to the object of the representation itself'. With these presuppositions I was able to define the point of view of individual characters as 'the semantic position which each character occupies in the text' (cited from Conte (1986*a*), 155 n. 10).

phenomenon; the programme of Callimachus and Theocritus had a limited number of followers in the third century and virtually none in the next, apart from Euphorion, Moschus, and Bion. And although the poetics of the *Aetia* experienced a real renaissance at Rome, the fashion for Callimacheanism was in fact limited to the period between Sulla and the Augustan age.[11]

The long epic poem, whether mythological, historical, or panegyrical, never went into eclipse but always remained dominant in contemporary literary practice. Cicero defended the poet Archias, author of historical epic poetry on the Cimbrian wars of Marius and the Mithridatic war of Lucullus, and expected as thanks a fine historical poem to celebrate his own consulate.[12] Some of these epics, mythological or otherwise, were large-scale poems (I leave aside that of Apollonius Rhodius),[13] for example the *Thebaid* in eleven books by Menelaos of Aigai, the *Perseid* in ten books by Musaeus of Ephesus, or the *Bithyniaka* in at least ten books by Demosthenes of Bithynia. Even at Rome, alongside the Callimachean poetry of the neoterics, there were monumental epicists like Volusius and Hortensius, mocked in Catullus 36 and 95; Caesius, Aquinus, and Suffenus are perhaps in the same category (Catullus 14 and 22); Varro of Atax wrote a *Bellum Sequanicum* in praise of Caesar's campaign of 58 BC against Ariovistus. Furius Antias wrote at least eleven books of *Annals* on the model of Ennius and even Furius Bibaculus, who had links with the neoterics, had written a historical

[11] Fundamental here is Ziegler (1988), an important modernization of the original German edition (1934). The Italian version has an instructive preface by M. Fantuzzi, who also offers a valuable *catalogue raisonné* of the epicists who cultivated the tradition of the (non-Callimachean) large-scale poem in the various forms of mythological, local, and encomiastic historical epic from the age of Alexander to the last century before Christ (pp. lv–lxxxviii). One should also read Kroll (1916), though it is less reliable on Naevius' historical epic. Most important is the recent study of Cameron (1995), especially 263–302. The provocative stance of this learned and brilliant book (easy to guard against) is better at opening and reopening problems than at indicating peaceable solutions. On the influence of the *Aetia* on the *Aeneid* and Augustan poetry see George (1974) and the useful compilations of Miller (1982) and Briggs (1981). On the Alexandrianism of Virgil in general see Clausen (1987).

[12] *Att.* 1.16.15.

[13] Apollonius' poem is in four books, perhaps not accidentally, if we recall that Aristotle (*Poetics* 24) called the poems of the ancients too long and wanted to allow only those comparable in length to a tragic tetralogy—see Vahlen (1914), 287.

epic on the Gallic war, perhaps to be identified with the *Annals* (these too in at least eleven books) of a certain Furius, from whom Macrobius (*Sat.* 6.1) cites some lines.[14] Was it the failure of such works as Furius Bibaculus' epic on Caesar's Gallic campaign that made Virgil renounce the project of writing a historical epic on Augustus? This epic is supposed to have been insistently demanded of him: he had even promised to write it in the 'proem in the middle' (cf. Conte 1976/1984*a*/1992*a*) of the *Georgics* (3.46–8): 'soon I shall arm myself to sing the impassioned battles of Octavianus Caesar and to transmit his name with the support of Fame, for as many years as lie between Caesar and Tithonus, his remote origin.' As we have said, the Ennian tradition rejected by the neoterics was not in fact dead, and epic was expected to celebrate contemporary deeds. Contemporaries must naturally have looked to Virgil for some kind of *Caesareid*. What they actually got will have astounded them.

What was Virgil's innnovative proposal? It is given twofold articulation by the commentator Servius (p. 4.11 Thilo–Hagen): his first aim was *Augustum laudare a parentibus*, that is to celebrate Augustus by retrojecting, into the mythical and heroic past, the encomium of his present achievements, so as to steer clear of the reef of courtly eulogy;[15] his second aim was *imitari Homerum*.[16] To transform Homer by disassembling his narrative structures in order to reassemble them in a new *ensemble* with a modern significance, contaminating but also continuing the two poems, as if the new poet were in fact Homer himself *redivivus*, now bringing to an end his interrupted work: this is Virgil's project.

---

[14] Cf. Courtney (1993), 192–200.

[15] The crucial point where myth joins history in a vertiginous exchange of inverted perspectives is in book 6. There the mythical past contains and narrates the national history of Rome as a succession of future events, when Anchises in the Underworld reveals to Aeneas forthcoming history: *quae postquam Anchises natum per singula duxit | incenditque animum fame venientis amore, | exim bella viro memorat quae deinde gerenda* (6.888–90). *Fama veniens*—History—itself becomes the child of myth, and conversely myth finds its validation by assimilating itself to past historical time. The tradition founded by Naevius and continued by Ennius is renewed here; the timing of events loses its linearity of development (the 'beforehand' of myth which in the sequence of the narrative should precede the 'afterwards' of history) to become a complex narrative plot.

[16] The classic article of R. D. Williams (1967) is still very helpful.

The beginning of the *Aeneid*'s plot (its *fabula*, as opposed to the beginning of the story in book 1) with the last night of Troy, when Aeneas is invested as founder of a new order willed by Fate, springs from the very heart of the *Iliad*. There the end of Troy was only an expectation and could be foreseen only in the form of a future tense: ἔσσεται ἦμαρ ὅτ᾽ ἄν ποτ᾽ ὀλώλῃ Ἴλιος ἱρή ('a day will come in which the holy city of Troy shall be destroyed') is the sorrowful prophecy delivered by Hector to Andromache at the Scaean gates (6.448). When the destruction of Troy is realized in the *Aeneid*, the future of the prophecy takes the form of completed action: *venit summa dies et ineluctabile tempus | Dardaniae* ('the last day and inescapable fate of Troy has come' 2.324–5), where the perfect tense declares the fulfilment of these expectations. In taking up the prophetic words of Homer's Hector, Virgil closes and completes the *Iliad*: the *Aeneid* programmatically defines itself as a fulfilment of Homer's text, its *anaplerosis*,[17] to use the expresssion of the ancient Homeric commentators, who discussed the function of the *Odyssey* in these terms, as a continuation and completion of the *Iliad*. Aeneas will move from the ruins of defeat (that is, from the full and completed ending of the *Iliad*) towards a new beginning.

Macrobius surely understood the complexity of Virgilian *imitatio*, if he could talk of a way of composing *de Homeri speculo* (*Sat.* 5.2.13). Did he mean merely to refer to the reprising of individual words and phrases? Or to the retrieval of sacrosanct material and atmosphere? Or did he mean that Virgil was appropriating rules of genre and codification? Long before the Augustan age, Latin literary practice had absorbed the emulatory technique of Hellenistic allusion (*Mitspielen*), but a critic using the simple terms of Alexandrian *zelos* would not understand much about the *Aeneid*.[18] The game of emulation would not suffice to account for the compulsive power of Homer's mastery, 'mother' and 'nurse' of Virgil, to borrow the expressive words which Dante so many centuries later applied to his own kinship with the *Aeneid*.[19]

[17] Here I repeat the substance of what I wrote in Conte (1992c).

[18] Cf. Barchiesi (1984), 93–5.

[19] In this connection we cannot fail to recall the famous remarks of that great romance philologist Gianfranco Contini, 'Dante come personaggio-poeta della "Commedia" ', in Contini (1970), 335–61.

More than just a literary text, the Homeric poems were a monument for Virgil: however remote, indeed precisely because of his remoteness, Homer is an authority. We could say, to use a banal expression, that for Virgil Homer is the quintessence of all that we understand by the term 'classical', an author given authority by the precious labour of an entire culture that has continually been forced to measure itself against him, and by the daily toil of the school, which has sanctioned his paradigmatic value by using him as the basis for every level of instruction. To be a classic, indeed, to be the classic text *par excellence*, meant that readers could extract from Homer immutable examples, always finding them verified in their own diverse experiences. For Virgil, to contemplate Homer was not to confront an enduring and well-preserved survivor, but to seek the company of one who had reached the goal before him. Through his peculiar way of imitating Homer, Virgil ascended to the same heights, he made himself into a literary monument, a new classic.

Thus Virgil did not limit himself to the showcasing, glossing, and variation of memorable Homeric phrases, as had been the practice of the schools and commentators and to a certain extent even of a modern Homerid like Apollonius.[20] Virgil produces his own Homeric text, imposing the same authoritative aspect, the same lapidary diction on all his utterances. He borrows from Homer the linguistic gesture needed to give himself authority. Even where Homer used a seemingly quiet tone, Virgil needs a solemn grandeur, a sublime intensification, as a vehicle for the text of his model. The canonical power of the model required that the *imitator* should be *Homerikotatos*, 'as Homeric as possible', in order to embody him in a new voice. Virgil seems to have known that he would be immediately compared to Homer, and therefore knew he had all the less time to establish himself as a classic.

Let us consider an example of this pointed intensification. Odysseus proudly introduces himself to the Phaeacians, but he speaks with the calm and innocent objectivity of someone presenting his credentials by way of identification (*Odyssey* 9.16 ff.): 'So I will tell my name so that you too may know it [...] I am Odysseus, son of Laertes, known to men for all my wiles, and my renown rises to

---

[20] See on this whole question the excellent work of Fantuzzi (1988).

heaven.' But when Aeneas presents himself at the beginning of the
Aeneid, he needs to add to the Odyssean model a pathetic note of
epigraphic solemnity, in order to express adequately his destiny of
past suffering and future responsibility (*Aeneid* 1.378–9): *sum pius
Aeneas, raptos qui ex hoste Penatis | classe veho mecum, fama super
aethera notus* ('I am pious Aeneas, who carry with me in my fleet the
gods snatched from the enemy, and my fame is known above the
heavens'). Virgil chooses a lofty voice for his text, a memorable tone,
something to give his words the same *auctoritas* as a classic. Linguistically he already aspires to be a classic. His words, even from a
stylistic point of view, show that his paradigm is the imperious
grandeur of Homer.

In this sense Homer bears for Virgil a value and function completely different from that of other epic predecessors, whether the
Alexandrians and Apollonius, or the poets of Roman historical epic.
Among such secondary influences I include even Ennius himself,
although he is an indispensable model for the elaboration of a
Roman national character, and it is true that Ennius is a primary
ingredient in the distillation of an idiom, such as that of the *Aeneid*,
that seeks to synthesize an archaic colouring within a stylistic mixture at once modern, noble, and elevated. For Virgil, to rediscover
Homer meant above all rediscovering the epic code itself; but his
ambition was not to imitate Homer in the sense of creating his
double, but rather to reformulate him so that the new work *replaced*
Homer's work according to the needs of his own time. This is why the
intertextuality that binds the *Aeneid* to the Homeric poems is constitutive, structural, inherent, coeval with its conception, coexistent
with the process of composition.

In previous work I have distinguished the different functions of
the intertextual relationship that binds Virgil to Homer in terms of
an exemplary model and a code-model.[21] That is, on the one hand
there was the Homer who is ready made, unsurpassable, complete,
needing only to be imitated; but there is also the Homer who is a
guide to behaviour, an eye that observes new facts 'Homerically',
Homer as the category and genre of epic writing. Homer is not
only the repertory of types, but a grammar capable of generating

---

[21] See especially Conte (1981), 148–50.

on each occasion a new *analogon*, a correlative that on each occasion is individually distinct but also similar in nature.

Imitari Homerum is a compositional practice functioning at every level of the text, from the most extended structures to the most minute details; it is like an internal form generating from itself every external form of the discourse. Virgil, for example, avoids the formulaic use of the Homeric epithet, but reserves for his protagonist Aeneas a small constellation of fixed epithets which sets the hero apart from other characters and so composes a quasi-formulaic system: *pater Aeneas, pius Aeneas, Troius Aeneas*. The reader can recognize a Homeric styleme in this, an index of his manner, but he is also led to see in it a sign of a particular status reserved for the protagonist.[22]

Starting at the most elementary level of Virgil's Homericity, let us linger over another pseudo-formulaic aspect. In epic diction like that of Virgil, which no longer depends on the functional use of stereotypical formulae and recurring lines,[23] the reader is struck by the

---

[22] On Virgilian formularity, Moskalew (1982) is accurate and often acute in interpretation.

[23] Certain sequences can be repeated even in Virgil as quasi-fixed structures, especially in the repetition of typical scenes (speeches, battles, deaths of heroes, conventionalized similes, etc.). I noted in Conte (1974*a*), 42 n. 26, that at times it is a matter of short cola of one or two words, at other times of hemistichs and even whole lines or pairs of lines (e.g. *Aen.* 10.745 f. = 12.309 f.). In a way distinct from that of the Homeric poems, their function is not connected with the modular requirements of oral composition, but is a procedure aiming to restore a mark of style. Indeed it sometimes seems that Virgil is afraid of the presence in his modern poetry of an unmotivated formular composition and seeks somehow to give even this procedure a function in the new dramatic purpose of his poetic art. Thus certain details are repeated, and motivated, each reclaiming the other as internal to the work, as samples of a strong consciousness of unity, as structural articulations that set the action in motion again or signal a significant reversal of the narrative situation. The case of 1.100–1 is exemplary … *ubi tot Simois correpta sub undis | scuta virum galeasque et fortia corpora volvit* ('where the waters of Simois will turn over so many bodies of heroes and shields and helmets') when compared with 8.538 ff. *quas poenas mihi Turne dabis! quam multa sub undas | scuta virum galeasque et fortia corpora volves | Thybri pater!* ('how you will have to pay for your savagery at my hands, Turnus! What brave bodies of heroes and shields and helmets your waters will turn over, O father Tiber!'). Cf. *Iliad* 12.22–3 καὶ Σιμόεις, ὅθι πολλὰ βοάγρια καὶ τρυφάλειαι | κάππεσον ἐν κονίῃσι καὶ ἡμιθέων γένος ἀνδρῶν· ('The Simois, where many shields and crests will fall in the dust and the race of heroes half-divine'). In the two Virgilian passages the verse is not repeated with a stereotypical formulaic function: it is enough to see how the second context is constructed as a mirror image and reversal

invention of unique linguistic combinations (this is how I describe single unrepeated structures) which seem to reproduce the appearance of a Homeric formula, but without being calqued on some precise formulaic phrase already to be found in the model. These are the pervasive and ubiquitous details of Homeric stylization, clausulae constructed by analogy that behave outwardly like formulae because they mimic the simple and bare objectivity found in the paratactic appositions which Homer often uses to round off a sequence ('his knees were slackened', 'death seized him'). I refer to such narrative tags as *fessos sopor inrigat artus* (3.511; cf. 2.253 *sopor fessos complectitur artus*) or *pugna aspera surgit* (9.677) or again *Teucri clamore secuntur* (9.636).[24] When the function of the formulaic system has been lost, its stylistic character remains, because it has been shaped to preserve a marked feature of the model—and the will to create a worthy match guarantees that the Homeric atmosphere penetrates the new text.

I have argued that Virgil expected his readers to consider the *Aeneid* as a modern work by Homer.[25] The evocation of this very distant model would have guaranteed a synthesis between the new

of the first. Here is the first context: in 1.90 a threatening thunderclap explodes in the sky during the storm with which Aeolus is trying to destroy the Trojan fleet; in 94–9 there follow the desperate laments of Aeneas, who invokes the bravest of his Greek opponents (*O Danaum fortissime gentis | Tydide*) as the man who should have killed him: thus Aeneas would have died as a warrior, in battle on the plains of Troy, where (100 ff.) 'the Simois overturns the corpses of so many heroes'. In the second case, in perfect parallel, the same triadic structure returns, but is reversed as a positive sign. Now Aeneas—such is the will of Fate—is not a defeated man as he was then, but prepares to become the victor. In 8.523–9 the thunderclap explodes in a clear sky (this is the *signum faustum* of divine favour); then there follow his words of triumphant defiance, calling on Turnus, chief of the new enemies (*Turne, dabis*) as responsible for the many deaths which the Tiber, a new Simois (but this time a benevolent father), 'will overturn in his waters' (538–9). The mechanical formula of the inner ear has become an intratextual allusion. And the new Aeneas is to be found entirely in the suggested opposition.

[24] Cf. Conte (1983*a*) [translated as Ch. 8 below].

[25] The *Aeneid* even includes a sort of 'repetition' of Homer. For example, the war in Latium between the Trojans and Italians is often seen as a repetition of the war at Troy (see e.g. 6.89, 8.538–40, compared with 1.100 ff., on which see n. 23 above). But this is not a passive mirroring, the same unfortunate destiny; at the end, At the beginning of the Trojans are besieged and near death, as if they were condemned to repeat their unfortunate destiny; at the end, however, the Trojans are victors, and Aeneas kills Turnus, as Achilles killed Hector in the *Iliad*. In the new *Iliad* the Trojans are destined to win. One can see that the repetition is also a surpassing of Homer; war, with all its struggles and suffering, will

'sentimental' style and the (lost) *naïveté* of the archaic, between the freedom of the new critical reasoning and the apparently simple necessity of the mythical world of heroes, producing a new, richer and more complex unity. In fact Homer was also a restraint preventing the new affective style from becoming predominant, the best formal corrective to moderate the intrusive subjectivity of a sentimental and dramatic poetics.

Homeric stylization (at all levels of the text: the construction of the narration, the staging of the action, but also the transplanting of marked structures, epithets, paraformulaic combinations) was a sufficient foundation to save the new epic text from collapsing into nothing but a meditative voice, and of losing itself in purely emotional effects.

Homer, who represented the world with a kind of detached stability, helped Virgil to establish an ultimate objectivity—that objectivity which, reached as it is through contradictions, was so necessary to the author of a national epic poem if he also wanted to offer his addressees the image of a positive truth. Critical doubt could be aroused, but its corrosive influence had to be controlled: it was also necessary, up to a certain point, to provide answers to the questions by holding out a constructive and reassuring vision. If it was not possible simply to celebrate History, it was necessary to find some way of 'edifying' the reader by providing a connection to some positive example and to a sense of hope.

To the external observer the *Aeneid* seems like the story of a mission willed by Fate, thanks to which the foundation of Rome and its salvation by the hand of Augustus are made possible; thus myth and history are associated and become mutually interconvertible. Aeneas is the bearer of this fated mission, and the poet is the guarantor of the project; in this Virgil reclaimed the inheritance of the Roman historical epic, turning his poem into a national epic in which the entire community could see itself reflected and feel united. But the *Aeneid* is not exhausted by this project. Beneath the 'objective' level represented by Fate, whose mouthpiece is the poet himself,

---

not lead to destruction, but to the construction of a new unity. In the end Aeneas reclaims in himself the image of the victorious Achilles and above all that of Odysseus who conquers his native land after many ordeals, and restores peace there. For an acute and innovative consideration of the repetition of Homer in the *Aeneid* see Quint (1989) [= Quint (1993), 50–96].

move characters who themselves act 'subjectively' in opposition to Fate; the narrative undertakes to represent their sentiments and contemplate their various conflicting motivations.

Thus the structure of the text appears to become polycentric: since each individual claim as it surfaces seems always to offer itself as the unique point of view, it always resists and will not let itself be stifled by the superior will of Fate. In the Virgilian mode of understanding reality and reconstructing it in an artistic medium, many individual manifestations of consciousness come into being, each with its own right to exist; thus a structure is generated that contains different autonomous rights within it. Every partial truth seeks to establish a standard of comparison, polarizes contradictions around itself and measures itself against the absolute truth (to succumb tragically in due course). Thus the epic text, rendered polycentric and manifold, comes to assume the divided language of drama: even in an epically narrated history the confrontation of different rights will give the reader the experience of participation and suffering.[26]

[26] The discovery of a tragic dimension converges with the most vital thread of Virgilian criticism in this century. In his famous study *Virgils epische Technik* (Heinze (1915), 321 ff., 467 ff.; translated as Heinze (1993), 252 ff., 370 ff.), Richard Heinze identified the presence of the tragic element with the concrete influence of the great Athenian dramatists, but also introduced the fruitful idea that the entire narrative technique of the *Aeneid* was in fact a dramatization of Homeric material, not only in the compression with which Virgil conducted the action, impressing upon it a strong progressive dynamism, not only in that the narration proceeds articulated by scenes, but also because from the beginning of the poem strong tensions are built into the poem which demand solutions and thus instal into the poem a teleological move-ment dramatic in type. Other more historically motivated critics have identified the tragic feeling of the poem with the sympathy turned on the defeated and the irresolute (Aeneas) which would be a sort of tearing of the Augustan ideological veil. Anyone who like Pöschl (1977) sees the unifying element of the poem in its tragic component, makes it consist in the opposition between the sense of history (*Römer-tum*) and the eternal tribulation of the individual, a price paid in the historical and political dimension of the *Aeneid*. The war in Latium is tragic because it is virtually a 'civil war' (ibid. 128 f., a very happy formulation): this tendency finds itelf in agreement with Augustan policy, concerned with re-evaluating the Italian (as we see there is much compromise in this solution). In German studies of the post-war period the concept of the tragic is implicated with a discouraging generic aspect (bibliography in Wlosok (1976)). There is little gained, I think, by refining the concept through a pedantic application of the categories, themselves quite disputed, as articulated in Aristotle's *Poetics*. On these tendencies see the above-mentioned work of Wlosok, and also von Albrecht (1970): he argues that the *Aeneid* would pass through all the phases of the Aristotelian definition to dissipate itself in an unspe-cified *Metatragisches* that would be peculiarly Roman.

In the age of conquest Roman epic and national historiography alike had represented the Punic wars as a conflict of opposites: Roman identity founded itself on its great opposition to Carthage. The enemy was treacherous, cruel, luxury-loving, addicted to perverse rites. For Virgil, on the other hand, war with Carthage was not born of a *difference*; when traced back to the time of its origins, the war was created by an excessive and tragic love between *equals*. The words with which Dido advances her hospitality to Aeneas speak of their kinship in suffering (*Aeneid* 1.630) *non ignara mali miseris succurrere disco* ('knowing suffering I learn from it to aid those who suffer'). This is the new fruit produced by the grafting onto epic of the grand experiences of drama. Dido, who learns from her own suffering to feel compassion for another's misfortune, repeats for herself the tragic principle that had been sententiously formulated in the *parodos* of the *Agamemnon* (177): πάθει μάθος ('from suffering comes learning'); the pregnant sense of 'learning' is truly alive in the present, inchoative verb *disco*. Dido, the fellow of the Trojans in the great law of suffering, will be defeated by destiny (as Carthage too will be); yet the text opens itself up to her rights, welcomes them, lets the readers listen to them and make them their own, as far as is possible. At this point truth is entrusted to a point of view that is dramatic and sentimental.

The case of Turnus is no different. The war which Aeneas is waging in Latium is not seen as a necessary sacrifice. The peoples divided by war are from the beginning substantially *similar*, even neighbours; to accentuate this point Virgil even claims that the Trojans have Italian origins through their ancestor Dardanus: and in this sense Aeneas too, like Odysseus, is 'one who returns'. The war is a tragic error willed by demonic powers, and essentially a *fratricidal* war. Towards the end of the poem, a little before the conclusive duel between Aeneas and Turnus, the poet concentrates his sorrowful theodicy in a cry of protest (12.503–4) *Tanton placuit concurrere motu, | Iuppiter, aeterna gentis in pace futuras?* ('and did you wish, Jupiter, that peoples destined to live in eternal peace together should clash with such violent passion?'). The death of Turnus, prepared for by the death of Pallas, seems necessary, but Virgil does nothing to make this choice easy. Turnus is disarmed, wounded, and begs for mercy. Aeneas has learned from his father to defeat the proud and spare those who submit; Turnus is a proud hero (*superbus*) but now he is also *subiectus*.²⁷ The choice is a difficult one. Aeneas kills him only because, at this crucial moment, the sight of Pallas' baldric sends him into a fit of deadly rage, and he must become the avenger.²⁸ Thus in the last scene of the poem, the *pius* Aeneas resembles the terrible Achilles who exacts his vengeance on Hector, whereas the *Iliad* ended instead with an Achilles filled with pity, who discovered his own human kinship with Priam.

Virgil makes a heavy demand on his readers. They must appreciate the fated necessity of victory, and at the same time must not forget the reasoning of the defeated; they must view the world from a superior perspective (Jupiter, Fate, the omniscient narrator) and at the same time witness and participate in the sufferings of individuals; they must accept epic objectivity, which beholds from on high the great providential cycle of history, and at the same time accept tragic subjectivity, which reflects and matches against each other personal motives and relative truths. Once Homeric *naïveté* is lost Virgil is more free, but also more complex: the divided language of drama is paradoxically his instrument for attaining a modern synthesis, a new world order.

His hero, positive in his triumph as he is, does not live only by his glory and virtue, but is forced to absorb the trauma of victory and the subjugated rights of the defeated. He could not have won without destroying other men's rights, thus making himself to a degree like his own enemies. Epic, through its modern nature as 'poetry of pathos', has ended by equipping itself with conflicting registers. Now that truth is divided, epic language too has become double, and cannot any longer be simply representative of the 'real' world: it must also

²⁷ *Aen.* 12.930–1 *ille humilis supplex oculos dextramque precantem | protendens.* See the subtle note of Traina (1997), 185 in his commentary on *Aen.* 12: '*humilis*, "from the ground", takes up with a reversed direction from low to high, *ad terram* of 927, but the etymological denotation (*humilis... tractus est ab humo*, Serv. Dan. *ad Aen.* 4.255) doubles itself with typical Virgilian polysemy, by a psychic connotation, activated by *supplex*; the proud one "humiliates" himself to supplicate. Thus the reversal is achieved, as is the redemption of Turnus' ethos, which will make Aeneas' resolution more dramatic and conflictual.'

²⁸ Cf. Cicero, *De Invent.* 2. 65–6 *naturae quidem ius esse, quod nobis non opinio, sed quaedam innata vis adferat, ut religionem, pietatem, gratiam, vindicationem, observantiam, veritatem; [...] vindicationem per quam vim et contumeliam defendendo aut ulciscendo propulsamus a nobis et a nostris, qui nobis cari esse debent, et per quam peccata punimus.*

convey suppressed desires and ideals. No longer just the glories of the conqueror, but also the grievous cost of his self-affirmation.

This polyphonic method of composition also emerges from an analysis of the lesser characters who are apparently treated as victims. Juturna appears in the poem in a subordinate role, as an intermediary between Juno and events on earth: her intervention at Turnus' side is to all appearances a copy of Apollo's appearance in *Iliad* 22, and echoes its failure. But in Homer Apollo abandons Hector in silence at the moment when his destiny has been weighed and sanctioned on Olympus. In the parallel situation Juturna is granted the narrative space for a monologue before she disappears (12.869–86), to blend her lament for her brother (who is paralysed by the Dira and cannot hear her) with protest against the commands of Jupiter, which naturally goes unheard. Her dramatic monologue assumes a perspective that is not only incompatible with the vision of Fate, but is openly critical of the traditional status of divinities. The gods are more wretched than mortals because they suffer just like them but cannot die (879–84 *quo vitam dedit aeternam? cur mortis adempta est | condicio? possem tantos finire dolores | nunc certe et misero fratri comes ire per umbras! | Immortalis ego? ... | ... O quae satis ima dehiscat | terra mihi Manisque deam demittat ad imos?* 'Why did he grant me eternal life? Why have I been deprived of the right to die? If only I could now, at least, put an end to my grief and follow my poor brother through the shadows! I immortal? ... Oh, what depth of earth could gape low enough for me and send a goddess down to the deepest shades?'). Here is a voice that cannot be reconciled with the ideological horizon of the poem.[29]

The polyphony of the *Aeneid* is constructed out of different points of view set alongside each other and kept distinct, partial affirmations of truth received within the text in order to complicate its fundamentally edifying vision. The individual characters, as they advance their own versions of truth, oppose themselves to a principal character, Aeneas; he for his part is unable to give way to the personal conflicts of the tragic genre, because he is forced to be the executor of Fate, and Fate, being the destiny of the world, is not open to challenge

---

[29] See the fine interpretation of Barchiesi (1978), Lyne (1987), 86–7, 139–44, O'Hara (1990), 114–16, and Perkell (1997).

from particular individuals. The point of view of Fate is superior, and operates from an exterior and suprapersonal plane; it does not allow itself to be tested, but triumphs over everything and everyone, while staying out of the conflict, without submitting to assessment. As a providential nexus of causes, Fate is a cosmic necessity, and at every moment of history it refers men to a predestined and immutable other world, an other world hostile to anyone not directly summoned to its service.

Republican epic and national historiography (for all that it was threaded through with critical pessimism) had put at the heart of its providential vision precisely this suprapersonal character of Fate: Rome accomplished her historic mission under the benevolent guidance of *fata deum*. Virgil reclaims this constitutive feature of the Roman cultural tradition, but he relativizes it within a picture composed of different perspectives. The resultant image is split into a multiplicity of fragments, as many as the individual visions—differing rights and truths—received into the text.

In order to reclaim from the depths of history these individual rights crushed by the burden of Fate, Virgil knows that he cannot provide an easy reconciliation in his final vision; these individual rights are welcomed into the text, find a space and an audience, but cannot be integrated into it. The non-integration of Dido, of Turnus, as well as of Mezentius and Juturna, the tenacity with which each of them resists until the end, maintaining a personal point of view in the text, signifies the impossibility of integrating individuals who claim to keep themselves undiminished and fully autonomous. Only at the last moment does Turnus show some willingness to acknowledge a model of behaviour other than that dictated to him by his own unbridled heroic individualism; but Aeneas does not answer this request for reconciliation, since, under an overwhelming obligation of *pietas*, he is forced to assume the role of the priest who sacrifices the victim and carries out the rite of punishment: *Pallas te hoc volnere, Pallas | immolat et poenam scelerato ex sanguine sumit* ('Pallas sacrifices you with this blow, Pallas, and exacts the penalty from your criminal blood' 12.946–7).[30]

---

[30] Note the brilliant observations on the killing of Turnus as a sacrificial act in Hardie (1993), 32–5. On the theme of sacrifice in the *Aeneid* see also Bandera (1981), O'Hara (1990), 19–24, 28–35, 82–4, 106–10 [also Hardie (1993), 33–4 and Dyson (2001)].

Even in the Underworld, after her death, when Aeneas tries to show Dido that the law of grief unites all men in the face of the superior reasoning of Fate, she wraps herself in silence and does not abandon the absolute assertion of her own rights (6.469 f.). It is possible that Virgil condemns the unilateral and exclusive passion of all the figures enclosed in their own proud isolation; but, as a sign of its own dramatic tendencies, the *Aeneid* does not conceal the grievous cost of the need to condemn the individual passions which clash with the ideological design of the poem; to reject them, to be forced to exclude them, is a serious deprivation. While he champions his own constructive vision of the world, Virgil takes on the burden of showing at the same time what human values must be painfully sacrificed to found and defend it. Besides all the *immaturi* who die in the poem there are many lesser shades who demand a reply from the poet: Laocoon and his sons, Ripheus (*iustissimus qui fuit unus*), Creusa, Palinurus, and others. The poet answers them all by constructing a text in which the contradictions are not evaded, still less smoothed over, but are instead left as open wounds, like a scandal that cries out to be dealt with. From this desire is born the hope of a world that does not yet exist.

We have alluded to the providentialism of Fate, to the strength of its inescapable and predestined truth. The Virgilian narrative, as we have just said, allows itself to be permeated by the subjectivity of individuals and adapts itself to represent their sentiments and take on their individual points of view. However, it anchors every criterion for judgement in the external objectivity of Fate, the historic destiny that measures everything and everyone. I wish to stress that such objectivity not only guarantees the poem's unity of design, but above all prevents the epic form from collapsing into drama.

In fact the Virgilian text, in order to increase its aesthetic and literary power, multiplies subjective points of view and gives a voice to conflicting rights. But in doing so it runs the risk of creating a dialectic that would be disruptive if it were not kept under control. The aspects of doubt and ambivalence would end up by dominating, and the narrative would become a dramatic clash of opposing rights, which would undermine the positive drive that makes the *Aeneid* into an epic poem. The *Aeneid* aimed to make itself the Bible of the

Roman people, and so had to celebrate the foundation of the cultural values which defined Roman national identity. Virgil, the epic poet so marked by the power of tragic poetry, could not make too many concessions to the structural pressure of the dramatic form. He could make room for dialectic between points of view, but on condition that they remained subordinate to an epic objectivity; he had to correct the effects of their fragmentation and provide a reunifying and positive vision. The universal dominion of Fate guaranteed a criterion of reference from outside the text, an ultimate, objective, absolute criterion.

Criticism over the last century (Heinze, Klingner, Otis) has established that Virgilian narrative opens itself stylistically to two equally significant modifications of epic objectivity. One of these is the 'subjectivity' of the poet who projects himself into the text, openly intervening with his own affective participation. The other is the product of subjective interpenetration (identification) between character and narrator. By this means the narrative appears to be saturated with the sentiments of individual characters in action; there is fusion rather than distance between the representation of characters and their own perception of the events in which they are involved. The first modification may be labelled *sympatheia*, the second *empatheia*.[31] For the most part, Virgilian criticism has been tempted to see in these two stylistic coefficients (different forms of subjectivity) two functions of one and the same expressive requirement: the one working in harmony with the other.

I believe that this has the effect of concealing from us the extraordinary difference between, on the one hand, the narrative style of Apollonius Rhodius and Latin epyllion (Catullus 64, and the Aristaeus epyllion in *Georgics* 4) and, on the other, that of the *Aeneid*. It is usually supposed that the form of Virgilian narration can be explained as an intensification of Alexandrian and neoteric subjective

---

[31] Heinze defined the first as 'Subjektivität', the latter as 'Empfindung'. Klingner (1967), 434, 451, and *passim*, talks of 'lyric insertions' to indicate 'Subjektivität', a rather inexact definition, which reveals its idealistic origins, dominated by the generic definition of all poetry of emotion (indeed of all poetry) as 'lyric'. Brooks Otis followed this path (Otis (1964), 49–52, 61–92, and *passim*), and rendered 'Subjektivität' by 'sympathy', and 'Empfindung' by 'empathy'. The term 'empathy' draws on the idea of identification with the thing represented which has had so much importance in studies of the psychology of art (see e.g. Wörringer (1975)). The problem is discussed more fully in Conte (1984*a*), 80–6.

technique. But resemblances in the superficial form of expression should not blind us to the significant differences in the construction of the narrative in the *Aeneid*. The process of 'sentimentalization' set in motion by Virgil cuts deep into the flesh of the text, and is no superficial colouring of the discourse, as in Apollonius and Catullus. The empathy of Virgilian narration, penetrating to the deepest levels of the dense text, determines the significance of his representation by giving form to the personality of different characters. Their subjectivities, free to display themselves as competing rights, are not skin-deep colouring of the narrative but affirmations of truth offered to the reader, affirmations seeking autonomous existence and aiming on each occasion to impose themselves with dramatic power. Here I use 'dramatic power' in its proper sense, referring to the opposition offered by each of these subjectivities to the ideological horizon of the poem. The multiplication of points of view, relativizing the absolute and objective view of the epic and historical tradition, enriches the *Aeneid* with problematic connotations, but undermines its epic quality and renders uncertain the nature of a work intended for collective edification. In fact a picture emerges of a world dissolved into autonomous fragments, as many as the partial truths that present themselves as potential adversaries to the order and positive meaning of the poem.

But there is a force opposing this pressure towards disunity, a force capable of correcting and diminishing it, so that the fractured elements can be reassembled. This is *sympatheia*, the mode of intervention based on the omniscience of the author and narrator, which upholds the *Aeneid*'s epic mission. Only the author knows the whole story he is telling and knows how to interpret its future perspective; only he, who has set out in his text all the incompatibility of these contradictions, can recognize in the hidden purpose of Fate the faint outline of hope and can simultaneously suggest a final meaning that will reconcile the divergent voices accepted into the text. If the disruptive elements opposing the fixity of the traditional epic vision were necessary to reconstitute the genre by reopening it to a freer capacity for meaning, it was also necessary to hold them restrained in a hierarchy of truth under the control of the author.

In this way the new articulation of contents is moulded into a form that is essentially a new form of epic. At the end of this combined process of decomposition and recomposition, the meaning of the text rediscovers its objective foundation, entrusted to the direct responsibility of the poet, that is, to his *sympatheia*. Thus the poet's affective participation in his narrative, while it presents itself as a subjective mode, paradoxically becomes the means of reconstructing objectivity, though it is a new kind of objectivity; the author refers every event he narrates to himself, to his own sensibility but also to his own authority, and makes himself the objective consciousness to which the different individual truths are related. A unifying axis of ideology, the poet with his gesture of *sympatheia* offers himself as an instrument powerful enough to redirect to an objective goal each of the subjectivities aroused in the text by his empathetic narrative.

Certainly the epic of Apollonius Rhodius and the narrative technique of the Latin epyllion were strongly tinged with subjective colouring; the poet's proximity to the narrated action had greatly reduced the distance that had made the Homeric model impersonal and detached. Their narration made room for the author and his affectivity, it even encompassed his gestures of excited participation. From the very first verses of the *Argonautica* the poet's *persona* shapes itself as a pervasive and strong presence: Ἀρχόμενος σέο Φοῖβε παλαιγενέων κλέα φωτῶν | μνήσομαι ('Beginning from you, Apollo, I shall record the famous deeds of men of old' 1.1). This is Apollonius' way of announcing that 'this is not Homer',[32] and when after many lines he mentions the Muses, it is obvious that they are no longer the source of inspiration but merely collaborators in the song which is under way.[33]

The relationship between narrator and audience now comes into the foreground. Jealously possessive of his leading role, Apollonius seldom agrees to abdicate it; in comparison with the Homeric model he reduces the frequency of direct speech and instead enhances the control of the narrating voice: he does not like to hand over the speaking role to his characters, but instead seems to award himself the space that he has taken from the agents in the episode he is narrating. Sometimes he apostrophizes them directly, at other times he intrudes his own judgement on their actions or their destiny (e.g. 1.616–19;

---

[32] Hunter (1993), 172.   [33] Cf. Faedo (1970).

1.1302–3; 2.65–6; 2.1028–9; 3.1133–4; 4.915–16; 4.1524–5). He does not hide his own bitter conception of existence but incorporates it into the narrative. Sometimes by using the associative first person plural he makes himself one of the great number of suffering mortals (2.541–3; 4.1165–7), even giving full vent to his own feelings when, in a combined evocation of the lyric and tragic traditions, he hurls his own apostrophe against destructive Eros (4.445–59). Often he declares himself openly and puts himself in place of the characters, so that the narrative 'I' steals their words and prevents their subjectivities from expanding too much within the text; he dominates and controls, a fellow participant, but really absolute master.

Above all the frequent intrusion of the narrator's *persona* attests a strong and confrontational poetic self-consciousness, and imposes a single strong point of view.[34] On the other hand Virgil, even when he alludes to Apollonius, radically transforms his model, allowing the sentiments of the characters in the action to invade the text. Consider in this respect the invective against Eros just cited (4.445–9):

Σχέτλι' Ἔρως, μέγα πῆμα, μέγα στύγος ἀνθρώποισιν,
ἐκ σέθεν οὐλόμεναί τ' ἔριδες στοναχαί τε γόοι τε,
ἄλγεά τ' ἄλλ' ἐπὶ τοῖσιν ἀπείρονα τετρήχασιν·
δυσμενέων ἐπὶ παισὶ κορύσσεο δαῖμον ἀερθείς
οἷος Μηδείῃ στυγερὴν φρεσὶν ἔμβαλες ἄτην

(wretched Love, great grief and loathing of mankind: | from you arise mortal struggles, | groans and suffering and again endless sorrows. | Come armed to the children of my enemies, Lord, as you thrust hateful ruin in the heart of Medea).

Virgil closely follows Apollonius, his dominant model throughout the fourth book, but he writes with a different intonation (4.412–14):

improbe Amor, quid non mortalia pectora cogis!
ire iterum in lacrimas, iterum temptare precando
cogitur, et supplex animos submittere amori.

What matters is not so much that Virgil, out of a sense of the sublime and a taste for decorum, omits Apollonius' exploitation of

---

34 On point of view in Apollonius see e.g. Fusillo (1985), 347–59, Knight (1995), index s.v. 'focalization'; on the relative incidence of direct speech and of poetic intervention in Apollonius see Farrell (1997).

the chance to vent his personal resentment against his enemies. Far more significant is the fact that Virgil, in expressing his pity for Dido,[35] allows the torment of her emotions to emerge directly in the text: 'pitiless Love, is there anything which you do not force upon mortal hearts? Dido is driven to melt again in tears, to try him again beseeching him, and to submit her proud spirit to love in supplication.' The repetitive structure, consisting of descriptive theme and successive pathetic variations, first presents the character framed in her exterior actions (tears and beseeching), and is then suffused with an overwhelming *empatheia*, as it foregrounds the queen's interiority (her feelings of pride and humiliation). Now that the narrative perspective has been entrusted to Dido's point of view, as if she were an actor moving on the tragic stage, only her own words, addressed to her sister Anna, can be allowed to emerge.

The narrated action is directly conveyed by the character. Similarly, a few lines later (450 f.) the representation is directed entirely from Dido's point of view, as she is tortured by terrible and grievous visions (453 *vidit*, 456 *visum*), anguished nightmares like those—the poet himself says so explicitly—that pursue the maddened Pentheus and Orestes on the tragic stage. Then comes her *Trugrede* to her sister Anna (478 *inveni, germana, viam—gratare sorori*, 'sister, I have found the way—share my relief'), the speech which enables her to hide her intention of suicide (550 *praetexere funera*), just as in the Sophoclean play[36] the hero Ajax chose to hide behind calm and confident words his decision to redeem his humiliation through suicide.

There then follow two authentically tragic rheseis. *Empatheia* takes over to the extent of making the text assume the actual form of drama, as Dido's feelings impose themselves with such violence that the narrated action necessarily becomes direct discourse. The second and final *rhesis* ends immediately before Dido drives the fatal blow into her breast, with the lament *felix, heu nimium felix, si litora tantum | numquam Dardaniae tetigissent nostra carinae* ('happy, alas, too happy, if only the Trojan vessels had never touched our shores': 4.657–8)—a lament that significantly repeats the lines which

---

[35] On authorial interventions in Virgilian narration see G. Williams (1983), ch. 7 'The Poet's Voice'.
[36] Cf. Lefèvre (1978).

open the *Medea* of Euripides: Εἴθ' ὤφελ' Ἀργοῦς μὴ διαπτάσθαι σκάφος | Κόλχων ἐς αἶαν ('Would that the Argo had never winged its way to the land of the Colchians ...' 1–2). In order to signal his imposition of a dramatic register, Virgil makes direct contact with the great tragic model; if Apollonius' Medea inspired Virgil's Dido, it is now the fierce grandeur of Euripides' Medea which prompts the last speech of the humiliated Carthaginian queen. At the same time there is an echo of Ennius' reworking of Euripides in his *Medea Exul*,[37] but it is Catullus, through the pathetic lament of the abandoned Ariadne, who puts his verbal imprint on Dido's words,[38] even if the queen's farewell gains its great pathetic intensity above all thanks to the original expressive figure, which we might call a '*makarismos manqué*', *felix, heu nimium felix*. Such is the cry of lamentation of the heroine so pointedly characterized in the poem by the quasi-formulaic epithet *infelix Dido*.

In short, the *empatheia* generated by the subjectivity of Virgilian characters is very different from the affective and psychological colouring typical of Alexandrian and neoteric poetry. Indeed in the *Aeneid* it determines a new configuration of epic discourse. Virgilian *empatheia* is not just a pose of the narrative surface to generate pathos, but rather a bold appropriation of the fractured and confrontational language of drama. The subjectivity of Virgilian characters introduces into the narrative a corresponding number of points of view, which constantly strive to take possession of the text, and so constantly endanger, with their dissociating effects, the objective vision which is at the base of epic narrative. From time to time the various characters—not just Dido and Turnus, but Andromache, Deiphobus, Palinurus, Amata, Evander, Mezentius, Juturna—claim the right to see events from their own point of view: each and every one of them demands that his or her own claims, once welcomed into the text, triumph over every other claim; but all that is granted to them is to express their grief at their inevitable defeat.

Empatheia is a feature that permeates the entire Virgilian narrative: for example, if we analyse a typically epic narrative structure such

---

[37] Enn. *Scaen.* 246–54 Vahlen (=208–18 Jocelyn) *utinam ne in nemore Pelio securibus* | *caesa accidisset abiegna ad terram trabes* ... (but see Jocelyn's comments ad loc.).
[38] Catull. 64.171–2 *utinam ne tempore primo* | *Gnosia Cecropiae tetigisset litora puppes*.

as that of the duel and compare Homer's technique of representation with Virgil's, it becomes obvious that even here *empatheia* has the power to condition the form of representation itself. In Virgil, perception of the phases of the duel is focalized through the eyes of the defeated; that is, the defeated party is allowed to orchestrate the scene of his defeat from his own point of view (10.439–509).[39] It is the defeated warrior (and not the victor, as in Homer) who speaks last and thus, through his words, makes himself the active subject and interpreter of his own death (10.833–908).[40]

In conclusion, *empatheia* in Virgil not only relates to the form of expression, but also affects the form of the contents of the poem. But its effects cannot be reduced to the same level of the text as that at which the *sympatheia* of the narrator functions. As different forms of narrative subjectivity the *empatheia* of the characters and the *sympatheia* of the narrator are genetically and functionally distinct factors, destined to work in opposite directions. While the empathetic multiplication of points of view generates a dramatic structure in which individual subjectivities fragment the text as they emerge in their various affirmations of truth, the *sympatheia* of the omniscient narrator is able to relate each fragment to the objectivity of a unitary vision. The sympathetic 'sentimentality' of the poet is certainly an act of solidarity with the many defeated figures in his poem, but above all it is an instrument of cohesion and a measure of judgement. The poet himself acts as guarantor of the existence of a truth above and beyond the individual. If the providence that rules history is blind, the gaze of the poet is able to see everything from on high, and every intervention on his part is an act of direct responsibility, a reminder directed at the individual characters—and at the reader—with the end of ensuring that every doubt receives acknowledgement and partial satisfaction. His *sympatheia* functions as a continuous element of contact with the epic addressee, an addressee who is in need of a vision with a single unifying meaning and who seeks a positive and constructive whole.

This final vision the epic poet is in a position to vouchsafe, but he also wants his reader to know the cost of historical providence, and not to forget how many personal truths must be sacrificed for the

---

[39] See Bonfanti (1985), 46–51.   [40] Cf. Conte (1984*a*), 143.

fulfilment of Fate. Now that the text has opened itself also to the possibility of doubt, the reader is led to ask questions in dramatic terms about the rights of the excluded. What the poet offers his reader is not a detached response, but one that comes with the experience of suffering: he too pays the price of grief in offering his own compassion. Even his Aeneas, in order to act as the agent of destiny, must pay a price: as one character among many he too is, at the end, overwhelmed just like the others; as protagonist and executor of Fate he has to suppress his doubts and personal desires.[41] He too must accept the law that the destiny of a people is paid for by the destiny of individuals.

---

[41] As I tried to show in Conte (1986*a*), 173–82, the figure of Aeneas has a double literary status in the text. Like every other character Aeneas has a personal and limited point of view, but he is also the representative of the will of Fate, executor of that cosmic will which suffocates the rights of individuals (and so also the subjective rights of Aeneas). In short, Aeneas fulfils two functions in the text: he is a character, possessor of a personal voice and a relative truth, but also the protagonist, bearer of an absolute and objective truth. Thus the vehicle of Fate's constructive will sometimes shows his personal features (as a character) marked by uncertainty and doubt, but he is also forced to shed his identity and repress his own subjectivity to take on his mission instead. As a character Aeneas can recover his subjective personality only by seeking a different dimension from that of Fate, but to do this he has to withdraw and turn back to the past. If he attempted to look in the future for paths other than those imposed by Fate, he would betray his own elect status, and merely live a life like his own memories, something only possible before he was called from on high. See *Aen.* 1.340–4 *me si fata meis paterentur ducere vitam | auspiciis et sponte mea componere curas, | urbem Troianam primumque dulcisque meorum | reliquias Compositor Name: RaKarthik colerem, Priami tecta alta manerent, | et recidiva manu posuissem Pergama victis.* Aeneas is unlike the other characters of the poem in the mission that has fallen upon him (and in this respect close to Fate and the omniscient narrator), but not unlike them in the defeat which his personal 'I' must undergo.

[Author's final note in first English publication [Conte (1999*a*)]: 'My warmest thanks go to Elaine Fantham for once again translating my original and to Philip Hardie and the referee for helpful comment.']

3

Anatomy of a Style: Enallage and the New Sublime

Aesthetic criticism has been left behind by historical and scientific criticism: it lacked the foundations. The knowledge that it is missing is the *anatomy of the style.*

Gustave Flaubert*

SOME writers write only in order to communicate; others are also creators of language—*Sprachschöpfer,* as the great German Romantics called them. Simplifying greatly, we could say that the former make linguistic expression a means, the simple vehicle for a discourse which considers itself neutral and referential, while the latter make linguistic expression an end, the instrument which makes the essence of language itself perceptible, almost tactile, and thereby intensifies its effects upon the reader.

For the former group, linguistic expression functions transitively: it acts in such a way that the words serve the thoughts and vanish into them, like transparent windows which let the light pass through them. For the latter, the expression has the capacity to become opaque, thick: it carries the thought but it also draws attention to itself, indeed it aims to double the force of the thought by adding its own reserve force, like a loyal shield-bearer who carries the hero's weapons but also wants to fight alongside him. The reader is captured by this agonistic use of language: he feels that he cannot limit himself to receiving inertly the discourse he is offered, but must in response commit himself to enhancing the possibilities of his

---

* *Correspondance: Nouvelle Edition Augmentée,* ed. Conard (Paris, 1926–33), III. 336–7 (7 Sept. 1853).

own language, that he must adapt his own linguistic potential symmetrically to the author's, colluding with him in combating the insufficiencies and lethargy of everyday language.

More than many other Classical writers, Virgil is an exceptional *Sprachschöpfer*. I do not wish to recall only that Virgil is an inventor of new and effective words, or that he is a linguistic experimenter as Ennius or Plautus had been before him; I mean that, for him, what is capable of being thought almost manages to become capable of being felt, it materializes, taking on a body and shape. The expressivistic interpretation of the style of the *Aeneid* (and with it also the expressionistic one as well) supposes that writers make use of rhetorical procedures in order to speak better, that is, that they create in order to express. Virgil seems rather to do the opposite: he expresses in order to create, arrogating the power of redescribing reality and redefining the relations between the elements that represent it linguistically. Indeed it is unproductive for the critic to believe in the existence, in some conceptual limbo, of simple structures of language—be they lexical, morphological, or syntactical elements—from which the verbal construct concretized in the text would derive: the task of the philologist is not to search for a 'substance' (let us say, a naked and literal meaning) of which every linguistically complex formation would be an 'accident'. It is less legitimate for Virgil's text than for any other poetic work that it should be translated (one might say: reduced) by means of a periphrastic exercise based upon the formula 'Virgil meant to say this.' Had he wanted to say it, he would have.

The poet wants to communicate, but in order to do so he is obliged almost to obstruct his discourse so that it does not slip away like an immediately communicative act, but instead comes to a stop in the recipient's ear and mind, taking hold there without dissolving, as though it had become reified. The metre, the formal constraints, and the rhetorical audacities act as an impediment to communication, but only because they thus manage to valorize it fully: they alert the reader and let him play along, making him an active collaborator. The reader, in order to be able to perceive the meanings which the poetic discourse communicates, must traverse a distance, overcoming the obstacles which lessen the discourse's transparency. Obviously, it is only partially that the rhetorical function renders the meanings opaque. The poet certainly does not want to obscure entirely the referential values of his discourse; he only wants to suspend them all for the reader so that a new system of reference can be established. The reader is summoned to confront dialectically this particular new universe, which is composed of words but arrogantly aspires to a full existential alterity.

Virgil lets the poetic word reveal itself before it reveals things, and in this way he ends up circumscribing and establishing a defamiliarized space. Within it, new norms can become valid, and these norms will be not only linguistic but also ideological ones; new means can be insinuated into it, rendered possible and acceptable precisely because they are enclosed within a space created for that very purpose. To demarcate this special place, Virgil's poetic discourse gives itself its own rules: it uses ordinary language but manipulates it, stretching and deforming it, restructuring it so that it can foster the creation of a parallel and alternative world, one which can be fairly near the real one but can also compete with it. Here, new things (ideas, hopes, anxieties, provocations) can find a home, precisely because they are welcomed by a space within which the established norms have been temporarily suspended.

To define Virgil's style for the young students who attended his unforgettable seminars on the *Aeneid* in the 1960s in Munich, Friedrich Klingner liked to repeat a little formula which was the simple condensation of his long and intense experience as a leading Virgilian scholar: 'maximum freedom in maximum order'. All the words in this precept must be given a strong meaning if it is not to be reduced to a banal generality; it must be paraphrased more or less in this way: 'there is perhaps no other poet who is as capable of liberties and audacities which are integrated into a context as clear and balanced, made up of composure and of decorum'. This is what Klingner thought, as I well remember: and it would probably be easy to find traces of this view in some of his writings on Virgil.

But I think that Klingner also wanted to communicate to those of us who listened to him his admiration for one aspect of the style of the *Aeneid* which never ceased to astonish him: that Virgil managed to write a continuous narrative of almost ten thousand verses—an extended narration of events, descriptions of things and characters—while filling every verse with the very same creative tension which the author of a short and compressed lyric composition would have employed, charging the form of the expression with an immense accumulation of linguistic energy, indefatigably enhancing the effects of every component of the verbal, phonetic, and metrical texture. As a result, every single means of communication bears impressed upon it the constant participation of the poet's I in the narrative of the facts: a mental and emotional presence which is always alert, an active *sympatheia* which the author imposes upon himself and demands in response from his reader. And it is precisely here, I think, in the daring intensification of the language, that we see the most evident result of that 'maximum freedom' which, according to Klingner, is coupled in the style of Virgil with 'maximum order'.

That said, I nonetheless do not wish to reduce Virgil's style to the systematic activation of a series of expressive deviations which would function like calculated infractions with regard to a supposed norm (and then, what is a norm? is it what ought to be generally the case? and according to whom? or is a norm that which conforms to the majority of the cases?). In this way the poetic text would easily be transmuted into a collection of morphological and syntactic *monstra*, a set of surprising experiments, an *Ausdrucksdichtung* (poetry of expression) whose contents would risk being completely extinguished for the sake of the verbal form. The term 'deviation' is ambiguous in itself, and I think even infelicitous, if only because of its evident teratological implications.[1] On the other hand, are not the conventions of epic diction—which are in fact constitutive of literary language—and all the other constant structures typical of it themselves deviations, even if codified ones? With respect to these, every new deviation would thus be a deviation from deviations: and if we went along this path we would never stop, except perhaps at infinity.

And yet the notion of deviation can be useful, so long as we attribute a purely functional value to it. It can be useful, if only to help measure the distance the reader must travel in order to reach

---

[1] I made a similar observation in Conte (1974a), 58 n. 36. Cf. Gruppo μ (1976), 27 ff., 60 ff., a book which deserved a wider audience and closer attention: perhaps it was harmed by its taxonomic anxiety (to which, as a negative counterpart, a certain essentialist positivism is not foreign).

the 'proprium' after he has started out from the 'improprium', which
is nothing other than the defamiliarized form assumed by the
expression. But the two ends of the linguistic trajectory must not
be imagined as though they were two fixed entities, belonging to
two substantially different languages, but rather as the poles of a
symmetrical and variable relation, as vanishing points. The reader
grasps them together, perceives them as though they were co-present,
seeing at the very same moment both the deviation and the norm,
the 'improprium' and the 'proprium'. The language that produces
them is the very same one: it is only one; what differs is the gesture,
and for this reason the function that the poetic usage imposes upon
the language differs too.

All this is fairly obvious. Repeating it, however, may serve to lay
upon clear and simple foundations an analysis of Virgil's style which
I intend to be above all empirical (and which prefers to renounce
any more complex theoretical discussion). For my part, I consider
somewhat banal the criterion which opposes deviation and norm to
one another, but the advantages that it presents in functional terms
save it to some extent from banality.

Virgil is an exceptional *Sprachschöpfer* above all because of one
virtue of his style: he confines words under tension. To create his
effects, Virgil does not need an aggressive language, nor does he have
any use for too strongly marked rhetorical colours; the most ordinary
words suffice, but they are suffused with an energy which reinforces
their meanings. One ancient critic of Virgil (his extraordinary success
immediately earned him many such critics) accused him of being
'the inventor of a new kind of stylistic affectation, neither swollen nor
meagre, but based upon ordinary words and therefore surreptitious'
(*eum . . . appellabat novae cacozeliae repertorem, non tumidae nec
exilis, sed ex communibus verbis atque ideo latentis*).[2]

---

[2] Very important in this regard is Jocelyn (1979), an article which, though remarkable for its erudition and intelligence, is not convincing in its basic idea. Some
observations useful for our needs can be found in Görler (1979); but it seems
impossible that the judgement of the detractor (whether this was the great Vipsanius
Agrippa or the otherwise unknown grammarian Vipranius) might have been directed
at the *Georgics*, and even less at the *Bucolics*: the accusation of stylistic affectation, as it
was made by the detractor, was aimed at the systematic use of a poetic language made
of common words, a stylistic feature which no one could in any way have considered
out of place in a work like the *Georgics* (I disagree in particular with the judgement

We can trust the nigglers, their irritation always provides a useful hint. Usually they are not good judges, but their very prejudice sharpens their sensitivity: they notice and censure precisely those fine points which they fail to esteem. So too in this case. They recognized correctly the defamiliarized effects of the Virgilian style, they vaguely perceived in him the elaboration of a refined art made up of effective deviations and innovations, but they wanted nonetheless to criticize that way of writing because it seemed culpably refined, artificial ('cacozelia' implies above all an accusation of excess, of extremism, as though Virgil were being condemned for posturing). Their greatest annoyance arose from the fact that the affectation he was accused of was not something evident (*latentis*), it lacked the ostentatiousness typical of 'cacozelia' and the easy emphasis of swollen or unusual words, indeed the discourse made use of a familiar language, of 'ordinary words'. This was the novelty of Virgil's style, all the more insidious because it was concealed.

Traditional Aristotelian theory, rigorously systematized by Theophrastus, had based the poetic character of a text upon the *ekloge* of the words, a perspicacious selection which blended ordinary words and forms with those extraneous to the current language and with rhetorical figures (a mixture of *kyria* and *xenika onomata* [proper and foreign terms]) so as to create the 'defamiliarization' of the poetic discourse, the *xene dialektos* [strange idiolect]. Starting in the second half of the first century BC, in polemic with the Peripatetic tradition, the attention of critics and philologists moved away from *ekloge* towards *synthesis*, towards the composition and combination of the words: the work of Dionysius of Halicarnassus, entitled precisely Περὶ συνθέσεως ὀνομάτων, is said to have been greatly appreciated at Rome from the first years of the Augustan age.

In fact, already some representatives of Stoic thought had begun to theorize the perceptible nature of artistic beauty (in the preceding

---

expressed by D. A. Russell, p. 205 of the discussion following the paper by Görler). It must instead have seemed scandalously strange that for a heroic poem (entrusted traditionally to an elevated and wholly special language) a diction was chosen which was constructed with a wholly common lexicon, even if it was diverted towards a formal defamiliarization: indeed, no one could have been scandalized by a king's being dressed in ermine and a peasant in rags.

century, particular distinction had been gained by Crates of Mallos, the *kritikos* of Pergamon who polemicized against the arid *grammatikoi* who were capable only of making classifications);[3] but Dionysius was certainly the first one to identify in the concreteness of verbal *synthesis* the aesthetic factor which reaches the reader's (or better: the listener's) soul and inflames his emotions.[4] The beauty of a poetic text is caused not by the *kala onomata* (fine words) but by their *syzygia*, their combination: even ordinary and humble words (*onomata mikra kai tapeina*) can produce poetry, thanks to their clever 'yoking together', their artistic combination.

It is not as though Aristotle, the founder of the opposite critical tendency, had not already had an occasional intuition on this subject: indeed, he had mentioned it himself, at least in the third book of his *Rhetoric* when he noted that Euripides had known how to confer dignity and poetic force upon words from ordinary language precisely by means of the combination of metres.[5] Aristotle, indeed, made the *ekloge* of the words the constitutive principle of poetic language, but still he was obliged to recognize the unusualness of a style like that of Euripides: the great tragic poet, impelled by his intellectualistic realism, could not resign himself to a selective and artificial language, and sought instead the simple spontaneity of ordinary language (we can recall here parenthetically that it was precisely the example of Euripides which in many regards would go on to be strongly influential on the Virgil of the *Aeneid*).

Thus, between the end of the Republic and the beginning of the Principate, two different conceptions of poetic language confronted one another in the literary culture of Rome: a traditional one of

[3] On Crates of Mallos as a critic of poetry one may refer to Asmis (1992) and Janko (2000), 120–34. The text of Philodemus re-edited by Janko is evidently important because it brings to light a whole series of Hellenistic literary critics, otherwise little known or completely unknown (Megacleides of Athens, beginning of the 3rd cent. BC; Heracleodorus, end of the 3rd cent.; Pausimachus of Miletus, end of the 3rd/ beginning of the 2nd cent.), who are predecessors of Dionysius of Halicarnassus in many regards. In particular, *synthesis* is considered to be primary by many of these critics in virtue of the phonetic effects created by the *synthesis* itself (and not in virtue of the *dianoia* of the verses).

[4] Cf. Lombardo (1988), 60–3; on the predecessors of Dionysius see Ardizzoni (1953), 79 ff., and Scaglione (1972).

[5] Arist. *Rhet.* 3, 2, 1404[b] 24.

Peripatetic origins and one that found in the work of Dionysius of Halicarnassus its most systematic formulation. But there was not a real theoretical contrast, and in practice a compromise was reached: the theory of *synthesis* (verbal combination) with the celebrated formulation of the *callida iunctura*, would go on to be championed in the *Ars Poetica* by the very same Horace who, faithful to Theophrastean precept, had insisted in his epistle to Florus upon a careful *ekloge* of the words.[6] In any case the discussion must have been lively, and already we can hear the first signs of another and even livelier discussion, one which a few decades later would count among its protagonists the anonymous author of the treatise *On the Sublime* who goes under the name of Pseudo-Longinus.[7]

It is not by chance that in that very treatise so much attention should be devoted to the subject of *synthesis*, indicated as one of the principal sources of the sublime: the author discusses it at the very point when he wishes to demonstrate conclusively that *ingenium* and *ars* belong reciprocally to one another; indeed, in order to indicate to what degree the effects of *synthesis* are constitutive of the sublime style, he declares that he has already dedicated to this important subject a special treatise in two books.[8] The critical path decisively opened up by Dionysius seems to have found in Pseudo-Longinus its point of arrival: *megalopsychia*, the spiritual vitality which can inflame thoughts and emotions and elevate them to sublimity, must necessarily be based upon *synthesis megaloprepes*, that is, it must find in the *compositio verborum* a grand form of expression which captures the reader and drags him/her off.

Pseudo-Longinus has no doubt: the sublime is not a matter of innate talent alone but is also a construction;[9] it does indeed have its own natural sources, but it also has other sources which are capable of being acquired. And among these, *synthesis* has the first place, as the one which shares both in the impetus of *physis* (nature) and in the procedures of *techne* (technique), combining inventive talent

---

[6] *Ars* 47–8; *Ep.* 2.2.112.

[7] Conte (1996*a*), 7–9.

[8] Cf. Lombardo (1988), 65.

[9] Almost at the very opening of his treatise (in chapter 2), the author polemicizes against those who believe that the sublime is only 'nature': passions are communicated by means of language, the sublime can be the object of teaching and learning.

and stylistic mechanism with one another.[10] Thanks to *synthesis*, the denotation of meanings is blended with the connotation of emotions: in this way the verbal language seems to bear, impressed within its forms, the signs which distinguish the pathetic excess of the sublime style.

Perhaps Pseudo-Longinus is guilty of a certain *naïveté* when, devoted as he is to the idea that art could be a mimesis of *physis*, he tries to make us believe that the procedures of poetic language serve the *direct* imitation of nature: he claims that the convulsive effects of the passions are reproduced in the concrete form of the discourse, that the emotions' disorder is mirrored faithfully in the disorder of the linguistic expression; 10.1–3 furnishes the exemplary analysis of Fr. 31 L.-P. of Sappho, the celebrated ode about the sufferings of love which Catullus translated. But iconic expressivity—structuring the words in such a way as, in the end, to give an almost physical image of the idea—is only one extreme possibility of poetic language, perhaps the most obvious one, certainly not the most characteristic one. Discussing the *figurae per ordinem* (figures of word order) which are of such importance for *synthesis*, Pseudo-Longinus writes (22.1): 'The greatest writers use hyperbata to imitate nature's mode of operation. Indeed art is perfect when it seems to be nature.' But a few lines earlier he seems nearer to recognizing the purely defamiliarizing (and not necessarily iconic) function which syntactic and expressive procedures fulfil in the text: 'It is a syntactical arrangement which detaches the words and concepts from their logical consequences and agitates them with the imprint of the most authentic pathos.'

This is a plausible judgement as long as it is free from the illusion that the signifiers, in order to have an artistic effect, must resemble the signifieds, or rather that the linguistic signs must take on the form of the thing or idea that they represent. It is evident that stylistic elaboration—with all its syntactical, rhetorical, metrical, and phonetic effects—serves above all to impose a special form upon the discourse, so that it will end up being different from ordinary communication; but it is erroneous to believe that this occurs by reason of the signifiers imitating the signifieds. And yet there is also

---

[10] Ibid., chapter 8.

an element of truth in this illusion. It is true that in every poetic text the signifiers are structured by creating an entirely functional linguistic system, and it is also true that this new linguistic structure adheres so perfectly to the signifieds as to appear to be a necessary emanation from them. Signifiers and signifieds are born together, produced by the same inventive gesture: for this reason they seem to resemble one another.

In any case, what is important in the thought of Pseudo-Longinus is the idea that the stylistic deviation characteristic of the sublime must be located above all in *synthesis*, in the syntactical structuring of the words, in the sequence of the phrasing. As Aristotle too had already remarked, Pseudo-Longinus notes that Euripides, like other poets not predisposed towards the sublime by an innate 'natural grandeur' (40.2–3), 'nonetheless achieved elevation of style, though only using common and ordinary words, precisely by virtue of the art of combining and harmonizing them with one another'. The sublime, so far from being an ineffable quality, is entrusted to expressive techniques and becomes visible by means of them. The syntactical figures, the anomalous construction, and so too the juxtaposition and separation of linguistic elements within the phrase, as well as the transpositions which disturb the normal sequence of the words and concepts—these are the ways in which *ars* makes *ingenium* function.

For Virgil too, the style is above all the creation of an 'artful syntax'. The sublime style, which appears to the reader as a perfect form or as an astonishing correspondence between expression and contents, was for the author merely one solution among the many possible, it was a labour of construction. And this labour of construction certainly includes procedures involving techniques of transposition, a syntax of pathos which replaces and overwhelms the syntax of reason.

Nonetheless we should not forget that, although the syntax of the sublime is produced in gestures of enhanced expressive intensity, it tends in fact to infect the whole discourse into which it is introduced, pervading it through and through and determining its movements and structures. Aiming to give vigour and grandeur to the language, it artfully moves the words and combines them in an indissoluble sequence of sounds; assonance, alliteration, parechesis, homoeoteleuton articulate the discourse by concatenating its parts with one another. The linguistic signs lose their arbitrary character, they no longer appear to be conventional but seem intimately motivated. This can be demonstrated by a Virgilian example chosen at random. In the second book of the *Aeneid* (2.210 f.), when the monstrous snakes which will kill Laocoon and his sons arrive from the sea, the poet's expressive manipulation creates a scene of intense pathetic horror: the words, structured in a sequence of syntactical and acoustic figures, acquire emphasis and corporeality:

> ardentisque oculos suffecti sanguine et igni
> sibila lambebant linguis vibrantibus ora.

The participle *suffecti* is a forceful linguistic choice: one could say that it takes the place of a normal *suffusi* (which perhaps would have been an appropriate term, but not an incisive one). The meaning which we must attribute to *suffecti* is that of 'dyed', and in fact Servius glosses the word with *infecti*. But it is not so important to notice how drastic the syntactic inversion contained in *oculos suffecti* (scil. *angues*) is— in fact it is obvious that, despite the inverted construction, it is the eyes of the serpents and not the serpents themselves which are literally injected with blood and fire. Rather, the important thing is to indicate that the innovative form *suffecti* is produced by the 'sigmatism' which determines the acoustic form of the whole pair of lines: notice the word-endings in arsis -*tis*, -*los*, -*guis*, and the alliteration *suffecti sanguine... sibila*. The sound has created the form, as Alfonso Traina would put it.[11]

There is more: an onomatopoeic exaggeration (did not Plato's *Cratylus* want signs to resemble things by nature?) also produces the new adjective *sibilus* ('hissing') by audaciously deriving it from the verb *sibilo* or from the noun of identical form and current usage.[12] The *sibila... ora*, 'the hissing mouths'—like the pictorial nexus *oculos suffecti sanguine*—are the emphatic signs of a linguistic impulse which drags the reader towards the emotion, distresses him/her by representing the horror of the marine monsters, and makes him/her sympathetic—remember that Dionysius of Halicarnassus

---

[11] Traina (1977).   [12] Cf. Traina (1988).

deemed an insistent sigmatism intolerable to the listener's ear: 'it belongs more to a savage beast than to a rational being'.[13]

Here the intervention performed by the stylistic deviations is energetic, indeed domineering. The expressive exaggeration, forcing the words and charging the sounds, results in a linguistic materiality which is resistant and as it were rough to the touch; the meanings do not rush past: intensified, almost coagulated, they come to a stop in the reader's ear and mind. But other deviations are also operating in the text which are more veiled, but which still suffice to produce analogous effects of defamiliarization. Even the unmarked words do not remain 'intact', but they too are affected by the alterations and artifices of the poetic form: thus the structure which assigns adjective and noun to the two ends of line 211 (*sibila . . . ora*) frames the phrase by a procedure familiar from Alexandrian technique; line 210 has almost the same framing structure, inasmuch as it opens with the adjective *ardentis* and closes with the noun *igni*, which is the logical (if not grammatical) complement to *ardentis*; the word *linguis*, rendered emphatic by the two caesuras which isolate it in the centre of the verse, is linked by alliteration to *lambebant* and by assonance at word-end with *vibrantibus*. There is more: the preceding verse (209), despite its semantic simplicity, is marked by strong expressive effects as well: it opens with an elegant movement reminiscent of archaic style, a return of the Ennian manner (*fit sonitus*), and it goes on to form a refined three-part alliteration, *sonitus spumante salo*, announcing the 'sigmatism' which will become dominant in the two following lines.

In short, the style of Virgil seems to leave no linguistic signal inactive. His sublime language is the result of a complex operation, a constant intervention which pervades the text in all its parts. Every phrase, every combination, almost every word is charged with an expressive energy which finds fuel in some individual element of the text, but can ignite other elements near by and thereby spread all around. The effects are produced by a shrewd dosage, a modulation which, in order to avoid uniformity and monotony, with a varied

[13] *De Comp. Verb.* 6, 14, 20 or 18, 40, or 14. The comic poets loved to make fun of Euripides' pretended sympathy for expressive *sigmatismos*: see D. L. Page on Eur. *Med.* 476; cf. also Conte (1988), 36.

touch sometimes restrains its gestures, sometimes heightens them. The tenor of the discourse produces a diffuse stylization, a modest degree of defamiliarization derived from slight linguistic deviations (energy is transmitted by lightness too); but it is capable of increasing its efforts until it attains climaxes of pathos—and then the language swerves and takes off. Virgil's epic style takes care to avoid the nakedness of a discourse which does not display the signs of the form; but it also knows how to attenuate immediately its flashes of expressiveness so that the effects of pathetic intensification do not become inflationary and disturb the reader by their excessiveness. We find a *klassische Dämpfung*, therefore, an art of measure and balance, in which the expressive requirements of 'maximum freedom' never overcome the complementary requirements of 'maximum order'.

We have said that Virgil's sublime style, precisely since it is a *synthesis megaloprepes* (grand combination), is also the creation of an 'artful syntax': this new syntax applies force to the usual syntax of the discourse and thereby modifies it. But this does not derive from merely superposing additional structures, that is, it comes not from outside the language, but from within it, like an endogenous impulse: it is nothing other than the very form of the communication, its gestural quality. Virgil's language succeeds in revealing itself only if it becomes 'figured'; this is the only way in which it also succeeds in shaping the thoughts it transmits. The syntactic modifications, the anomalous constructions, all the procedures that disturb the order of the phrase and the normal relations between words are the material signs of a creative tension which exerts pressure upon the language and generates a chain of defamiliarizing effects.

The most powerful of these effects are obtained by means of the simplest figures. Nothing is more simple and at the same time more effective than enallage (or, if one prefers, hypallage), that is, the trope which exchanges the syntactic relations among words: one element of the phrase, often the adjective, is referred not to the element to which it belongs by a logical or grammatical connection, but to another one more or less near by. The language becomes 'difficult', renouncing transparency and refusing to dissolve itself in the act of communication; from this source arises a style which is dense and tense (*hadros*, in the terminology of Pseudo-Longinus and Dionysius of Halicarnassus). The violence may appear to infringe only the coherence of the syntax, but in fact it reaches and violates the semantic coherence as well: the deviation involves the reader's senses, engaging his/her mind and kindling his/her reactions. Obviously, the defamiliarizing effects produced by enallage can vary in intensity, increasing with the violence applied to the language.[14] In elaborating his own sublime style, the author of the *Aeneid* makes ample use of this syntactical figure, sometimes with results that are surprising and extreme (indeed, this is one of the ways in which Virgil succeeds in inventing highly defamiliarized expressions although starting out, as his detractor said, from quite usual words); but he almost entirely avoids it in the *Georgics*, and even more in the *Bucolics*. This is an evident sign that by its vocation enallage is at the service of the *hypsos* (sublime); indeed, we may suspect that no other stylistic audacity is as characteristic of the *synthesis megaloprepes* (and as exclusively so).

The very few cases that can be recalled from the *Bucolics* and the *Georgics* do not have the same expressive energy demonstrated by the very many examples offered by the *Aeneid*. Consider line 46 of the ninth *Eclogue*: *quid antiquos signorum suspicis ortus?*, where *antiquos* has taken the place of *antiquorum*: the syntactic exchange (perhaps also due to the sudden elevation of the stylistic level demanded by a new and quite lofty poetic theme, the prodigious appearance of the comet and the catasterism of the divinized Caesar), is above all a response to metrical considerations, avoiding the heavy double spondee *antiquorum*[15] which would have created an unpleasant homoeoteleuton with *signorum*.

The stylistic deviations which enallage manages to produce in the *Georgics* are just as moderate, rare examples for the most part limited to the purple passages which close the poem's various books, where the diction is maintained at a higher level, close to the *grandiloquentia* of heroic epic. Thus, in the gloomy finale of book 1, a passage of

[14] Precious materials in Bell (1923), 315–29, but the whole book (excepting some imprecisions and some exaggerations) remains an inexhaustible goldmine for serious study of Latin poetic language: indeed, it ought to figure among the tools which are absolutely indispensable for every Classical philologist.

[15] Traina (1997), 31: '*antiquorum* è la sola forma di *antiquus* assente in V'.

epic poetry which condenses into a few majestic verses all the horror of the civil wars, a peasant working the soil sees empty helmets, rusty weapons, and human bones come to the surface: line 496 *grandiaque effossis mirabitur ossa sepulcris*, where *effossis* would have to refer literally to *ossa* (in that case *effossis* would mean 'brought to light by digging'); the enallage reverses the image and imposes upon *effossis... sepulcris* the new meaning of 'tombs uncovered by digging',[16] so that the ploughed fields implicitly become a huge cemetery, every furrow of the plough a tomb.

So too, the syntactic exchange in lines 534–5 at the close of the second book produces a defamiliarization which is fundamentally moderate: *facta est... Roma, | septemque una sibi muro circumdedit arces*, where *una* refers as predicate to *Roma* rather than to *muro*: here the grammatical displacement aims more at elegance than at expressiveness, and produces a meaning almost equivalent to what the normal syntactic construction would have had, that is, it does not produce a true semantic violation. Even slighter is the intervention produced by the transference of the epithet in cases like *Georg.* 1.143 *Bacchi Massicus umor* 'the liquid of Bacchus (=wine) which comes from the slopes of Mount Massicus': this is a traditional feature of Latin poetic diction, frequent above all when two proper nouns, either of persons or of places, come together in a phrase (e.g. Lucr. 1.474 *Alexandri Phrygio sub pectore*; Hor. *Carm.* 2.12.22 *pinguis Phrygiae Mygdonias opes*); this is a type of enallage which, though it can boast as its stylistic merit an origin in Homer (e.g. *Il.* 2.54 Νεστορέῃ παρὰ νηῒ Πυλοιγενέος βασιλῆος),[17] almost always responds to practical considerations imposed by metrical constraints or by euphony.[18]

---

[16] Traina (1997), 35 and 43. It should be noted that the verse in question belongs to a passage which as a whole is conceived under the impulse of great expressiveness: the preceding verse too bears the signs of linguistic defamiliarization, marked as it is by the *sigmatismos* that dominates in it: 495 *aut gravibus rastris galeas pulsabit inanis*. The language is charged with a strong expressive energy which also reveals itself in the syntactical torsion created by the enallage.

[17] Cf. a similar enallage in Valgius Rufus: *... Pylio profluxerit ore | Nestoris* (fr. 2, vv. 3 f., in Courtney (1993), 288).

[18] See e.g. Lucr. 2.501 *Thessalico concharum tacta colore* (the transference of the epithet serves above all to avoid the heavy homoeoteleuton of the feminine plural genitive of the adjective).

In the *Aeneid*, on the other hand, enallage operates to create very drastic expressions: here it is a strong coefficient of the sublime style. By its means, the manipulation of the syntactic relations ruptures the semantic coherence between the words and thereby radically restructures the language, making it more difficult and less common, elevating its stylistic level. The semantic incongruity produced by the syntactical incongruity renders the meaning of the new construction problematic and thereby individualizes the meaning of every single one of the words involved, heightening each one's specific value. In a certain sense, enallage, by virtue of its intrinsic economy, can be considered the most representative procedure of Virgilian classicism: in fact it privileges lexical sobriety and ordinariness, but it engages the reader's intellect and mind agonistically, demanding that s/he confront the syntactical incongruity. The maximum of expressive tension is obtained with an extreme parsimony of linguistic elements.

As has been said, there are many devices which can give form to poetic expression and serve to qualify it: from alliteration to assonance, from phonetic symbolism to metrical effects, from the elevating use of archaisms to the invention of incisive neologisms—devices which are all intended, individually or synergistically, to defamiliarize the language, to give it value in itself: the poetic expression, made 'intransitive', persists in the listener's ear and is not dispersed in the act of communication. But enallage does more, or it does it with more force: it requires the expression to use common words, the ones least remote from customary usage, those which would be readiest to slip away unnoticed—but it distorts them from current use; it binds them in inappropriate combinations. The newness, or rather the heat of newness, arises from the tepidity of age, almost like a flare-up which rekindles the smouldering fire of language each time. Behind the deviation one glimpses the normal combination, like a repressed presence: within the text the 'inappropriate' meaning imposed by the form of the expression dominates on the surface, but the 'appropriate' meaning kept in the background tries to come forward; the reader has a double perception of the meaning of the words, or rather a doubled, a more intense perception.

Let us begin with an extreme case, but one which is also more instructive than others. In book 9, Nisus and Euryalus massacre the sleeping enemy during a night-expedition, then they themselves fall heroically, overcome by the enemy. The poet-narrator has just finished pronouncing his emotional eulogy (a solemn apostrophe addressed directly to the fallen youths and proudly uttered 'ex voce poetae'), then the narrative point of view shifts to the camp of the Rutulians. They discover with horror the mighty massacre performed by Nisus and Euryalus: their extraordinary horror is an indirect tribute to the extraordinary exploit of the two Trojan warriors (454–6):

> ingens concursus ad ipsa
> corpora seminecisque viros tepidaque recentem
> caede locum et pleno spumantis sanguine rivos.

The Rutulians rush into the camp and pass in anguish from corpse to corpse: their frenzy and agitation find an immediate expression in the enjambment which bridges the syntactic sequence and dilates the representation of space: *concursus ad ipsa | corpora*. The whole period is constructed with the greatest simplicity, and makes use of parataxis so as to pile up, one by one, the horrifying details as they present themselves to the eyes of the Rutulians. Prominent amidst the simplicity of the syntactical construction is *seminecis*, a compound adjective of archaizing flavour, probably invented by Virgil, or else taken over by him from Roman tragedy. But after this come only ordinary words, among the most common ones in the current lexicon, those which ought to say, with a purely denotative value, that 'the place is still warm from the recent massacre'; and yet the syntactic relations are interchanged, and the meaning of the phrase hangs suspended, hesitating as it were between the new connection and the expected one. The denotation 'warm' does not refer to the noun 'place' but is replaced by 'recent', a feature connoted by it, since the fact that the 'place' is still 'warm with the massacre' implies also that the massacre is 'recent'; analogously, 'recent' ought to be the natural denotation of 'massacre', but in its place figures the connotation 'warm': the massacre was done only a little while ago and the blood has not yet gone cold. The marginal and implicit meanings have been captured and rendered distinct, the connotation has been superimposed upon the denotation. The double enallage functions here as a double metonymy (a displacement triggered by the contiguity between the cause and the effect), but it also brings with it a discontinuity in the logical syntax. The group of words is congealed into a new concreteness in which every element ineluctably implicates all the others; the thought no longer flows along the linear path of the discourse (it no longer observes the normal grammatical and logical agreements), but instead becomes turbid, thickened.

As has already been observed, the lexicon of the phrase is constituted only by common words, ones which are marked in no way at all. Against such an intrinsic 'poverty' of the language, the semantic incompatibility produced by the enallage reacts almost as a corrective which redeems the lexical ordinariness by injecting an unusual energy into the form of the expression. In this way the common language leaves the colourless space of limbo and becomes defamiliarized, qualifying itself as a poetic language and rising to the level of art; the style too acquires further intensity and is elevated. The deviation engages the senses of the reader and compels him to make himself into a 'sublime reader', that is, a reader ready to yield, in mind and spirit, to the appeal of the expressive pathos.

Exactly the same thing might be said about the group of words which immediately follow in the verse—quite common words, like *pleno* and *spumantis*, or like *sanguine* and *rivos*, ordinary designations which, all together, are supposed to describe 'streams of water full of foaming blood'. This is the literal meaning which the phrase is supposed to communicate, but the defamiliarization of the form alters the expression. The adjective *pleno*, referring to *sanguine*, acquires a physical connotation and comes to mean 'abundant', almost 'big', 'full-bodied': the image becomes materialized and is charged with a pathetic note of horror; the emotion is accompanied by repugnance. The syntactical displacement has elevated the common language to a new stylistic grandeur.

The reader here experiences hesitation between the new form and the normal form, since both the (implied) norm and the deviation present themselves to the reader at the same time. Sometimes, indeed, s/he notices only the more banal meaning, that is, the one which we could call 'literal', and unconsciously s/he is led to cancel out the figure which the syntactical 'impropriety' introduces; in the two cases which I have just discussed, one part of the tradition (both the direct and the indirect ones) presents normalizing constructions:

instead of *pleno spumantis sanguine rivos* we also find the reading *plenos spumanti sanguine rivos*,[19] and instead of *tepidaque recentem | caede locum* we also find transmitted *tepidumque recenti | caede locum*.[20] These are isometric variants, or rather isoprosodic ones, in which the 'easy' form has dethroned the 'difficult' one (it is precisely the fact that the two different readings are isometrical that has permitted the corruption which aims to regularize the constructions). Once the linguistic deviation has been eliminated, the expression remains flat and loses its impetus; once the verbal torsion has vanished, so does the pathetic intensification, which was aimed at redeeming the language from its ordinariness and elevating it to the sublime style.

The syntax of the sublime is above all a transpositional syntax, as we said earlier when we recalled Pseudo-Longinus and his statements about *synthesis megaloprepes*. It is a boldness of the material expression, which transforms the syntax of reason into a syntax of passion; in fact, the principal mediator of *pathos* (emotion) is *megalegoria* ('expressive grandeur'), which is above all the art of putting words together and therefore loves the figures of syntactical transposition (Pseudo-Longinus 39). Among these figures, enallage seems to be the most economical and at the same time the most effective one: the most economical one, because it can allow itself to use a 'poor', unmarked lexicon, like the one which recurs in ordinary language; the most effective one, because by combining those words in anomalous syntactical constructions it produces enormous results in expressive defamiliarization.

The language of Greek tragedy, the *tragike lexis* of great Attic drama, was quite familiar with enallage and knew how to make use of it as a qualifying stylistic means.[21] A good many examples could be

---

[19] pleno MP[1]ω, *Mynors, Geymonat*: plenos PRγ, *Serv., Tib., Mynors*: spumanti ωγ[1], *Ribbeck, Sabbadini, Geymonat*, spumantem *DServ.*

[20] tepidaque ωγ[1], *Macrob.* 6.6.3, *Serv., Tib.*: tepidamque M, tepidumque M[2]PRγ; 'tepidaque recentem caede locum *hypallage est, tepidum locum recenti caede; unde multi legunt* tepidumque recenti caede locum' *Serv.*

[21] Useful, even if unsatisfactory in many regards, is Bers (1974)—see also Hoesktra (1976). Still worth consulting is Kühner–Gerth (1898), 263. I suspect that the cases of enallage discoverable in the language of Attic tragedy might well be more numerous than those which actually appear in the texts of modern critical editions: many cases

given, for the most part from the lyrical parts of the tragedies, that is, at those points where the linguistic expression aims to take on a tense form or to seem less usual. Let us take a look at some instances. Towards the beginning of the *Seven against Thebes*, Aeschylus shows us a chorus of virgins who in their anxiety ask for help from the gods who protect the city: κλύετε παρθένων κλύετε πανδίκως | χειροτόνους λιτάς (171–2) 'hear (us) virgins, hear, with a full sense of justice | the prayers which stretch their hands to the heavens'. The epithet does not refer to the virgins (it is they who stretch out their hands while they pray) but is transferred to their prayers: in this way an unusual phrase is created which violates the usual meaning of the adjective (literally it would mean 'who raises his hand to vote', 'who declares his vote in an election'). The new phrase lends force to the image, but it also creates a new meaning, one charged with emotion.

In the same tragedy, anxiety about the imminent sack of the city finds a voice in the painful words of the virgin chorus which describes intolerable atrocities. These are the lines most daring in expression: βλαχαὶ δ' αἱματόεσσαι | τῶν ἐπιμαστιδίων | ἀρτιτρεφεῖς βρέμονται (348–50), literally: 'bloodied bleatings of the (babies) clasped to the breasts moan, just now suckled'.[22] It is obvious that the adjective 'bloodied' belongs literally to the babies, just like the

have been eliminated by the intervention of normalizing corrections or else have been concealed by banalizing interpretations (this is probably due in part to the influence exercised by the exceptional authority of E. Fraenkel, who showed himself more inclined than other critics to limit enallage in the language of Aeschylus). I can cite as examples a couple of normalizing corrections which eliminate enallage and its effects of expressive defamiliarization. In Soph. *Antigone* 980 μᾱτρὸς ἔχοντες ἀνύμφευτον (ἀνυμφεύτου Meineke, Lloyd-Jones) γονάν, where reference is made to the sons of Cleopatra 'who have a badly married birth from their mother', i.e. were born from a mother who had an unfortunate marriage; Griffith (1999) keeps ἀνύμφευτον. In Eur. *Hel.* 72–3 ἐχθίστην (ἐχθίστης Dingelstadt, Diggle) ὁρῶ | γυναικὸς εἰκὼ φόνιον, ἥ μ' ἀπώλεσεν | πάντας τ' Ἀχαιούς 'I see the murderous image of the woman who destroyed me and all the Achaeans'. Cf. Diggle (1994), 95 n. 13, and (1981), 48. The correction ἐχθίστης would only be necessary if γυναικὸς received no specification ('I see the murderous image of the woman / of a woman' would not specify who was in question: this is Teucer's first contact with Helen); but with the specification introduced by the relative clause there are no reasons to make the change: the conjecture aims to blunt the impact of the enallage (it should be noted that enallage is present anyway in εἰκὼ φόνιον.)

[22] According to another (well-attested) reading, 'just now born', ἀρτιβρεφεῖς. Cf. Bers (1974), 52, who cites W. Headlam, 'Metaphor, with a Note on Transference of Epithets', *CR* 16 (1902), 434 f.

adjective 'just now suckled'; instead, both adjectival formations refer to 'bleatings' (βλαχαί, which becomes the grammatical subject) and not to the logical subject, that is, to the suckling babies who cry while they clasp the breasts of their mothers. The enallage creates a synthesis of the blood of the massacre and of the children's bleating: the new combination gives a visual and auditory concreteness to the harsh metaphor which treats the slaughtered newborn children as though they were bleating lambs. The syntactical manipulation has created an extraordinarily audacious verbal mass whose elements are closely connected with one another and hence enhance one another, producing grand effects of defamiliarization and of stylistic enhancement.

The torsion which Aeschylus imprints upon the tragic language here must have seemed extraordinary to the audience of his drama; indeed this must have been one of the most memorable expressive inventions in all his theatrical production, if it is true that Euripides parodied it in his *Cyclops*, when the chorus of satyrs makes an entrance pushing ahead their flocks: ποθοῦσί σ' ἁμερόκοι | τοι βλαχαὶ σμικρῶν τεκέων (lines 58–9), literally: 'it is you they demand, sleepy by day, the bleatings of little children' (in the parody too, just as in the model, this is a lyric passage, characterized by elevated language). The clue that indicates the parodic allusion is provided precisely by the enallage of the adjective 'sleepy by day', which here too, with an analogous syntactical displacement, refers to the bleatings and not to the lambs.[23] It is as though Euripides intended jokingly to correct Aeschylus, who with a tragic metaphor had identified with one another bleating lambs and newborn children killed in war: in the parody the bleatings are no longer metaphorical but belong to real lambs, and for that reason they are not 'bloody' bleatings, as was the case in the grand model, but instead 'sleepy by day': this is what is demanded by the satyr-play's anti-sublimity, with its humble good sense.

But Aeschylus' expressive audacity can also be whetted to extreme acuity, in the form of sharp syntactical contrivances in which enallage manipulates the language, stretching it to the point of obscurity. It should suffice to recall a lyrical passage from the *Suppliants*

---

[23] A brief hint in Bers (1974), 67.

(539): 'I have moved towards the ancient imprint, the flower-gathering supervisions of my mother, the field nourisher of cows, from which Io fled tormented by the gadfly', ματέρος ἀνθονόμους ἐπωπάς, that is, 'towards the places where my ancestor (Io) was supervised (by the watchdog Argus) while she gathered flowers'. This daring phrase, in which syntactical deviations and rhetorical metaplasms are condensed, is explained by the apposition and relative phrase, which together serve to solve the sublime linguistic puzzle.

Obviously the effects of deviation which enallage produces in tragic language can vary in intensity: the greater the degree of distortion to which the syntax is subjected, the greater the daring, indeed the insolence, of the stylistic expression. Often the enallage affects only the verbal surface without violating the logic of the expression: even so, the result is a slight effect of defamiliarization which aims only at distancing the tragic language from the language of normal communication.[24] In Sophocles, for example, there are many cases in which the syntactical alteration is barely hinted at, as in *Ajax* 860 ὦ πατρῷον ἑστίας βάθρον, 'O paternal foundation of the hearth' instead of 'foundation of the paternal hearth', or *Trachiniae* 656 πολύκωπον ὄχημα ναός, 'many-oared vehicle of a ship' instead of 'vehicle of a ship furnished with many oars'. In such cases, the epexegetic genitive forms an entirely solid nexus with the noun that governs it, as though the whole phrase constituted a single compound word; in this way the impropriety is slight, since the adjective might seem in appearance to have been transposed but refers in fact to the entire verbal combination and not to only one of its elements.

These adjectival transferences too form part of the more general tendency (a tendency typical of *tragike lexis*) to produce compounds and to privilege a synthetic, condensed mode of expression. The style of the *Aeneid* will know how to derive an ample profit from the example of superficial enallages like these: the two elements of the verbal group formed by a noun and a genitive of specification make up a unified semantic complex, which makes it easy to transfer

---

[24] See the fine notes of Friis Johansen and Whittle (1980), Aesch. *Suppl.* 64 (II. 61), 933 (II. 242), 956 (II. 257), 1028 (II. 315).

the specifying attribute to the governing noun.[25] Thus in 3.294 *incredibilis rerum fama*, where the transposition barely modifies the usual construction which would literally apply the adjective *incredibilis* to *rerum*;[26] in 3.421 *imo barathri... gurgite*, a phrase in which *imo* would be an appropriate attribute for *barathri* rather than for *gurgite*.[27]

In these cases a modest, almost imperceptible syntactical deviation is produced, since the new construction contravenes the linguistic norm only slightly and in any case creates a meaning which is acceptable in itself and not unnatural: in short, the deviation does not commit a real semantic infraction but serves only to emancipate the language from the banality of the usual formulation. This structure privileges above all phrases in which the adjective is a proper noun of a region or person: 6.2 *Euboicis Cumarum... oris*; 8.526 *Tyrrhenus tubae... clangor*; 12.739 *arma dei... Volcania* (cf. Hor. *Carm.* 3.29.1 *Tyrrhena regum progenies*; 1.12.34 *superbos Tarquini fasces*).[28] An analogous enallage (in a certain sense, a complementary one) can connect the genitive of specification with the adjective which would literally belong to the governing noun: this too is a form of slight enallage, a measured alteration of the expressive form, nonetheless capable of defamiliarizing ordinary language and reanimating it with effects of a new intensity: thus in 2.150 *molem hanc immanis equi*; 2.302 *summi fastigia tecti*; 2.801 *iugis summae... Idae*; 3.411 *angusti... claustra Pelori*; 6.285 *variarum monstra ferarum*.

It can also happen that recognizing this type of enallage permits the philologist to interpret correctly certain passages which otherwise resist interpretation or at least are ambiguous. See for example *Aen.* 2.713–14, where Aeneas exhorts his companions to split up in flight and to meet again later all together, by different paths, at the temple of Ceres, just outside the city: *est... templum... vetustum | desertae*

---

[25] Still useful for the recognition of this particular mode of verbal structuring in Greek tragic poetry is Schneidewin–Nauck (1899), 7. Cf. also Wilamowitz-Möllendorf *ad* Eur. *Herc. Fur.* 468; Mastronarde *ad* Eur. *Phoen.* 30.

[26] It is almost too banal to note that the enallage is favoured by the metrical impossibility of using *incredibilium*.

[27] It is superfluous to recall that *callidae iuncturae* generated by this kind of transference are also frequent in Horace's lyric poetry: e.g. 3.30.4 *innumerabilis annorum series*; 1.2.26 *ruentis imperi rebus*.

[28] See Norden *ad Aen.* 6.2.

Cereris. Interpreters ancient and modern[29] have had trouble understanding why the adjective *desertae* is attributed to Ceres. Is it because she was abandoned by her daughter Persephone? Or because (as is said at 6.484) her priest Polybetes is dead? Or is it because after a ten-year siege no worshippers go any longer to pray to the goddess in her temple? To me it seems likely that Aeneas chooses the temple of Ceres as a meeting point for his companions in flight precisely because it is 'solitary', a secure refuge far from the menace of the Greeks: *desertae* refers to Ceres by enallage, but literally it should be connected to *templum,* as though Virgil had written 'templum vetustum et desertum Cereris'. The new syntagm performs a metonymic displacement with respect to a hypothetical unaltered construction: 'solitary Ceres' obviously means that the goddess's temple, situated outside the walls of Troy, is 'not visited by crowds'.[30] The improper syntactical connection not only gives a welcome emphasis to the adjective *desertae* (an important idea for Aeneas' strategy of regrouping his companions in a remote place) but also avoids the inartistic accumulation of two attributes (*vetustum* and *desertum*) referring to a single noun.[31]

As was said above, the cases we have just examined are all ones of moderate syntactical distortion, in which the enallage modifies only the surface of the verbal constructions. But deriving an example from *tragike lexis,* which knows both slight and intense cases of enallage, Virgil succeeds not only in producing a series of modest linguistic deviations which punctuate the epic diction and defamiliarize it, but also in experimenting with extraordinary stylistic audacities which upset the form of the expression and even its logic. Even for Virgil's most audacious constructions one can indicate some precedent in the extreme use of tragic language which Sophocles dared to attempt. But the two poets, though they are both exceptional *Sprachschöpfer,*

---

[29] Serv. *ad l.* 'DESERTAE CERERIS utrum a sacerdote, qui in sexto <484> exstinctus inducitur, ut *Cererique sacrum Polyboeten:* an 'desertae' belli tempore propter decennalem obsidionem? an 'desertae' a filia, ut *nec repetita sequi curet Proserpina matrem.*

[30] Vitruvius (1.7.2) noted that, according to the Etruscans, a temple of Ceres had to be placed in a remote position, outside of the city, where men would have to go on purpose to make sacrifice in honour of the goddess; cf. R. G. Austin *ad Aen.* 2. 714.

[31] On the prohibition against *duo epitheta,* a regulation of Augustan and post-Augustan poetry, see Quint. 8. 6. 43 *duo...uni adposita ne versum quidem decuerint;* important is Timpanaro (2001), 62 f. and especially n. 106.

are very different in their modes of procedure: the great tragedian associates his syntactical inventions (which for the most part are contained within the lyrical parts of his dramas) with a lexicon which is select and unusual, stylistically already marked in itself. On the contrary, when Virgil recurs to enallage he tends to associate it with a language which is not remote from the usual one: indeed, for him enallage functions as the stylistic corrective for a lexicon which is entirely common, a lexicon which enallage succeeds in elevating stylistically by combining its elements in structures which are anomalous and charged with effect.[32]

A good example is provided by a passage of the *Electra* (492–3) in which Sophocles involves his chorus in arduous syntactical contortions: Ἄλεκτρ᾽, ἄνυμφα γὰρ ἐπέβα μιαιφόνων | γάμων ἁμιλλήμαθ᾽, literally: 'conflicts of homicidal weddings without a nuptial bed, without a conjugal promise'—an exchange of elements which can be paraphrased in this way: 'bloody conflicts for weddings without a nuptial bed and conjugal promise'. Despite the syntactical connections, each attribute looks towards the referent appropriate for it: the individual verbal elements stand out more clearly, as though the one sought autonomy from the other in order to impose with greater force its own individual meaning; taken as a whole, the disconcerting syntactical tangle engages the listener's mind and spirit. A similarly rare and precious language (in which once again abstract nouns are linked with privative or compound adjectives) characterizes another Sophoclean lyric sequence marked by the presence of an enallage:[33] *Antigone* 862–5 Ἰὼ ματρῷαι λέκτρων ἆται κοι- | μήματ<ά τ᾽> αὐτογέννητ᾽ | ἐμῷ πατρὶ δυσμόρου ματρός, 'Oh the horror of the maternal bed and the embraces which united the unfortunate mother to my father, her son.' The adjective 'maternal', which ought to refer literally to the genitive of specification, becomes an attribute of the governing noun (literally 'the maternal horrors of the bed'): the linguistic deviation heightens the monstrous nature of the incest, a theme which is so dominant that it is reiterated redundantly in the

---

[32] In this connection it seems pertinent to recall a very acute observation made by T. S. Eliot in *The Music of Poetry*: 'Every revolution in poetry is apt to be, and sometimes to announce itself as, a return to common speech' (Eliot (1957), 3). Good use is made of this suggestion by Lyne (1989)—see especially 1–19.

[33] See Long (1968), 52, 89, 97.

following words. One more example: in the same part of the tragedy, a little earlier (793–4), another basic idea of the drama—the violated blood kinship—derives an expressive emphasis from enallage of an attribute: νεῖκος ἀν- | δρῶν ξύναιμον, literally 'the consanguineous strife of men'. And in this case too, as is customary in Sophocles' style, the syntactical deviation is applied to a language which is already refined in itself, to a lexicon which bears Homer's personal imprint.

We have said that the syntax of the sublime bases its expressive gestures upon the transposition of words; we have also said that the syntactical displacements produced by enallage make language tense and defamiliarize it. We have seen that these stylistic effects arise from violating or altering normal constructions; but until now we have considered only the verbal figures which are produced in the syntax of nouns when the adjective is attributed improperly. Even more drastic effects, however, can be obtained by enallage when the syntax of the verbs is manipulated. Perhaps it is imprecise to use the same term to indicate linguistic procedures which are applied to different parts and functions of the discourse, but it is certain that ancient rhetoricians, and with them many of their modern counterparts, have customarily understood under the single label of enallage (or hypallage) the most varied syntactical violations, provided that the usual construction of the words ends up being inverted in some way.[34] In the end, this is acceptable for us too. What counts, in fact, is that the boldness of the material expression violates syntactical normality; whether the infraction applies to the syntax of nouns or to that of verbs is secondary.

It really does not need much for the text to show the signs of linguistic defamiliarization: even in fixed lexical structures, which might seem destined for transparency and inalterability, the elements can be simultaneously preserved and recombined in unusual forms. Thus in 2.712, in the line immediately preceding the example examined above of *templum... vetustum desertae Cereris*, Aeneas says to his followers, 'Pay attention to what I will tell you'—a verbal cliché of the sort that easily occurs in an epic narration, hence a formulation which is entirely functional and not predisposed to be charged with expressive connotations. But here the cliché takes on an unusual form: *Vos, famuli,*

---

[34] Quite useful here is Torzi (2000), 119–83.

quae dicam animis advertite vestris, literally 'turn to your minds the things that I shall say.' As is apparent, the lexicon is the common one, the most current one; even the syntactical construction is not too strange, since it is helped out by the more usual construction of the verb *adverto*, with the dative; and yet the final effect, without wanting to be risky, seems daring. We would have expected the normal construction *animos advertite vestros*, but Virgil avoids the stereotype; indeed it is as though the usual compound verb *anim(um)advertere* had been decomposed into its constitutive elements and inverted in its construction. This is an artistic syntax which works to create an effective deviation, but it is also a gesture of linguistic inventiveness which seeks to re-elaborate an entirely banal phrase by imitating a Homeric motif. In the *Iliad* and *Odyssey*, in fact, the formula ἐνὶ φρεσὶ βάλλεο σῇσι, 'fix in your hearts', recurs over a dozen times: clearly, the same word order and the same construction as in the Homeric formula are suggestively reproduced in the Virgilian phrase *animis advertite vestris*.

It is precisely the aspect of syntactical inversion which Servius notes when he comments on an example which is analogous (even if it is of greater linguistic boldness): 1.9–11 *quidve dolens regina deum tot volvere casus | insignem pietate virum . . . | impulerit*, 'incited by what rancour the queen of the gods drove a man, who was so full of reverence and sense of duty, to struggle in so many mishaps'. Commenting on the phrase *volvere casus*, Servius writes, 'id est casibus volvi. et est figura hypallage, quae fit quotienscumque per contrarium verba intelleguntur'. What he means is that if the words in hypallage are to be understood correctly their construction must be reversed: *casibus volvi* 'to be overwhelmed by mishaps' becomes *volvere casus* 'unroll mishaps' and hence 'confront them'. Perhaps in this specific case Servius' interpretation is a little mechanical, perhaps even simplistic (certainly, the expression contains a verbal figure which apparently reverses the usual syntactical structure, but the new construction still succeeds in capturing an additional meaning implicit in the active form of the verb *volvere*, that of 'confronting *one after another* mishaps *which follow one another in time*');[35] in any case

---

[35] In fact the nexus *volvere casus*, 'unroll the mishaps' in the sense of 'confront them, endure them', is an enallage by reason of the syntactical form of the construction, but it was probably inspired by a particularly effective Homeric expression. In *Il.*

the criterion of syntactical inversion provides a pretty good interpretation for this linguistic gesture which animates Virgil's expression in this case and in other similar ones.

Thus, in the construction *dare classibus Austros* (*Aen.* 3.61), it is certain that ancient readers must already have been struck by the inversion, if Tiberius Claudius Donatus felt himself obliged to defend passionately this Virgilian invention: 'not only should this expression not be blamed, on the contrary, it is splendid: it would have been natural to say "give the ships to the winds", but in order elegantly to revitalize the expression the poet says "give the winds to the fleet", so as to suggest that the ships are eager for flight. Indeed, to give the wind to a ship means to expose it to the gusts in such a way that the ship sails more quickly, impelled by the breezes it receives in its sails.'[36] By inverting the construction the poet attains a notable expressive intensity without having to give up an entirely common lexicon: the enallage defamiliarizes the language and frees it from ordinariness.[37]

24.6–8 Achilles turns over in his bed 'mourning the force of Patroclus and his noble fury | and how many *pains he had unrolled and suffered with him* | amidst the wars of men and the dangerous waves': τολύπευσε . . . καὶ πάθεν ἄλγεα seems to be the model which Virgil has suggestively copied. It should not be forgotten, on the other hand, that the Homeric gloss τολυπεύειν, 'unwind' in the sense of 'confront, endure', often has πόλεμον as object. It only remains to mention that the verses quoted from the *Iliad* (24.6–9) were athetized by Aristophanes of Byzantium and by Aristarchus: I wonder whether Virgil, with an erudite and playful Alexandrian technique, might have intended to allude to the problem and to take sides with those philologists who had harshly criticized this athetesis: cf. *Scholia Graeca in Homeri Iliadem (Scholia Vetera)*, rec. H. Erbse, vol. v (Berlin, 1977), p. 513. This takes away nothing from the fact that the final result of the enallage is to have the effect of adding a concrete notation to the expression: cf. A. Traina in *Enc. Virg.* v* p. 626, who sees the *casus* as masses which must be rolled along with great effort, and thus attributes to Aeneas 'una partecipazione attiva allo svolgersi delle vicende, lo sforzo di portarle avanti'.

[36] Ti. Claudi Donati *Interpretationes Vergilianae*, p. 272 Georgii: *locutio non tantum non vitiosa, verum etiam splendida; simplex enim fuerat dicere dare navis ventis, sed ut novitatem induceret eloquentiae, ait dare classibus austros ut ad fugam paratas navis efficerent. Dare enim ventum navi est flatibus obicere, ut agi possit auris exceptis et velocius currere.*

[37] Virgil often uses constructions with the simple verb *dare* when we might expect a more definite and less general verb: in these cases it happens that the syntactical inversion of the construction serves to redeem the ordinariness of the verb, to defamiliarize it. In the same way, Euripides uses forms of the verb δίδωμι construing them with an enallage: cf. Dodds *ad Bacch.* 621; Di Benedetto *ad Or.* 42; Kannicht *ad Hel.* 688–70 banalizes this.

Thus syntactical inversion aims to distance the language from current usage and to charge it with expressiveness: but sometimes it can also achieve effects which might be called impressionistic. And then the syntactical torsion transforms the unusual construction into a subjective suggestion: the form of the expression determines the form of the perception, the reader must accept the very immediacy of the statement. In the fifth book, for example, the encouraging shouts that greet the ship-race resound from shore and forest behind: *consonat omne nemus vocemque inclusa volutant | litora: pulsati colles clamore resultant* (149–50). By an impressionistic effect 'the hills rebound, struck by the cries', whereas it is obviously the sound that rebounds against the hills—precisely this is the flat form in which Virgil represents the echo of a voice in *Georg.* 4.50 *vocisque offensa resultat imago*, where, because of the difference in stylistic level, the language adheres simply to the basic idea and does not seek an expressive enhancement in an enallage.

The same effect of impressionistic defamiliarization recurs in *Aen.* 8.305 *consonat omne nemus strepitu collesque resultant*: here the enallage exploits the symmetrical arrangement of the verbs which frame the verse (a pattern of which Virgil was very fond) and figuratively suggests the immediate response of the echo. In these two cases the impressionistic reversal is applied to the perception of sounds; elsewhere it is instead visual perception that is affected in this way, as in 5.287 f. *gramineum in campum, quem collibus undique curvis | cingebant silvae*, where the landscape itself is perceived in inverted terms. Servius observes that Virgil has reversed the construction when he says that 'from every side the forests surrounded the field with curving hills': in fact (Servius continues) 'it is not the forest that has the hills, but rather the forest is upon the hills '; hence he should have said 'the field that the hills surrounded with forests'.[38] Here too Virgil gives a new arrangement to words derived from ordinary language; but the lexical normality is compensated by the activation of various expressive factors which conspire together to produce a sublime effect, above all enallage, which makes the image perceptible as a whole; then the triple alliteration (*collibus... curvis | cingebant*)

---

[38] '*Collibus undique curvis*' *mutavit: non enim silva colles habet, sed est in collibus silva. Debuit ergo dicere, 'quem colles cingebant silvis'.*

which contextually motivates the concatenation of the words; and finally, in enjambment, the adverb *undique*, which enlarges the represented space and implicitly suggests the gaze's circular movement along the forested arc of the hills.

It seems obvious that syntactical inversion cannot be considered in any way as an additional discursive figure, a decorative supplement of the form: instead, it is the move that lends style to the expression, the manoeuvre that grants the poet the felicitous conciliation of opposed requirements: to give naturalness and authenticity to epic language thanks to the use of an ordinary lexicon, and at the same time to distance the language from normality, to redeem it with interventions capable of revitalizing its constructions. 'Nove dixit': this is how Servius comments on the syntactical deviation with which Virgil inverts the expression in *Aen.* 6.353 f. *quam tua ne spoliata armis, excussa magistro | deficeret... navis.* We would have expected a phrase like *excusso magistro* ('the helmsman thrown overboard'), but the reversal of structure improperly attributes the verb to the subject *navis.* The daring invention *excussa magistro... navis* lends intensity and grandeur to the linguistic form; but on the other hand, with an admirable sense of measure, the poet tempers the syntactical daring by assimilating the unusual phrase to the preceding *spoliata armis,* which is entirely plain and normal. The symmetry lessens the deviation and absorbs it into an ordered structural parallelism. One recalls the formula, quoted earlier, with which Klingner liked to define Virgil's classical style: maximum freedom in maximum order.

It is as though Virgil 'smuggled' in his infractions: he continually permits them in order to lend defamiliarization and expressiveness to his language, but just as continually he attenuates them in their context so that they do not disturb the totality of the discourse. Symmetry and parallelism are the procedures which collocate deviations and anomalies once again within an ordered frame. As for example in *Aen.* 4.506: *intenditque locum sertis et fronde coronat*: Dido, who is preparing her own funeral pyre, covers the place with garlands and adorns it with funeral crowns, that is, she stretches festoons from one wall to the other; Servius paraphrases, 'intendit serta per locum'. The enallage *intendit... locum sertis* is a gesture that challenges ordinary language; but the excess of the linguistic gesture is immediately calmed down in the parallelism of the phrase, a

balanced syntactical structure in which *locum*, the improper object of
the verb *intendit*, is in recompense an appropriate object for the verb
coronat. The symmetry attenuates the expressive exaggeration, or at
least disciplines its effects.[39]

In every case, the syntactical torsions with which Virgil defamiliarizes poetic expression are disciplined by the caution of a
Sprachschöpfer careful not to offend linguistic common sense: his
acts of daring revivify the linguistic means, but for every 'improper'
formulation they also suggest the possibility of a 'proper' signification, one which in itself would be admissible, we might say reason-
able. And this brings us back to the idea of a style conceived in the
form of contraband, a move which is irregular but also surreptitious,
not flaunted. Finally, this brings us back to the judgement of the
detractor who spoke of a 'new kind of *cacozelia*', a stylistic elegance
constructed without exhibitionism, indeed well concealed behind the
appearance of linguistic ordinariness. Thus in *quae te, genitor, sententia vertit?* (1.237), where the syntactical construction is reversed,
Venus is accusing Jupiter of not maintaining the promises he had
made regarding the destiny of the Trojans. The new expression, while
it evokes 'in absentia' the phrase which normally would be expected
('what, father, has changed your opinion?'), formulates a meaning
which in any case would be natural ('what opinion, father, has
changed you?'). It is obvious, in short, that *sententiam vertere*
would have been the usual construction; but it is no less evident
that, thanks to the improper syntactical structure, the language here
acquires defamiliarization without having to submit to being
arrogantly outraged. The effects of enallage show themselves to be
even stronger some lines later (1.260), when the same reversed
construction reappears in Jupiter's answer to Venus: *neque me*

---

[39] The same syntactical inversion in 5.403 *ferre manum duroque intendere bracchia
tergo*, 'to hurl fists and to wrap the arms in hard leather', where the normal construction would have required *tergum* and not *bracchia* as the object of *intendere* ('to
stretch the hard leather around the arms'): the parallelism between the two coordinate phrases *ferre manum* and *intendere bracchia* attenuates the syntactical
impropriety. On the other hand, we find the normal syntactical construction in
2.236 f. *stuppea vincula collo | intendunt*, where the procedures of linguistic defami-
liarization of the expression are not syntactical ones (particularly remarkable is the
effect of the double enjambment, marked by the rhyme at the beginning of the verse,
in the verbs *subiciunt* and *intendunt*).

sententia vertit: the verbal structure, even more naked here, makes the syntactical inversion stand out (a perfect parallelism between Venus' question and Jupiter's answer would have required a phrase like *neque ulla me sententia vertit*). The expression has become incisive and the meaning of the sentence has taken on a strong form and a clear structure; the words of the father of the gods become fixed, lapidary, as peremptory as the divine will.

In Virgil's use of syntactical inversion there is one feature which more than all the others is distinctive of his style: we might summarize it in the formula 'simplicity of interventions, complexity of effects'. I am referring once again to the fact that the syntactical modification is often obtained with the lightest of touches, with barely perceptible deviations, without the language having to exhibit the signs of abuse. It is easy to note the most obvious cases, those in which the expressive intensity reveals itself by means of torsions and inversions of constructions; but it is more difficult to measure the effectiveness of a style which is *dérobé*, one which achieves its effects 'stealthily' because it grasps them with a concealed left hand while the right hand is displaying a perfectly correct and irreprehensible behaviour. In short, it is easy to notice the strong deviations, those which we might define as the gestures of language; it is more difficult to notice the subdued deviations, those which give the style a continuous form and which determine the character of an entire artistic language, constituting its constant bearing. The root which nourishes both kinds is always one and the same: but the one kind are occasional, the others persistent and systematic.

For example, what could be more measured and restrained than the intervention which generates a verse like 12.187 *sin nostrum adnuerit nobis victoria Martem*? If we consider that 'Mars' is a normal metonymy meaning 'combat, battle', and that 'Victory' can also be the personification of the goddess celebrated by the victor in a war, the formulation can appear relatively ordinary for a text in an elevated language: it means more or less 'if the victory will approve our battle'. But, given that *adnuerit* properly contains the idea of the assent which is willingly expressed in favour of one of the sides in combat and that the favourable will belongs precisely to the god Mars, one has the impression that Virgil has somehow reversed the normal construction, which would have had to be *sin noster Mars adnuerit nobis victoriam.* This is what Servius thought, for he argued, with scholastic rationalism: 'nam Martem Victoria comitatur', meaning thereby that the victory should only be considered a companion of Mars, a follower of his favourable will, not someone capable of causing it. It is clear that Virgil's intervention is sober, but its effects are remarkable: while the syntactical alteration is compensated for by the possibility of a plausible new meaning, the basic idea (in itself one that is quite banal: 'if we win') finds a defamiliarized form thanks to an improper construction which rhetorically obscures the natural relations of the phrase and thereby stimulates the reader's attention.

No less sober, indeed even less flagrant, is the reversal of the expression in 4.385 *cum frigida mors anima seduxerit artus,* so much so that one might perhaps even deny that there is an enallage in this case; in fact, the syntactical impropriety is almost imperceptible. But to say that 'death detaches the limbs from the soul' is not exactly the same thing as to say that 'death detaches the soul from the limbs': this latter would have been the proper formulation, since according to the epic stereotype it is the soul that departs and leaves the cold body behind when death arrives (*frigida* has an emphatic force and a causative meaning here: referring logically to *artus,* it is instead connected with *mors*). The expressive enhancement lends energy, while the logical and syntactical violation is extremely slight. Of the same kind is the intervention in 12.64–6 *Lavinia...|...cui plurimusignem | subiecit rubor et calefacta per ora cucurrit*: shy Lavinia blushes out of maidenly shame in front of Turnus and Amata. In literal terms it ought to be the fire of her emotion that sets her heart aflame and rises to her face: like Servius *ad loc.* we would expect a construction like *cui ignis animi subiecit ruborem.* But the normality of the current phrase *subicere ignem*[40] prevails, and thus *rubor* takes the place of the subject, that is, it becomes the cause of the fire instead of its effect: the impropriety is attenuated by the parallelism with the second member of the 'dicolon abundans' (*et calefacta per ora cucurrit*), in which *rubor* is a perfectly appropriate subject. The expressive defamiliarization is assured, thanks to the slight syntactic violation; but the natural logic is rescued at the very moment when *ignis* and *rubor* become interchangeable by metonymy.

[40] Cf. 11.186; 2.37; cf. also *Georg.* 4.385.

It happens, too, not only that the syntactical exchange serves to charge the phrase with expressive force, but also that the new construction effectively compresses a complex thought by leaping over the intermediate articulations through a daring condensation. At *Aeneid* 4.477, Dido has decided to die and tries to conceal from her sister her true plans, tricking her with calming discourses: *consilium voltu tegit ac spem fronte serenat* (recalling Ajax in Sophocles' tragedy before his suicide in the 'false speech' he addresses to his wife Tecmessa): 'she conceals in her face her plan and makes her forehead serene, displaying hope': but Virgil's invention *spem fronte serenat* reverses the construction which we would have expected, something which, for the sake of normalization and simplification, might be *spe frontem serenat*.[41] The word *spem* (simulated by Dido: but the fact that Dido is simulating is dramatically suppressed) becomes the object of a verb which is used literally in a physical sense and which therefore could refer to 'forehead' but not to 'hope': *serenare* is the verb that indicates that the sky clears up again when dark clouds have been scattered: cf. 1.255 *caelum tempestatesque serenat*.[42] It is well known that in a certain sense 'dicolon abundans', one of the most characteristic features of Virgil's diction, repeats in the second member the meaning expressed in the first one, so that a sort of parallelism is easily established between the two members: the former phrase proposes the theme, the latter one provides the variation; indeed it often happens that the former has a purely narrative function, while the latter mostly adds descriptive touches. Here too the parallelism acts in such a way that *consilium* corresponds to *spem*, *voltu* to *fronte*, *tegit* to *serenat*, so that the perfectly symmetrical course of the two phrases facilitates the syntactical boldness of the construction *spem ... serenat*. But if *voltu tegit* corresponds to *fronte serenat* (in the sense that for Dido *serenare* is a way of *tegere*), *spem* is instead opposed to *consilium*, indicating its cancellation. Out of this syntactical tension arises an additional meaning which grows until it becomes a dramatic contrast: the reader, knowing the false serenity of

---

[41] The Virgilian nexus will stick in the ear of Silius Italicus who will eliminate the audacity of the enallage, writing *tristia fronte serenant* (11.367).

[42] *Serenum* is the normal designation for a clear and luminous sky; *caeli serena* is a Lucretian nexus to indicate the sky free of clouds.

the speech with which Sophocles' Ajax concealed his plan to kill himself, is caught by the pathos of that tragic prefiguration.

Thus, as I was saying, we see sober use of syntactical displacement, capable nonetheless of producing an effective intensification of the language. But I must add that, since Virgil's syntactical modifications involve linguistic efforts that for the most part are restrained or subtly disguised, there is also the risk that these can sometimes get lost: in other words, it can happen that the reader does not fully notice certain violations of the language only because they are devised with moderation or resolved with apparent naturalness. It can even happen that part of the Virgilian textual tradition suppresses some deviant construction by normalizing it. At 10.857 *quamquam vis alto volnere tardat*, there can be no doubt that the meaning of the phrase must be 'even if the deep wound hampers and slows Mezentius' force (i.e. his physical force, his martial impetus)': the Etruscan king has been wounded in the groin by Aeneas' spear and hence has sustained a bodily injury; he has been made weak and sluggish in his movements. But the cause of this impediment—the deep wound—is not indicated as the subject of the sentence but instead appears as an ablative of cause, and in consequence *vis* becomes the subject. Because of this inversion of the syntactical functions, the verb necessarily takes on an intransitive value: thus *tardat* means 'comes late, arrives slowly, with difficulty', a meaning which is possible but uncommon[43] and which would properly require the passive form *tardatur*. The syntactical reversal forces the language towards a meaning which exists only potentially but which is not the normal one. Its expressiveness is thus much increased.

But in part of the Virgilian textual tradition this unusual construction has disappeared: the syntactical anomaly has been normalized, or at least misunderstood. The two most notable textual variants are *tarda est* (from which derives Sabbadini's *tardast*) and *ardat*: the former restores the more predictable construction (a banalization whose meaning is quite close to that of the passive), the latter

---

[43] Cf. Publ. *Sent.* A. 43 *audendo virtus crescit, tardando timor*; *CIL* 6.18385 PRAETERIENS GRESSV TARDANTE VIATOR. See Feltenius (1977), s.v. *tardare*, who also recalls Cic. *Ad Brut.* 26.1 *at illa rettulit quaesivitque ... an tardare ac commorari te melius esset*; Plin. *Nat.* 11.27 *tardantes sine clementia puniunt*; Apul. *Met.* 5.27 *nec vindictae sequentis poena tardavit*.

interprets the phrase *vis alto volnere* in the sense of 'violent pain for the deep wound', since the wound 'burns' (*ard(e)at*). Servius and Tiberius Donatus too tend to suppress the enallage and to interpret *vis* in the sense of 'violent pain'. But this is unacceptable.[44]

In short, only a systematic interpretation which treats syntactical inversion as an essential feature of the Virgilian manner is capable of recognizing certain expressive audacities which continuously and constantly mark the sublime style of the *Aeneid*.[45] This is a style (this bears repeating) which is nourished by an 'artistic syntax' invented by Virgil in order to lend defamiliarization and intensity to ordinary language. One more case, no less controversial than the preceding ones, will suffice to convince the reader. At 11.830–1 Virgil tells of the death of Camilla, a slow loss of consciousness which overcomes the heroic ardour of the virgin warrior, who is still eager for life and combat: *et captum leto posuit caput: arma relinquunt | vitaque cum gemitu fugit indignata sub umbris*. The direct tradition has lost the reading *arma relinquunt*, replaced quite early by banalizing readings like *reliquit, relinquit, relinquens* (of which Camilla

---

[44] Serv. *alti vulneri violentia*; Tib. *licet tardaretur alti vulneris violentia*. The oscillations of the manuscript tradition can be seen in Geymonat's critical apparatus, without question the most reliable and richest one. Certainly worth less attention is the corruption *quamvis*, which represents the attempt in some way to save *vis*, which was perhaps disturbing in the sense of 'physical force' (probably it was easier to expect a plural *vires*), together with a misrecognition of the syntactical inversion.

[45] It is only if one sees in enallage a peculiar feature of Virgil's expressive defamiliarization, that is, only within the framework of a systematic interpretation of enallage, that one can grasp the effects of stylistic intensification which it is called upon to produce and which otherwise can pass unnoticed. In 11.18 *arma parate animis et spe praesumite bellum* I believe that the first hemistich (before the caesura) must be understood as an inversion of great stylistic effectiveness: these words are contained in the speech with which Aeneas exhorts his men to battle. The ardour of his speech has reversed the formulation which we would have expected: it is enough for the sake of contrast to compare the normal construction in 10.259 *atque animos aptent armis pugnaeque parent se*, a dicolon abundans in which the same encouragement 'to prepare yourselves for battle' is repeated. In *arma parate animis et spe praesumite bellum* too the dicolon abundans has the effect of repeating in the latter member the same idea which has been expressed in the former one. The editors oscillate between two different interpretations and two different possible punctuations: one which connects *animis* to *parate* (as seems to be suggested by the metrical pause) and another which coordinates *animis* with *spe*. Already Servius had his doubts: 'aut hypallage est pro armis parate animos aut certe est mutanda distinctio, ut sit *animis* et *spe*—*bellum*'. Considering the entire stylistic phenomenon which I am trying to delineate, I would not hesitate very much to side with enallage.

herself would be the subject).[46] Only the indirect tradition,
represented by Servius Danielis and probably also by Tiberius Claudius Donatus, preserves the inverted construction *arma relinquunt*
(scil. *eam*, where the subject is *arma*): 'the weapons abandon (her),
slip from her hand'.[47] Whether the nexus should be considered a
hypallage (or 'contrarium'),[48] as Servius Danielis observes quoting
Probus, or whether it should be interpreted differently, certainly the
most obvious way to construct a phrase with the verb *relinquere*
would consist in making Camilla the subject and *arma* the object.
In a certain sense, therefore, the combination *arma relinquunt* can be
considered the inversion of the most obvious construction, but
without any real syntactical violence. But there is indeed violence,
inasmuch as the linguistic representation of this scene is different
from what we might reasonably have expected. The weapons (as has
been said) slip from Camilla's hand at the moment when the mortally
wounded heroine loses her strength; it is not she who leaves
her weapons, but the weapons that leave her (*relinquunt*). And
together with the weapons, life too leaves Camilla: the copula *-que*
in the nexus *vitaque cum gemitu fugit* has the function of holding
together, in close connection, the two-part addition *arma relinquunt*
| *vitaque . . . fugit.*

Before *arma relinquunt* there is a pause, a break which interrupts
the continuity with the preceding sentence: the new syntactical
movement is completely autonomous, marked as it is by asyndeton
and a change of subject. This is a structure which has been stylized on
the basis of a Homeric model (the asyndetic coordination with a
change of subject is typically Homeric), a structure not different from
other 'paraformular codes'[49] with which Virgil likes to reproduce
those formulae which Homer places as a seal upon a narrative
sequence, clichés that are added as an appendix to a death scene,

[46] There are excellent treatments of the many problems connected with this
reading in Timpanaro (1986), 94–9, and Delvigo (1987), 69–81. I entirely agree
with the arguments of these two scholars, to whom I refer for the details.

[47] DServ. *Arma relinquens*: 'alii *arma relinquunt* legunt; Probus hypallagen vult
esse, vel contrarium, ut ipsa relinquat; alii *arma relinquunt* cum laude dictum
accipiunt, id est illa decidebant e manibus Camillae exanimis'; Tib. 'ceciderunt et
arma, cum haec ulterius tenere non posset' (II. 534, 26 ff. Georgii).

[48] Cf. above, p. 84; cf. also Timpanaro (1986), 94 n. 26.

[49] This is what I called them in my article (1983*a*): see Ch. 5.

like for example *Iliad* 12.386 λίπε δ᾽ ὀστέα θυμός 'life left his bones', 7.12 λύντο δὲ γυῖα, 'his limbs were loosened', 21.114 λύτο γούνατα καὶ φίλον ἦτορ, 'his knees and heart were loosened'. Perhaps we could compare the combination *arma relinquunt* with the Homeric stereotype (placed at the end of wounding scenes as a conclusive addition) 'from his hand fell the bow, from his hand fell the firebrand': τόξον δέ οἱ ἔκπεσε χειρός (8.329; 15.465), δαλὸς δέ οἱ ἔκπεσε χειρός (15.421).⁵⁰

Some ancient critic, or some scribe, did not understand the inversion *arma relinquunt* and normalized the stylistic deviation, banalizing the text.⁵¹ But now, this inversion too can be placed in a series with other analogous occurrences and accepted in a survey that considers syntactical inversion as a recurrent means of expressive intensification, and it can thereby be recognized as a genuine fruit of Virgil's creativity. Once more we must give thanks to that ancient detractor, grateful for a judgement founded upon antipathy but extraordinarily perspicacious: the *cacozelia* which he criticized in Virgil emerges as nothing other than a novel form of expressive defamiliarization, thanks to which words derived from ordinary language are set dynamically into reciprocal tension. Here resides the secret of a revitalized epic language. From this root, a new sublime style develops and draws strength.

Pseudo-Longinus would have approved of our efforts at stylistic analysis, especially because of a deeply rooted conviction of his: that the sublime, although it is produced by *ingenium* and is the fruit of spiritual grandeur, is always substantiated by *ars* and is necessarily entrusted to expressive techniques. As was remarked

---

⁵⁰ For the typicality of the scene we might also compare *Il.* 13.542–4 (or 14. 419 f.): 'while he was turned towards him, he struck him in the throat with the sharp spear: his head inclined to one side, but the shield and the helmet remained tied on; death which weakens the spirit fell upon him' (here too we find the description in three phases: the wounded man bends his head, his weapons remain uselessly attached, and then the final verse that announces his death).

⁵¹ Already Ribbeck (1866), 140, argued that, faced with a tradition offering only a plain and pacific reading like *relinquens* or *reli(n)quit*, no one would have thought of conjecturing *relinquunt*. 'Dunque,' concludes Timpanaro (1986), 99, 'Probo conobbe almeno un manoscritto che recava *relinquunt*, la *lectio difficilior* che, non capita da altri copisti, fu banalizzata'.

earlier, in his view the grandeur of ideas and images cannot be separated from *megalegoria*, that is, it never remains outside of language. The sublime style that brings the reader to exaltation is nothing other than a labour of verbal construction performed by the author. Transpositional syntax is the means which modifies the normal linguistic structures and saves the language from the danger of entirely passive consumption, that is, it frees it from the defect of instability, but in exchange it imprisons it, imprisons it within the form. Artistic syntax is different in this regard from normal syntax: it pretends to serve the language, but in reality it imposes itself upon it; it makes a show of pushing the words gently towards the meaning, but in reality the result is that the meaning drags the words along and arrogantly subordinates them to itself. Virgil knows how to temper the arrogance of his transpositional syntax: he allows the language to rise up in search of intensity and the words to be charged with an expressive gesture, but he also knows how to dilute that gesture within the ordered totality of the verse and how to recompose it in a new equilibrium.

Even when the deviation seems more marked, the new syntactical formulation finds a new meaning which is acceptable, that is, contextually tolerable. At 6.268 *Ibant obscuri sola sub nocte per umbram*, Aeneas and the Sybil are represented while they enter the subterranean realm of the dead. The verse moves along softly and fluidly; words of common usage repeat a single idea: that all around darkness hangs heavy and a silent obscurity covers everything. To describe two solitary wayfarers travelling across a world deprived of light, a hypothetical syntactical normality would have had to say *ibant obscura soli sub nocte per umbram*: this would have been a regular formulation, perfectly isometric and interchangeable. But the syntactical exchange of the two adjectives suffices to make the phrase acquire a strong expressive defamiliarization: the obscurity which belongs literally to the night (one cannot help but recall the Homeric cliché ἐρεβεννὴ νὺξ | ἐρεβεννῇ νυκτι, *Iliad* 5.659, 13.425) refers to the two wayfarers, while their solitude refers to the night. All the verbal elements which serve the gloomy representation survive in the new arrangement, but the logical unnaturalness foregrounds descriptive features which otherwise would have been secondary and thereby imposes a new logic, plausible too but at the same time stronger. It is plausible, in fact, that if the night is obscure the two wayfarers too should appear 'obscure'; and it is just as plausible that if they are alone on their path the night too should be 'solitary'. The new meanings, redistributed differently, impress themselves upon the reader's consciousness and inflame his perception by adding a note of emotional subjectivity. The language—the lexicon and the constructions—is the most ordinary possible: the enallage reacts to this ordinariness with an expressive flash that burns up the slag of a language intentionally poor in pomp and thereby sublimates it.

But not only does the syntactical deviation produce a strong stylistic heightening: by its effect the dominant idea, the darkness of the night, also emerges with greater intensity. In fact, if one considers the nine lines 264–72 which contain at their centre line 268, which we are discussing, it cannot escape notice that they are an insistent variation upon the theme of the obscurity which pervades the subterranean realm of the dead: *loca nocte tacentia late* (line 265), *caligine* (267), *sub nocte per umbram* (268), *caelum condidit umbra* (271), *nox...atra* (272). And in line 264 the same word *umbra* recurs in the phrase *umbraeque silentes*, this time to indicate the inhabitants of the infernal world themselves. In short, the lack of daylight which characterizes the Underworld is emphasized by the enallage *ibant obscuri*, a syntactical impropriety which concentrates in a single sharply focused point the idea of darkness diffused throughout the whole passage.

One more thing needs to be added. It needs to be added that, if the enallage which has just been examined produces a marked deviation, so too the following verse already reveals another expressive audacity, but one which is almost imperceptible this time yet still capable of transforming the construction of the words: *inania regna* of line 269 are literally not 'the empty realms' but 'the realms of those who are evanescent because they lack a body'. The syntactical figure barely strains the meaning, yet it is enough to make the language new. It is a delicate gesture, which forms part of the indefatigable process of defamiliarization by means of which Virgil succeeds in sublimating even the smallest details of poetic expression. This is the pertinent feature of Virgil's style: that no connection of words, or almost none, is left inert, without the signs of art.

But to create an artistic language means above all to know how to relax or increase the expressive tension according to a measured rhythm which not only respects the order of the whole but also sparks individual effects of detail. The agonistic use of language actively engages the reader and thereby makes him/her a sublime reader, that is, a reader who participates in, and almost shares responsibility for, the emotions which s/he acquires from the emotional intensity of the text. Thus it comes about that the tenor of the epic discourse is maintained on the threshold of a constant vibration. And when it is not the turn of alliterations, assonances, and the other figures of sound or versification, to make the language more expressive, it is instead the elaboration of the syntax, that is, the form of the constructions, that gives impetus to the diction, elevating the style and rendering the combination of the words new and 'difficult'. The deviation of enallage, as has been seen, is perhaps that which most felicitiously fulfils a double, contradictory requirement: to intensify effectively the construction of the phrases and to construct the verses according to a normal, apparently well-ordered profile.

We shall see that syntactical displacement can sometimes manifest itself in successive verses as well, or in ones that are very close to one another: it can act as a diffuse expedient and not only as an occasional one, functioning as an almost systematic corrective for an ordinary and 'easy' lexicon which thereby becomes defamiliarized, enhanced, more intense. Let us consider 4.356–9:

> Nunc etiam interpres divom Iove missus ab ipso
> (testor utrumque caput) celeris mandata per auras
> detulit: ipse deum manifesto in lumine vidi
> intrantem muros vocemque his auribus hausi.

Aeneas is telling Dido about the profound religious horror with which he reacted to the appearance of Mercury; Jupiter's divine messenger has harshly called him back to his duty and ordered him to leave Carthage immediately. Two enallages in successive verses, *celeres . . . per auras* and *manifesto in lumine*, revitalize the normal constructions. In fact, 'rapidity' would belong literally to Mercury or to the verb, not to the air through which the god has flown: strictly speaking we would expect *celer* or *celeriter*. The adjective *celeres*, even if it refers to *auras*, nonetheless communicates the idea of extremely rapid flight; but the syntactical displacement creates a new expressive emphasis which indirectly suggests Aeneas' petrified terror at the sight of this flight, which seems to him to be instantaneous and miraculous; indeed, fearing that he might not be able to persuade Dido of this incredible prodigy, he feels the need to add a strong oath to lend credibility to his words: *testor utrumque caput*. Incidentally, it should be noted that the transposed adjective *celeres* acquires even further emphasis in the verse by its isolation between two strong pauses, at the penthemimeral and hepthemimeral caesuras. And this provides further confirmation of a principle of considerable import-ance in every stylistic analysis, namely the convergence of expressive factors: metrical expedients and rhetorical expedients often conspire together to intensify the meaning, given that both kinds of features are born out of that very meaning and are its confluent effects.

A similar enallage recurs elsewhere, and with the very same stylistic effectiveness: not only a few verses earlier, when Jupiter imparts his decision to Mercury, at 4.226 *celeris defer mea dicta per auras*;[52] but also at 5.502 f. *primaque per caelum... sagitta | ... volucris diverberat auras*, where we should let ourselves be guided by the same syntac-tical figure and understand *volucris* by enallage with *auras* and not with *sagitta*, which has its own balanced complement in the adjective *prima*. Analogously at 5.128 *apricis statio gratissima mergis*, where 'sunny' is a perfectly appropriate adjective for defining a place; even if the deviation is slight, the new phrase succeeds in enhancing the meaning of the attribute. Analogously again at 5.211 f. *agmine remorum celeri ventisque vocatis | prona petit maria*, where *prona*, which is applied to the sea, should strictly speaking be applied to the rowers, curved forwards by their exertion, who are implicitly mentioned in *agmine remorum*:[53] the syntactical violation is consid-erable, and just as considerable is the expressive density which the construction succeeds in attaining (and which is also reinforced by the double alliteration *ventisque vocatis, prona petit*).

The enallage *deum manifesto in lumine vidi | intrantem muros* (4.358 f.), contained in the line following the one analysed above, also repeats the numinous horror which strikes Aeneas at Mercury's appearance. The syntactical alteration *deum manifesto in lumine*,

---

[52] Cf. also 4.270 *ipse haec ferre iubet celeris mandata per auras.*
[53] Cf. 3.668 *verrimus et proni certantibus aequora remis.*

instead of a predictable *deum manifestum in lumine*,[54] distorts the adjective towards a new, more intense meaning: 'in a brilliant light'; this new meaning represents the point of view of Aeneas, whose eyes are stupefied by the appearance of a superhuman light. The narration has become subjective and has allowed itself to be permeated by the speaker's emotional reactions; the form of the expression is unexpected and above all it acquires a pathetic (or, more exactly an empathetic) resonance. Virgil often reaches sublimity merely by allowing his language to take on the form of the emotions.

The transference of the adjective, in short, not only gives expressive enhancement and tension to the language, it also succeeds in capturing implicit suggestions and making them evident. An entirely analogous case is presented by 7.9 *splendet tremulo sub lumine pontus*, where the trembling would belong literally to the water of the sea, but by being transferred to the moonlight becomes an element of visual impressionism: what is more, the assonance (*-le, -lo, -lu*) insinuates musical effects into the whole sequence *splendet tremulo sub lumine*. This is another evident case of the accumulation of expressive factors: in fact, the words gain in intensity thanks to a construction in which syntactical displacement and phonetic recurrence converge with one another.

The same impressionistic suggestiveness characterizes 11.601 f. *late ferreus hastis | horret ager campique armis sublimibus ardent*: the whole *ager* seems *ferreus*, so many are the spearpoints that cover it like standing stalks of corn. The adjective need only be transferred from the spears to the field to create a syntactical impropriety which generates a deviation and thereby enhances the image. But what is involved is not only this violation of the verbal concordances: the whole sentence acquires expressiveness from an elaborate artistic structure. There is above all the effective redundancy of the 'dicolon abundans' of which Virgil was so fond, which lets him represent the same scene according to different and complementary perceptions: first the stretch of terrain 'seems

---

[54] Beyond the defamiliarizing function which the enallage performs by 'deforming' the more usual formulation, we may note on the other hand that Virgil's gesture of expressive liberty reconfirms the order and balance of the whole: *manifestum* would have created an accumulation of indications around *deum*, to which *intrantem* already refers, while *in lumine* would have remained without an adjectival complement.

to bristle with spears' (*hastis horret*); then the same terrain seems to 'catch fire' from the iron that glitters in the sunlight (*armis . . . ardent*). Then there is the elegance of the framing structure which arranges the two verbs (*horret* and *ardent*) at the opening and close of the verse and thereby lends balance to the sentence and restores order to the syntactical disorder produced by the slight enallage of *ferreus*. Finally one notices upon closer inspection another very slight syntactical violation, almost another enallage, only hinted at and yet still capable of adding an impressionistic touch to the picture: *sublimibus* is connected with *armis*, even though the descriptive notation should properly be connected with the verb *ardent*: 'they catch fire upwards'. Strictly speaking we might perhaps have expected an almost adverbial phrase, something like *campi in sublime ardent*, to indicate that the battlefield sends up tongues of flame towards the sky: the function of the nexus *armis sublimibus* is properly that of compressing this whole image in a single summarizing gesture. In this case too we find a clever arrangement of the words and an alteration of the constructions concurring with one another in a synergy which succeeds in defamiliarizing a thoroughly ordinary lexicon. Order and rhythm lend elegance to a balanced composition, while here and there gestures of syntactical freedom, more or less sharp points of linguistic innovation, render the expression more intense.

It has already been said more than once that Virgil likes to compensate for any syntactical violation, be it slight or prominent, by arranging a meaning which, however new it might be, also appears to be possible, almost natural: in this way the shrewd *Sprachschöpfer* tends to disguise the violation by constructing the semblance of a new logical and semantic normality. Although it has been rearranged in an acceptable form, the innovation nonetheless creates its defamiliarizing effect, but without offending the reader's linguistic common sense or seeming too provocative. The reader touches the deviation and notices its roughness, and yet he is not at all disturbed, since a new order of linguistic acceptableness—a poetic one—welcomes the new construction and immediately justifies it anew. Thus at 11.624 ff. *pontus | . . . scopulosque superiicit unda | spumeus*, although the adjective *spumeus* (which seems to be a Virgilian coinage)[55] refers

---

[55] Serv. *ad Aen.* 2.419; cf. Norden *ad Aen.* 6.281; Bednara (1908), 224 and 228.

improperly to *pontus* it only superficially violates the logical and semantic pertinence which would require it to refer to *unda*[56] (or else, if one wishes, to *scopulos*).[57] Indeed, the slight syntactical violation lends an expressive autonomy to the adjective and almost individualizes its meaning (the enjambment too contributes to this effect: by being displaced to the beginning of the following verse, *spumeus* is made to seem an addition which is marked inasmuch as it is unexpected). But upon closer inspection one notices other verbal effects as well which contribute towards defamiliarizing the whole context in which this syntactical deviation finds a place. An energetic alliteration (*scopulos, superiicit, spumeus*) deprives the individual words of any appearance of randomness and makes them seem the necessary elements in a harmonious chain in which the sounds themselves appear to generate the meaning and to be generated in turn by it. In this case too as in others, the defamiliarization due to phonetic and metrical effects and the defamiliarization produced by syntactical alteration conspire with one another to make the language more expressive.

Welcomed into a new order of linguistic acceptability, the syntactical deviation not only does not disturb the reader: indeed, it attracts her/him, for s/he finds the pleasure of an increased expressiveness and at the same time the comfort of a logic which may well be different but in any case is plausible. The two aspects cannot be separated from one another. Often, indeed, the linguistic ordinariness is not completely severed from the syntactical alteration but is merely evaded. Often, moreover, the memory of that ordinariness survives in the immediate juxtaposition of words which ought together to have formed a thoroughly familiar construction, if only the poet had not intervened so as to avoid connecting with one another verbal elements all too easily destined to be connected. What I mean is that behind a group of words like *ferreus hastis* or *unda spumeus* we catch a glimpse of the shadow of a normal construction which is absent (*ferreis hastis* or *unda spumea*): that construction seemed prosaic or gave the impression of being a cliché, so it ran the risk of banality, of expressive ineffectiveness.

---

[56] Cf. Catull. 68.3 *spumantibus aequoris undis*; Virg. *Georg.* 4.529 *spumantem undam sub vertice torsit*; Aen. 3.268 *fugimus spumantibus undis.*

[57] Cf. Cic. *Arat. progn.* fr. 3.3 Soub. *saxa . . . salis niveo spumata liquore.*

So too at 9.66 *ignescunt irae, duris dolor ossibus ardet*: the verse expresses the intolerable burning of anger, and the adjective, which means 'cruel', should literally refer to *dolor* (cf. e.g. *Aen.* 5.5 *duri... dolores*, 4.488 *duras... curas*). Instead, the new syntactical combination lends the adjective an entirely physical meaning ('in the hard bones') and at the same time gives the image a harsh force not at all possessed by the bare individual words—words which are among the most ordinary ones. In the sequence *duris dolor* we can still recognize the trace of the normal nexus *durus dolor*, the very combination which the enallage has dissolved. Once the reader's normal expectations have been frustrated, the meaning is as it were redoubled: the expected meaning persists alongside an unexpected one. Two meanings somehow coexist, one normal and one abnormal, one absent and one present: neither one can entirely eliminate the other. To try to eliminate it (or at least to try to reduce the anomaly to normality) is a mistake for which the price is banalization—precisely what the scribe of one of the oldest manuscripts of Virgil, the Palatine, did when he normalized *duris dolor ossibus ardet* into *durus dolor ossibus ardet*. Did he do this without noticing, or could he not tolerate the syntactic deviation?

We have seen that a syntactical violation can recur in verses which are close to one another or even sequential: this is a sign that violating normal phrasing is an attitude inherent in Virgil's style, a pervasive feature of his artistic language and not an exceptional procedure. The search for expressive intensity spontaneously accompanies every act of linguistic formulation. See 3.581 f., where Virgil describes the giant Enceladus who was struck by Jupiter's lightning bolt and now, crushed beneath the weight of Aetna, vomits forth fire: *et fessum quotiens mutet latus, intremere omnem | murmure Trinacriam et caelum subtexere fumo*. The image that concludes this pair of lines is as it were reversed: the usual construction, the most obvious and most logical one, would have required instead *caelo subtexere fumum* 'to weave together a curtain of smoke under the vault of heaven'. Ovid, for example, uses the very same image but respects the appropriate construction: a veil of clouds woven in the middle of the air covers the sky at *Met.* 14.368 *et patrio capiti bibulas subtexere nubes.*[58] In the Virgilian passage, the enallage permits the verb to release all its pent-up semantic charge and the image of *subtexere* becomes more incisive: the phrase suggests the viewpoint of the spectator who looks upwards and from below sees the vault of the sky as though it were interwoven with threads of smoke. But the preceding verse too conceals a slight syntactic deviation. *Mutare latus* is a stock phrase to indicate 'to turn over onto one's other side': cf. Ov. *Met.* 13.936 f. ... *coepit mea praeda moveri | et mutare latus*; Stat. *Theb.* 3.594 f. ... *ubi temptat | Enceladus mutare latus* (this whole passage is dependent upon Virgil). The Virgilian construction, which incorporates the adjective (*fessum* ... *mutet latus*), extrapolates an idiomatic phrase: one might more properly have expected *fessus* ... *mutet latus*. The intervention is minimal but nonetheless produces its effect.

At 12.738 it is once again the transference of the adjective that has the effect of defamiliarizing the language in two contiguous, strictly successive cases: *dum terga dabant palantia Teucri | ... postquam arma dei ad Volcania ventum.* The first syntactical violation is barely perceptible, but it is enough to reanimate a construction that otherwise would be flat and prosaic: *terga dare* (in the sense of 'flee') is an idiomatic expression complete in itself, one not open to further modification, so that the more predictable construction would have had to be *terga dabant palantes Teucri*; but metrical convenience and a taste for linguistic innovation have combined to modify the regular syntactical structure. The second violation contains one of those enallages which make the language supremely elaborated: in the phrase *arma dei ad Volcania* the adjective *Volcania* belongs properly to *dei*: the new nexus (an artifice of the 'ornatus difficilis') serves to render the naked verbal sequence more precious; cf. 10.113 *Stygii per flumina fratris.*

In short, the syntactical alteration is manifested in the text with great frequency; even if it does not appear in lines which are actually sequential, it can still do so in lines which are not too distant from one another. It thereby reveals its vocation for figuring among the procedures which are best adapted to Virgil's contradictory poetics

---

[58] But cf. Lucr. 6.482 *et quasi densendo subtexit caerula nimbis*; 5.466 *subtexunt nubila caelum*: 'the clouds interweave the sky' (almost stretching a grey veil under the heavens).

and which best put into practice his ambitious stylistic project of constructing an original and intense artistic language, but only using an entirely ordinary lexicon. See 5.45–8:

> 'Dardanidae magni, genus alto a sanguine divom,
> annuus exactis completur mensibus orbis,
> ex quo reliquias divinique ossa parentis
> condidimus terra maestasque sacravimus aras.'

At line 45, *genus alto a sanguine divom* is not in itself a very daring combination, even if *alto* ought to refer literally to *divom* (or, less probably, to *genus*): the deviation is made almost imperceptible by the fact that the new meaning which the attribute receives ('noble') is implicit to a certain extent, by connotation, in the meaning of 'origin, birth' which *sanguine* can also normally have. Three verses later, the expected predicate *maesti* is instead absorbed into the nexus *maestas . . . aras*, creating a singular syntactical reformulation which perhaps also aims to reinforce the 'sigmatism' which marks the verse expressively.

Precisely the opposite happens at 11.871 *(Rutuli) tuta petunt et equis aversi ad moenia tendunt*, where strictly speaking we would expect the combination *equis aversis*. Aside from its metrical convenience, the unexpected nominative *aversi* emphasizes the adjective in the verse; referring to the subject, it seems in fact to express the subjective intention of the verb, as though it were introducing an implicit psychological note: the Rutulians, terrorized by Camilla's death, choose flight *(aversi)* to seek safety *(tuta petunt)*. Five lines earlier, in another enallage, Opis, the divine executor of the goddess Diana's will, has just avenged Camilla's death by piercing with an arrow the man who slew her: line 865 f. *illum exspirantem socii atque extrema gementem | obliti ignoto camporum in pulvere linquunt.* Properly speaking, *ignoto* should refer to *illum* (=*Arruntem*); the slayer of Camilla had asked Apollo to be allowed to strike the virgin warrior and to return alive to his fatherland after that exploit; but his destiny is to remain, dead, on the battlefield, indeed not only dead but also unknown, without fame, without identity (a further punishment for his offence). This is a meaning which should have been expressed by the phrase *illum . . . socii . . . obliti ignotum . . . linquunt*, yet it is recovered somehow by the new formulation.

But the recovery is achieved only indirectly: in fact, while the adjective 'unknown' actually refers to the dusty battlefield, the text suggests that it is literally Arruns who is destined to remain 'unknown', since it says that his companions abandon him without taking thought for him (*obliti*). The enallage takes with one hand and gives with the other, as though next to the rhetorical 'improprium' one could also glimpse the suppressed 'proprium': not only what is explicit but also what remains implicit: *illum... socii... obliti (ignotum) ignoto camporum in pulvere linquunt*. Thus the idea receives an ambiguous formulation: the meaning remains as it were suspended and tries to complete itself almost without paying attention to the new syntactical arrangement. This thus benefits the form of the expression, boldly stretched taut between what is said and what is not said.

Once again, let us consider another pair of enallages which follow one another in the course of only a few lines: 8.542 f. *Herculeis sopitas ignibus aras | excitat...* and 548 f. *pars cetera prona | fertur aqua segnisque secundo defluit amni*. In the first case, Aeneas, with an act of religious devotion, revives upon the altars of Hercules the fires which were kindled in the solemn ceremony of the preceding day and which are now dying down; clearly, *sopitas* should refer properly to *ignibus* and *Herculeis* in turn to *aras*: the transference of the adjectives revitalizes the verbal sequence without committing a true semantic abuse. For the new meaning is made plausible by the contiguity of meaning existing among the words: if the sacred fire dies down, so too the altars (upon which it burns) can be said to die down; if the altars are consecrated to Hercules, so too the fire (which burns upon them) can be said to be consecrated to him.

Six lines later, in the lines 548 f. already cited above, a 'dicolon abundans' works an elegant variation upon the (symbolic) motif of the water of the Tiber which transports the Trojans, welcome guests of Evander, in its propitious and serene course. The redundancy is rendered emphatic by the perfect parallelism between the two members, *prona fertur aqua* and *secundo defluit amni*: 'Aeneas' remaining companions (while messengers from Aeneas are going to Ascanius) sail along, carried by the current, and move slowly along with the favourable motion of the river.' Strictly speaking, the adjective *segnis* should refer to the river, which literally flows 'lazily': but the syntactical transposition (*pars cetera...segnis...secundo defluit amni*) produces an effective expressive deviation: in this way, the Trojans become themselves participants—subjectively participants—in the atmosphere of quiet, of serene 'tranquillity', which rules Evander's rural world and which affects them too. But the text also contains a contrast, since this atmosphere of rural quiet is destined to disappear, destroyed by the imminent explosion of war. The contrasting effects supply a tension to the narrative and make it dramatic; the narrative thus becomes dramatic and thereby agrees to represent the characters' emotionality too: in this way the *Aeneid* constructs itself as a subjective epic.

Strong deviations and subdued ones, both serve to defamiliarize the language, to prevent the words from escaping without remaining in the reader's ear and mind. Enallage's most constantly creative function, that which succeeds in giving a form to the expression and a character to the style, consists in producing syntactical violations which can even be only slightly marked yet are diffused throughout the whole continuity of the text. Most often, in fact, the new linguistic formulation takes on the appearance of a choice which is justified in and of itself, as though it were one possible choice among others. In fact there is not a true violation of the linguistic norm if one says, 'every propitious oracle has predicted for me the route (towards Italy)'; and this is just how Virgil expresses himself at 3.362 f. *omnis cursum mihi prospera dixit | religio*; and yet there can be no doubt that *prospera* ought properly to refer to *cursum*. In short, the innovation must be discovered behind the soothing appearance of normality: the deviation tends to camouflage itself by entering into a new syntactical arrangement and adapting itself to a linguistic order which has been opportunely reframed.

This is particularly the case when the enallage involves a simple transference of the adjective; but even when the deviation is produced by an inversion of the syntactical construction, the move ends up being almost clandestine: it does not seek to be conspicuous; it avoids affectation. For example, what degree of violation can we sense in a combination like *ne tanta animis adsuescite bella* (6.832)? One might say that the requirement of linguistic defamiliarization has literally inverted the more predictable formulation (which would have had to be: 'do not accustom your spirits to such terrible wars');

but the violation is almost neutralized by being fitted into a syntactically regular structure.[59] But it is not only the form of the expression which ends up being revitalized; it is above all the meaning which is enhanced. Anchises, in a prophetic vision of the future history of Rome, exhorts his descendants not to accept the monstrosity of the civil wars as a habit of the spirit: *ne, pueri, ne tanta animis adsuescite bella | neu patriae validas in viscera vertite vires.* The syntactical reversal transmits a dynamic impulse to the construction and sharpens its meaning: that habituation to civil hatred should not penetrate so deeply into the spirit of the Romans that it determines their character; in other words, that the painful experience of civil strife should not become a perverse education in error.[60] Anchises' heart-felt intonation lasts into the whole following line, where a marked alliterative cadence solemnly articulates the (historiographic and tragic) topos of a great people brought by inner hatreds to destroy their own country. Syntactical inversion and expressive alliteration act next to one another as different modes of the same pathetic intensification: both of them are expedients intended to transform ordinary language into an artistic language aimed at the sublime.

As we were saying, this is the power of the stylistic expression and its expressive intensification: the words are defamiliarized by enallage and thereby rediscover the original freshness of their meaning. Indeed, they can even derive a surplus of meaning—an increase in their signification—from the logical and syntactical tension which pervades the constructions. At 5.478 ff. Entellus, who wants to sacrifice to the divine memory of Eryx the young bull he has received as a prize, strikes a deadly blow between the animal's horns with his right hand, covered by the boxing glove: *durosque reducta | libravit dextra media inter cornua cestus | arduus, effractoque inlisit in ossa cerebro.* The whole sentence is marked by cleverly arranged expressive effects. (*a*) *duros* is placed at the beginning of the sentence and its

---

[59] Analogously, one should not forget the double syntactical possibility normally offered by constructions like *donare aliquid alicui/donare aliquem aliqua re*, or *circumdo aliquid alicui/circumdo aliquem aliqua re* (the construction with the dative is the archaic one).

[60] Cf. Serv. *ad l.* 'mire dictum: ab ipsis enim quasi consuetudinem facit populus Romanus bellorum civilium'.

substantive *cestus* is delayed until the end of the following verse; the pulling apart of the two syntactically linked elements represents very well the movement of the fist which is first raised high (*reducta libravit dextra*) before suddenly descending. (*b*) *arduus* is pushed by enjambment to the beginning of the next verse, where the caesura leaves it isolated in an emphatic position: it represents Entellus stretching up in order to get a running start. (*c*) The verb *libravit* and its predicate *arduus* are placed with perfect correspondence at the opening of two successive verses: a single protracted effort, a construction sustained by a single breath.

But it is only with the enallage contained in the last verse that the maximum degree of expressive intensity is attained: *effractoque inlisit in ossa cerebro*. The more logical formulation, the one more appropriate for the normal sequence of the meaning, would have had to be: *effracta ossa inlisit in cerebrum* 'he shattered the bones (of the skull) and drove them into the brain'.[61] The anomalous syntactical combination has driven the expressiveness almost to excess, but it has also succeeded in imprinting an extraordinary power on the whole image. By refusing a usual and prosaic arrangement, every single element of the phrase becomes defamiliarized and acquires its whole original *vis significativa* anew.

Of necessity, the reader of Virgil must be vigilant. To notice these stylistic effects, to adapt him/herself to the expressive signals with which the poet animates the language, the reader must show him/herself to be continually circumspect. Anywhere in the text, behind an appearance of formal composure, behind the polished semblances of normality, can be hidden the sharp point of the linguistic deviation. Only if the reader's ear has been trained on the usual syntactical combinations—those which are normally and logically valid—can the deviation from the norm reach the desired effect. But Virgil's art knows how to attenuate its violations: it is enough if they are not made too evident. *procella velum adversa ferit* (1.103) or *serpens... quem obliquum rota transiit* (5.274): here are two cases in which there is, and at the same time there is not, a syntactical violation. Strictly speaking, we would have expected *velum adversum ferit* and

---

[61] Cf. Serv. *ad l.* 'hypallage: effregit ossa et inlisit in cerebrum'.

obliqua rota transiit, since this is what the logic of a plain and normal phrase would have required. But metrical convenience and, above all, the requirement of expressive defamiliarization have modified the construction, even if only slightly. Each of the two transpositions is like a roughness which is well disguised and yet is perceptible to the touch (I believe that there really is such a thing as a linguistic sense of touch). Slight thought they are, the two enallages produce an effect: in the former case, in fact, the storm seems to strike the sails with a more active force (*adversa ferit*); in the latter, the snake seems more conspicuously to be divided in two by the wheel which has passed over it at an angle (*obliquum... transiit*). In short, there is an increase in expressiveness and at the same time an increase in the style: not only is the meaning intensified, the language too increases in elevation, becoming an artistic language.

At 5.857 *vix primos inopina quies laxaverat artus,* the god Sleep deviously seizes the helmsman Palinurus, who tries to keep himself awake at the helm of Aeneas' ship, and hurls him into the sea. It is evident that the transference of *primos* to *artus* constitutes a syntactical 'improprium': properly it should refer to *quies*.[62] Indeed, the reader knows that the normal phrase, *prima quies,* is a cliché dear to Virgil, the 'inner ear' of his versification (cf. 1.723; 2.268; 8.407); but here Virgil separates himself from it, with a major gain in expressiveness. The first effect of the enallage is that it attracts attention to the suddenness with which sleep falls upon Palinurus; a secondary effect is that the words recombined in this way form an elegant framing structure (*primos... artus*). Finally, there is a balance in the adjectives: just as *quies* is completed by *inopina,* so too *artus* finds its completion in *primos*. The whole phrase, in short, finds a new equilibrium, but above all is charged with greater intensity.

As we have seen, Virgil does not flaunt his interventions, instead he disguises them: only a reader who is alert and attentive to expressive deviations can recognize and appreciate them. For example, everything might seem quite regular in the phrase *confusae stragis acervum* (6.504); but would not the more proper formulation have

---

[62] It remains true that *vix primos... laxaverat artus* has an implicit temporal connotation which indicates the suddenness of the sleep which falls upon Palinurus, so that, behind the transposition *vix primos,* we can perhaps glimpse the missing adverbial nexus *vix primum*.

had to be *confusum stragis acervum*? The same applies to *Idaeae sacro de vertice pinus* (10.230): even admitting that there is no violation in calling the peak of Mount Ida 'sacred', is it not the case that strictly speaking *Idaeae* should be the adjective for *vertice* and *sacro* instead the adjective for *pinus*? Likewise at 5.151 *effugit ante alios primisque elabitur undis*... *Gyas*: the meaning of the verse is perfectly clear, and yet Virgil's formulation is not at all equivalent to what we might consider normal, *primusque elabitur undis* (which would have been entirely equivalent from the point of view of the metre).[63] The meaning is in any case made certain by the redundancy of the 'dicolon abundans': *effugit* returns, varied, in *elabitur*, and by parallelism *ante alios* would lead us to expect *primus* rather than the new phrase *primis... undis*. The same thing happens at 8.596 *quadrupedante putrem sonitu quatit ungula campum*, where the adjective *quadrupedante* refers to *sonitu* and not, as it ought to, to the subject *ungula*: the enallage expressively reinforces the sound symbolism of the assonance (thus *sonitu* becomes a marked word, indeed the explicit sign of the strong sonority which the verse is imitating).

But there are also opposing examples,[64] in which the adjective is transferred from the adverbial phrase to the subject: 4.303 *nocturnusque vocat clamore Cithaeron*. In some cases considerations of metrical convenience may also play a role, as at 9.269 f. *quibus ibat in armis | aureus* (the cretic *aureis* was not capable of being used in a dactylic hexameter;[65] in any case the visual impression which is produced by the syntactical displacement—and which is reinforced by enjambment—is that of a brilliant blaze of light); so too at 11.695 *eludit gyro interior* or 11.786 f. *cui pineus ardor acervo | pascitur* or 10.785 f. *(hasta)... imaque sedit | inguine*. Hence it is not the case that Virgil is trying out possibilities unknown to ordinary language; rather, he tends to take apart the most obvious combinations, the ones which are nearest to the normality of prose. Thus at 12.267 *sonitum dat stridula cornus*, where the syntactical modification gives a strong meaning to the adjective *stridula*, turning it almost into an

[63] Baehrens (often infelicitous as a conjectural critic) banalized the text with *primusque*.

[64] Some indications in Kroll (1924), 258 ff. (generally rather reductive).

[65] In fact, it could be used, by synizesis: cf. *Aen*. 1.726 *laquearibus aureis* (at line-end).

echo chamber for the whole verse; for if we read the following phrase, *et auras certa secat*, the whole sequence of sounds seems dominated by a sigmatism which suggestively reproduces the hiss of the forcefully thrown spear.[66] So too at 11.739 *dum sacra secundus haruspex nuntiet*, where *secundus* ought properly to refer to *sacra*. An analogous, but expressively perhaps more marked, case is provided by 6.521 f. *tum me... | infelix habuit thalamus*.

Obviously, it is easier for the reader to perceive the effect of expressive defamiliarization when the new construction presents itself as the exact reverse of the expected syntactical structure: so at 1.195 *vina bonus quae deinde cadis onerarat Acestes* or at 3.465 f. *stipatque carinis | ingens argentum*.[67] Modest though the degree of the violation might be, the image is still revitalized and the expression rendered more incisive. There is an analogous syntactical reversal, with an analogous gain in expressiveness, at 7.72 f. *Lavinia... visa... longis comprendere crinibus ignem*: the quite ordinary lexicon is combined in an unusual (even if perspicuous) construction; the words are defamiliarized and thus seem to adapt themselves to the viewpoint of those who are impressed by the prodigy they witness: Lavinia's hair blazes with harmless flames, a mighty fire which seems to spread to the whole royal palace.

A similar descriptive impressionism characterizes 10.268 f. *versas ad litora puppis | respiciunt totumque adlabi classibus aequor* ('turning to look, they see the ships sailing towards the beach and the whole sea move towards the shore with (the motion of) the fleet'). The 'dicolon abundans', with its doubled and almost tautological structure, helps interpret correctly the meaning of the phrase: the ships cover the whole surface of the sea and rush together quickly towards the shore. A plain formulation, one not altered by syntactical defamiliarization, might have been *totum per aequor adlabi classes*. But in the perception of the Italians standing on the land, the approach of the fleet guided by Aeneas appears as a disturbing prodigy:[68] so quickly

---

[66] Similar is the verbal and syntactical construction of 11.458 *dant sonitum rauci per stagna loquacia cygni*, regarding which Servius (with a certain degree of scholastic rigidity) notes '*stagna loquacia* hypallage: in quibus habitant cygni loquaces'.

[67] Obviously *cadis* and *carinis* are datives.

[68] Cf. the preceding verses (267 f.) *at Rutulo regi ducibusque ea mira videri | Ausoniis*. Among other things, Aeneas' helmet, struck by the rays of the dawning sun, reflects a blinding gleam, as in a divine apparition (lines 261 f.).

do the Trojan ships rush upon the water, impelled as they are by the Nymphs' miraculous intervention, that the sea itself seems to hurl itself against the shore together with the ships. The impressionistic character of the image has been reflected in the construction and has inverted the syntactical form of the phrase.[69]

Only a very attentive reading, inspired by almost incessant suspicion, can perceive simultaneously the norm and the deviation from the norm. To appreciate the innovation, the reader must also know how to reconstruct in his/her own memory the normal linguistic form which has now been replaced by the deviation: he/she must be ready to use his/her common sense and at the same time ready to accept the meaning which the poet has in mind. But the distance between the 'proprium' and the 'improprium'—it is precisely in this distance that the stylistic deviation resides—can also be imperceptible. Is there, or is there not, a syntactical alteration at 1.117 *(navem) rapidus vorat aequore vortex*? Apparently there is not, and yet I believe that the more appropriate formulation, neglected for reasons of expressive intensity, would have had to be *vorat aequor rapido vortice*. At 2.565 f. *omnes . . . corpora . . . ignibus aegra dedere* and at 5.58 *laetum cuncti celebremus honorem* would we not have had to expect respectively *aegri* and *laeti*? Obviously, no one will ever think s/he can impose standardized forms of writing upon Virgil; yet at the same time it is true that it is only by employing such an indiscretion and measuring his language by the standard of the norm that we can have access to his most secret stylistic originality.[70]

The transference of the adjective usually does not have effects as drastic as those that accompany the enallage of the verb, yet it too is no less productive for the style, inasmuch as it too succeeds in injecting a new expressive tension into ordinary constructions. At 12.859 *(sagitta) . . . stridens et celeris incognita transilit umbras* it is evident that *celeris* is an ornamental adjective referring improperly to *umbras*; the

---

[69] Harrison (1991), *ad loc.* seems rather banal: 'A bold poetic hyperbole: to the astonished Italians the sea itself seems to be gliding towards them bearing multiple fleets'. The interpretation of Ladewig–Schafer–Deuticke (1912), *ad loc.* is mistaken '*adlabi* hat nicht *puppes* zum Subj., sondern "man" wie VIII 108.—*aequor* Akk. der Ausdehnung wie I 67.'

[70] Cf. e.g. 2.1 *Conticuere omnes intentique ora tenebant* and 11.121 *conversique oculos ora tenebant*.

syntactical displacement transforms a decorative element into an illustrative element, if we may be allowed to use the words of a celebrated critic of pictorial art: in fact, the idea of movement is enhanced. The same effect of expressive power is probably to be found at 5.503 *sagitta... volucris diverberat auras* if, as I suspect, the adjective (which strictly speaking would belong to the arrow) is connected here with *auras*: in this way a closed syntactical nexus is created, balanced in its elements, but improper and for this reason defamiliarized.

Sometimes, then, the enallage of an adjective seems to obey no other imperative than that of formal function, since the combination of adjective and substantive, however unusual, would seem to have no other intention than to produce a balanced syntactical structure; but one need only be a bit more attentive to discover that the procedure always has expressive implications. There can be no doubt that at 7.341–3 *Allecto... tacitumque obsedit limen Amatae* the transference of *tacitum* renders Allecto's hidden intervention more insidious, far more so than if Allecto herself had been called *tacita*, as a normal logic would have suggested. The same effect is found at 4.363 f.*... totumque (Aeneam) pererrat | luminibus tacitis*, where Dido's offended silence is made even more profound than it would have been if Virgil had referred that silence to Dido and not (improperly) to her eyes.[71] On the other hand, the adjective can be detached from its substantive and made autonomous, thereby breaking a proper combination and revitalizing the expression: so at 7.659 f. *quem Rhea sacerdos | furtivom partu sub luminis edidit oras*, instead of *furtivo partu... edidit* ('gave to the light with a clandestine birth').

It is evident that in constructing improper syntactical combinations, enallage is obliged to omit from them linguistic elements which would have been proper: in this way it creates extremely condensed formulations which can find an explicit meaning only if the reader adds what has been elliptically suppressed. At 6.674 *prata recentia rivis* the meaning of the phrase can easily be reconstructed as 'fields which are always green because they are traversed by brooks which have just now watered them': this is a topical feature of every

---

[71] The same effect in 12.219 *incessu tacito progressus*; cf. 10.227 *eminet ac laeva tacitis subremigat undis*.

locus amoenus and here it serves to characterize as such the region of the Elysian Fields; but the proper term ('always green'), expelled by the new adjective, remains understood, comprehensible but unexpressed. The balanced morphology of the construction (substantive plus adjective followed by a complement)[72] lightens and compensates for the syntactical audacity.

I have said that the reader of the *Aeneid* must be vigilant, almost suspicious. To be sure, it would be a mistake to be too much so: an obsessive hunt for enallages would constrict the range of Virgil's stylistic virtues and would also suffocate his readers' hermeneutic virtues. But to be sufficiently so is useful, for otherwise certain artifices of expressive defamiliarization and intensification run the risk of passing unobserved: a veil of naturalness seems to cover them and camouflage them within their context. One need only be a little circumspect to notice that, in the curse uttered by Dido before her suicide, the line *vos... stirpem et genus omne futurum | exercete odiis* (4.422 f.) contains a combination which in fact reverses the usual construction *exercere odium, amicitiam, iram, dolorem;*[73] or that at 8.266 f. *vultum villosaque saetis | pectora semiferi atque exstinctos faucibus ignis* a normal prosaic construction would have required *exstinctis ignibus fauces.*[74]

Certainly, one must not exaggerate one's suspiciousness; but if the words are weighed carefully and the proper meaning is sought with precision, one cannot be insensitive to certain violations, however disguised they may be, as as 9.325 f. *Rhamnetem adgreditur, qui forte tapetibus altis | exstructus toto proflabat pectore somnum*: already Servius noted that the usual construction would have had to be *tapetibus altis exstructis;*[75] and it must be added that *altis* too betrays a syntactical alteration, inasmuch as the adverbial form *alte* would

---

[72] Cf. for the same effect and the same structure (but without the same expressive condensation) 3.626 *membra fluentia tabo* (Serv. '*fluentia tabo* pro fluenti tabo').

[73] Cf. e.g. Cic. *Ver.* 5.145; *Flac.* 88; Liv. 25.6.19; Ov. *Met.* 12.534. But it should be noted that for the phrase *exercere genus* together with an instrumental word there also exists the possibility of the meaning 'to torment, make suffer': cf. *Georg.* 1.453; *Aen.* 7. 441, as well as the phrases *exercite fatis, exercite curis.*

[74] Cf. Kroll (1924), 258 f.

[75] *exstruere* properly means 'to heap up, to pile up', even if here, in Virgil's novel combination, *exstructus* takes on the meaning of 'raised, elevated'.

perhaps have been more appropriate. It may be added that
the construction *proflabat... somnum* ('exhaled sleep' in the sense
of 'snored') is an original Virgilian synthesis too, the expressive
conclusion of a phrase which aims in its entirety to reinvent the
syntax in order to revitalize the language.[76]

In this way we can see that at 1.392 *ni frustra augurium vani
docuere parentes* there is a pleonasm, since *frustra* and *vani* repeat
the same idea; perhaps *augurium vanum* might have been expected,
but the poet has avoided a disagreeable homoeoteleuton in arsis; in
any case it is certain that the fact that the verb has become predicative
lends *vani* a new expressive emphasis (the prominence of the adjective is also supported by the metrical pauses that isolate it in the line).
Another homoeoteleuton in arsis is avoided at 10.426 *caede viri
tanta* by displacing the attribute from *viri* to *caede*: Halaesus dies as
a great warrior while defending Imaon. At 7.533 f. *sub gutture volnus
et udae | vocis iter* we would have expected *udum vocis iter* to signify
metaphorically the throat, which had already been indicated by
gutture: notice how here too an absolutely ordinary lexicon is
defamiliarized and rendered precious by means of the syntactical
transference. At 9.534 *perque cavas densi tela intorquere fenestras*
there can be no doubt that *densa tela* would have been the proper
combination;[77] but it is also true that the displacement of the adjective *densi* not only revitalizes the expression but also lends the image
stronger perceptibility: the Trojans seem to show themselves, dense
and numerous, at the openings from which they hurl their spears.

A similar visual quality is displayed also by line 11.654 *spicula
converso fugientia derigit arcu*: the Amazon Camilla is forced to flee,
and as she withdraws she shoots arrows backwards; but the one who
is fleeing is obviously Camilla herself, not her arrows.[78] The effect of
the syntactical displacement is to give the verse a balanced structure,

---

[76] It is not improbable that Virgil chooses his tense and defamiliarized formulation in order to lend expressive *decorum* to a 'low', almost comic content (Rhamnes is
snoring, overcome by wine and sleep); the *aprepeia* of the representation is redeemed
by a linguistic elaboration of a sublime register.

[77] Cf. Sabbadini (1887), *ad loc.*

[78] Similarly, the adjective, by reason of the syntactical transference, intensifies its
meaning in 2.544 *sic fatus senior telumque imbelle sine ictu coniecit*: cf. Serv. '*imbelle
ipse imbellis*'.

inasmuch as each substantive receives one attribute (*spicula...*
fugentia, converso... arcu, in chiasmus): the deviation might seem
to be due only to considerations of metrical convenience, yet it also
becomes an instrument of balance and formal elegance. A similarly
balanced structure, this one too produced by an enallage of the
adjective, is found at 12.622 *quisve ruit tantus diversa clamor ab*
urbe? It is likely that *diversa... ab urbe* means 'from different parts
of the city', but in any case the attribute *diversa* ought to refer to
clamor,[79] the syntactical transference not only lends intensity to the
expression but also gives the verse a harmonious form by distributing
the words in symmetrical pairs.[80]

Not every time that one suspects the existence of a syntactical
violation can one be certain that it occurs. This is above all the
case when the context reabsorbs the deviation within a new coherent
structure: Virgil's tendency towards order and measure is so deeply
rooted as to attenuate every scar on the verbal epidermis until
it becomes almost imperceptible. Servius himself, though fully
convinced that syntactical violation is one of the indispensable
elements of Virgil's style, sometimes displays a degree of uncertainty
and prefers to indicate in enallage only one exegetical solution next to
other possibilities.[81] Indeed, sometimes Servius is even too cautious:
for example, although he declares himself undecided, nonetheless
there can be no doubt that 6.214 f. *pinguem taedis et robore secto* |
ingentem struxere pyram contains an enallage, seeing as strictly speaking we would have to expect *pinguibus taedis.*[82] Here the syntactical
deviation lends force and expressiveness to the language, but it
also creates an elegant parallelism between *pinguem taedis* and
robore... ingentem: an occasional disorder in the syntax ends up
submitting to the principle of order and symmetry. In the *Bucolics,*

[79] Cf. e.g. an appropriate combination in 2.298 *diverso interea miscentur moenia*
luctu.

[80] The whole context is extremely pathetic: the preceding verses describe the
citizens' grief for the death of Amata and express Turnus' terrorized lament when
he hears the cries of mourning.

[81] Cf. e.g. *ad* 10.418; 10.513; 11.18; 12.620. Servius, indeed, is so convinced that
Virgil loves enallage (or at any rate syntactical alteration) that he even finds it where it
is not: e.g. *ad* 1.403; 2.362; 4.385; 6.419.

[82] Cf. Norden *ad l.* '*pinguem taedis* für *pinguibus taedis*, in kühnem parallelismus
zu *ingentem robore*'.

on the other hand, where the plain style did not demand such a syntactical deviation, we naturally find the normal combination *taedae pingues* (7.49).

All in all, the enallage of the attribute seems to be so innate to Virgil's style as almost to constitute one of its distinctive features, an evident signature. So much so that whoever wished to defend the Helen episode in the second book of the *Aeneid*, which is notoriously suspected of being an interpolation, might refer to this stylistic feature as plausible evidence for its authenticity.[83] At line 576 *ulcisci patriam et sceleratas sumere poenas* the two-part structure of *dicolon abundans*, as in other like cases, demands from the former member the 'theme' (vengeance) and from the latter one the 'variation' (punishment of Helen for her crimes). So there can be no doubt that the clause *sceleratas sumere poenas* contains an enallage and means 'inflict punishment upon the wicked woman, take vengeance upon the accursed woman'. This is, quite evidently, the very same formulation with which Aeneas condemns Turnus to death at the end of the poem: *poenam scelerato ex sanguine sumit* (12.949): the same expressive alliteration and the same sigmatism, but this time a plain and normal syntax. In Aeneas' discourse against Helen, on the other hand, a true *rhesis* with strongly dramatic tones, the intensity of the pathos drives the linguistic elaboration to the very limits of tolerance; the extremely audacious enallage exasperates the idea of the crime (*sceleratas*) and impresses it more forcefully upon the reader's mind and spirit. In certain cases, as Pseudo-Longinus knew well, the syntax of the emotions is a syntax of excess.[84]

But it is not always the case that enallage makes such claims upon the reader. For the most part, Virgil is satisfied with asking of it only

---

[83] I have sided with those who defend the authenticity of this passage, recognizing in these verses a first draft which did not receive its author's *summa manus* and which for various reasons was not included in the definitive text of the *Aeneid* as it was published by the first editors after the poet's premature death: see Conte (1986*a*), 196–208 (I hope to return to this problem with new arguments).

[84] Another bold syntactical violation, and once more in order to express the same idea (the idea of punishment that obsessively dominates the whole passage), is found several lines later: *sumpsisse merentis | . . . poenas* (585 f.). Whether *merentis* is a genitive singular or (more probably) an accusative plural, the syntactical deviation is of great expressive effect. This too is evidence both for the Virgilian paternity of the passage and for its lack of final polishing. A good note is that by R. G. Austin *ad loc.*

effects of stylistic enhancement: the task assigned to it is above all that of creating a language parallel to the usual one, similar enough to it but at the same time substantially more intense. It is up to the reader to prove him/herself attentive to the deviations. At 8.3 *utque acris concussit equos utque impulit arma* the meaning of the phrase presents itself as normal without the expressive innovation standing out conspicuously; and yet *concussit* would be appropiate for *arma* and *impulit* instead for *equos*:[85] the exchange of the verbs has created an impropriety, a slight one but still sufficient to reawaken the reader's attention and to make him/her feel the unusualness of the expression.[86] So too at 8.680 f. *(Augustus) stans celsa in puppi, geminas cui tempora flammas | laeta vomunt*: the plain meaning of the phrase, once it is deprived of the syntactical artifice, would be 'both of whose temples emit flames promising victory';[87] by reason of the double enallage the two adjectives *geminas* and *laeta* exchange their substantives of reference, and yet the new combination creates a total meaning which is just as evident, indeed more evident because it is rendered emphatic by the defamiliarization.[88] The expressive surplus derives from the tension established between the words of the construction (*geminas... tempora flammas | laeta*): metre and syntax dissociate every adjective from its proper substantive, but the contiguity of the words reminds the reader anyway of what would have had to be the appropriate pairings: behind the deviation the avoided norm shows through.

The same expressive intensity animates the verbal combinations at 10.898 f. *ut auras | suspiciens hausit caelum*: Mezentius has fallen to the earth from his horse, but raises his eyes to the heavens and, panting, catches his breath. The syntax is inverted; it is evident that *auras* would require *hausit* and that *caelum* in turn would be appropriate for *suspiciens*. It is instructive to compare *Georg.*

---

[85] Cf. Virg. *Aen.* 12.333 *immittit equos*; 5.146 f. *immissis.../... iugis*; cf. also ThlL s.v. *concutio*, vol. IV, i, p. 118, ll. 57–60.

[86] Cf. Bömer (1965), 130 f.; Burkhardt (1971), 412 ff.

[87] Cf. Radke (1964), 89.

[88] It may be of interest to compare the enallage of Catullus 51.11 f. (the translation from Sappho): *gemina teguntur nocte.* The adjective *gemina* refers not to the substantive *lumina* but improperly to *nocte*; but the transference is not balanced by a second adjective which would complete *lumina* and thereby create a double exchange. So the intervention is less drastic, the deviation more restrained.

1.375 f. *bucula caelum | suspiciens patulis captavit naribus auras,*
where the calf, just like Mezentius, looks up at the heavens and
with his nostrils breathes in the air heavy with rain. The image
seems the same, indeed some of the lexical elements are identical in
both passages, but the linguistic attitude is completely different: in
the *Georgics* the formulation is realistically simple, entirely plain and
linear; in the passage from the *Aeneid,* on the contrary, the double
enallage exchanges the syntactical relations with one another and
nervously stretches the connections between the words. The pathetic
sublimity of the scene has forced itself upon the language, violating it
in a compressed form, like a spring which releases energy when it
expands.

   Little by little we have traversed the path that leads to the conclusion, but before attempting a conclusion (one already sketched out
anyway in the course of these pages) I would like to attempt an
invitation: let every reader of the *Aeneid* equip him/herself with an
ideal seismograph and stand ready to register all the tremors of the
text and of its linguistic crust.[89] She will see a trace which is not at all

   [89] In the Latin Literature seminar which I gave at the Scuola Normale Superiore di
Pisa in the academic year 2001–2, several students accepted my invitation to reread
the text of Virgil in order to track down examples of enallage and syntactical
distortion. I give in what follows some further examples selected from their rich
collection of material: 1.4 *saevae memorem Iunonis ob iram*; 2.135–6 *limosoque lacu
per noctem obscurus in ulva | delitui*; 2.168 *virgineas ausi divae contingere vittas*; 2.508
medium in penetralibus hostem; 2.569 *dant clara incendia lucem* (*claram* Ribbeck);
2.381 *[anguem] attollentem iras et caerula colla tumentem* (for the normal construc-
tion see 5.27–8 *sibila colla | arduus attollens*; Sen. *Phoen.* 352 *tumet animus ira*);
3.356–7 *aurae | vela vocant*; 3.418 *Hesperium Siculo latus abscidit* (Serv. 'hypallage est,
nam minora a maioribus segregantur; sed contra dixit'); 3.246 *infelix vates, rumpitque
hanc pectore vocem* (Serv. *ad Aen.* 2.129 'h.e. erumpit in vocem,... nam si "silentium
rumpere" est loqui..., "vocem rumpere" est tacere'); 3.472 *interea classem velis
aptare iubebat*; 4.641 *illa gradum studio celerabat anili*; 5.302 *multi praeterea, quos
fama obscura recondit*; 5.137–8 *exsultantia haurit | corda pavor pulsans*; 6.202–3
liquidumque per aera lapsae |...gemina sub arbore sidunt; 6.405 *ad genitorem imas
Erebi descendit ad umbras*; 7.28 *in lento luctantur marmore tonsae* (for the normal
combination see Catull. 64.183 *lentos incurvans gurgite remos*); 7.141–2 *hic pater
omnipotens ter caelo clarus ab alto | intonuit*; 7.689–90 *vestigia nuda sinistri | instituere
pedis, crudus tegit altera pero*; 8.68–9 *surgit et aetherii spectans orientia solis | lumina*
(Serv. 'pro "orientis solis lumina"'); 8.520 *defixique ora tenebant*; 9.35 *et maestum
Iliades crinem de more solutae*; 9.618 *ubi adsuetis biforem dat tibia cantum*; 9.756
diffugiunt versi trepida formidine Troes (contrast 9.169 *trepidi formidine portas |
explorent*); 10.418 *ut senior leto canentia lumina solvit* (Serv. 'pro "ipse canens"');
10.463 *victoremque ferant morientia lumina Turni*; 10.713 *sed iaculis tutisque procul*

linear, but desultory, showing various peaks of intensity. The verbal combinations—I would not say all, but certainly many of them—will display the signs of an intense mobility: behind a profile of ordered structures, it will be possible to perceive the vibrations of a free and inventive language, one made up of dynamic elements captured in the very instant of their creation, almost still moving. It is not by choice that the reader must be alert, ready to grasp in Virgil's stylistic expression every possible flash of artistic vitality; rather, s/he must do so because this is how s/he has been programmed by the author himself, who has entrusted his extraordinary capacities as a *Sprachschöpfer* above all to the tremors of the expression. In those tremors is concealed the secret of his style.

The secret (by now we should have understood this) consisted in procedures of expressive enhancement, in the invention of a new sublime composed of linguistic intensity and fundamentally foreign to the antiquated, tired forms of conventional epic. The epic poetry which was coming into being just then needed authenticity above all else if it was to appear live and modern. For this reason it had need of a language made up of words not remote from ordinary speech; but that language also had to be 'elaborated' in order to acquire artistic form and dignity. In short, precisely in order to guarantee a warm contact with its readers, the poet's language had to be similar enough to the language of everyone; but since it was intended to serve as an instrument of sublime poetry, it had to lose every feature of ordinariness: only after it had been freed from the stain of its origin could it be reborn to new life. Virgil felt the need for a 'noble vulgate': the language of his poem had to brush against the ordinary language, and in recompense it had to assume the attitudes of uncommon gestures, to derive force and grandeur from unusual constructions, in short, to defamiliarize itself.

Obviously, such defamiliarization was already provided for by the metre, which separated epic discourse from the dominion of ordinariness by means of an aura of distance; and, together with

---

clamoribus instant; 10.738 *conclamant socii laetum paeana secuti*; 10.785–6 *transiit intextum tauris opus imaque sedit* | *inguine* (Serv. 'hypallage est "ima hasta" pro "in imo inguine"'); 11.35 *et maestum Iliades crinem de more solutae*; 11.189–90 *ter maestum funeris ignem* | *lustravere* (Serv. 'maestum, id est funebrem, nam maestus non potest esse ignis'); 11.628 *[pontus] saxa fugit litusque vado labente relinquit* (Serv. 'hypallage pro "labens ipse per vadum"').

the metre, by the whole series of phonetic effects, alliterations, and assonances. But even more than from the metre and the chains of interlacing sounds, the rush of the sublime could come from the form of the phrase, from the combination of the words, from the tension of the verbal constructions, from the rhetoric of the material elocution. This is a technique of expressive sublimity, of *megalegoria* (the technique so well analysed by Pseudo-Longinus) and in it the syntax has the greatest weight. It was precisely the elaboration of the syntax (transferred words, inverted or violated constructions) that was supposed to lend pathetic grandeur to the language of the *Aeneid*. The creation of an artistic syntax coincided with the creation of a new narrative style willing to let itself be penetrated by the poet's emotions and by those of the characters: readers would accept the 'deformation' of the syntax as the trademark of a new sublime style.

I hope it is clear from my whole argument that the style could no longer be merely a labour of the chisel, composed of elegant touches learned from the Alexandrian masters. For Virgil, the style felt the effects of the urgency of grand and domineering emotions: it had become the form of a content which demanded intense participation. The centre of Virgil's poetic project lies in his style: to adopt ordinary language—not the language of everyone but a language close to every-one—in order to make of it the constitutive material of a modern sublime. If Virgil can be a new Homer, it is because his ambition is to be the poet of an entire community, like his distant model: in this sense he finds himself in the front rank among the most active creators of that Augustan ideology which aimed at a new foundation for the national identity. But the poet who took on the task of representing a collective destiny knows that language is the true means for establishing a bond with his ideal readers. By adopting a current lexicon, the poet seems to speak with the voice of everyone; but in this voice he always mixes in his own: his own voice does not leave the common voice in peace, but instead forces it, stretches it, revitalizes it. This is a conflict which reproduces the agonistic challenge to which the text of the *Aeneid* continually summons its readers. The choice of the form is also—or, to put it better, is above all—a response to an ideological need.

4

Aristaeus, Orpheus, and the *Georgics*: once again

> The critic is a reader who ruminates: he should have more than one stomach.
>
> Friedrich Schlegel

SOME years ago I proposed an interpretation of the story of Aristaeus and Orpheus, and I was quite satisfied with it.[1] Quite—but I still felt a little like the rabbi in the joke Arnaldo Momigliano once told me. One rabbi goes to see another rabbi and finds him immersed in the reading of the Torah. 'What are you doing?'—'I'm trying to interpret a passage that I've been studying for years and can't explain completely to myself.' 'Let me see: I'll try to explain it to you myself.' 'That won't do any good. I can explain it to *other* people; what I can't do is explain it to myself.'

I would like to see whether this time I can explain the close of the *Georgics* to myself. This time I shall try to be less elliptical, more nuanced, more open to the difficulties. Even if, in a certain way, with adjustments and additions, I end up offering a second time the basic outlines of my first interpretation, I would still prefer to be considered not an inveterate sinner (*perseverare diabolicum*), but only a stubborn rabbi.

More or less simultaneously with my own interpretation, which appeared in 1980, Jasper Griffin published a fine essay on the subject,

I am grateful to Glenn Most for once again clothing my thoughts in the decency of English and for discussing these interpretative problems with me without renouncing his customary obstinacy. The article has greatly benefited from the suggestions of Mario Labate, Giuliano Ranucci, Michael Reeve, and Gianpiero Rosati.

[1] In an introduction to Barchiesi (1980), later revised in Conte (1986a).

remarkable for his balanced discussion of the problem and his solid erudition.[2] The simultaneity prevented either of us from knowing of the other's work. When I look back, Griffin's article always appeals to me more than the numerous studies others have devoted to the passage. I find a significant harmony between us above all in the aim which underlies his whole interpretation: he too is looking for an *organic* interpretation, one that connects the *fabula Aristaei* with the whole system of ideas which sustains the *Georgics*. Setting aside all other methodological considerations, this is certainly the way to proceed, the method which treats Virgil's text as an entity delimited by a 'classical' closure, as an organic construction composed of various parts, whose closure in fact constitutes its seal of significance.[3]

For my own part, I cannot help but consider unsatisfactory the interpretations of those scholars who prefer to read these verses as a decorative exploit on the part of the poet, an ornamental *tour de force* to which he has given the form of an aetiological narrative (even though such readings can of course be appreciated for individual felicitous observations). For these critics the final narrative of the *Georgics* is nothing more than a highly elegant and fascinating appendix, an excursus which is structurally almost autonomous, introduced with the simple aim of furnishing an *aition* for the 'Bugonia', the birth of bees from the corpse of a bull.[4]

It is simply not true that the bees' miraculous reproduction has the same prominence in relation to the poem's doctrinal substance, which is made up of instruction and description, as does 'an *aition* in analogous cases in Ovid's *Metamorphoses*'.[5] On the contrary:

---

[2] Griffin (1979). One can find here a practically complete list of the principal studies on the epyllion.

[3] Some scholars have resolutely taken this path: cf. in particular Segal (1966), Parry (1972), Putnam (1979), 270 ff., Miles (1980), 257 ff.

[4] A striking example is provided by Wilkinson (1969), 108–20, who, with a truistic minimalism, concludes: 'To sum up, I believe that Virgil would have thought an *aition* for "Bugonia" a suitable ending for a book, Aristaeus a suitable hero for this *aition*, and epyllion a suitable form for it' (p. 120). In an appendix (325–6), Wilkinson discusses earlier contributions from his point of view.

[5] So A. La Penna, 'Introduzione' to Canali (1983), 101. This whole interpretation is in fact a good example of paraphrastic criticism. It recounts the story of Aristaeus and Orpheus; the quantity of information does not increase, but here and there a tender note of commentary is added to testify to the critic's admiration.

Ovid, who constructs a linear, homogeneous collection of *aitia* by linking one story to another and by inserting one story within another, is one thing; the Virgil of the *Georgics*, who sets his seal upon a didactic exposition—a genre which, properly speaking, is descriptive and not narrative—by means of an appropriate story, is quite another. If one wishes, one can invoke Ovid for a comparison of the *surface technique* (the story of the 'Bugonia' is contextually motivated as an *aition*: a custom is explained by reference to its mythic antecedent); but the literary function performed by Virgil's narration cannot be compared with that in Ovid's stories. For the relations of context differ too much, at least as much as the *Georgics* and the *Metamorphoses* differ from one another. In Virgil the aetiological move with which the epyllion is introduced is merely an 'Alexandrian' garment (a fashionable garment) superimposed upon an impressive story which serves to provide a significant conclusion for a doctrinal exposition.

Servius (on *Buc.* 10.1) claims that Virgil revised book 4 of the *Georgics* on the death of Cornelius Gallus (27 or 26 BC), eliminating praise of his recently disgraced friend and substituting the story of Aristaeus (or the section about Orpheus, according to a much less plausible version). This information cannot be simply accepted as a fact, but on the other hand it cannot be rejected with absolute certainty. If Servius' information is accepted as a whole, two large problems remain unsolved. (*a*) What happened to the original passage if it was deleted after circulating freely in the years between 29 and 27/26? Must it not have been a highly desirable sacred relic for the legions of Virgil's admirers? What abyss swallowed up the copies already in circulation? That the *Georgics* were not 'published' until Gallus' death seems most unlikely: the work had been finished for three years, it was already known to Augustus and to Virgil's circle of friends, and it was being imitated by other poets. Why then keep it in the drawer? (*b*) Virgil is alleged to have devoted to Gallus (perhaps in his role as prefect of Egypt) an encomium lengthy enough to have to be compensated and replaced by an epyllion more than 200 verses long, and this in a poem which grants only a few dozen verses to the celebration of Augustus and four brief mentions to the addressee and patron Maecenas. But if the praise of Gallus was brief—like, let us suppose, that of Pollio in the *Bucolics*—then what else did the fourth book contain? On the other hand, one can imagine that Gallus was praised less as a political figure than as a poet, perhaps in an elaborate poetic reflection like the one offered us by the Tenth Eclogue.[6] But in that case the necessity of deleting him becomes less intelligible, unless one wishes to regard the Augustan regime (even in its very first years) as a quasi-Stalinist tyranny.[7]

One can add—even if only as an initial suggestion, which we shall try to substantiate later—that the Aristaeus epyllion, as we read it, presents a strong internal organic unity and above all is linked by a profound thematic continuity with the rest of the poem. This renders more unlikely the idea that in essence it is merely an improvised

---

6 Cf. Conte (1986*a*), 100–29.

7 Cf. Griffin (1979), 180 ff. The supporters of Servius' notice sometimes use arguments of doubtful value. For example, they try to trace out a large number of narrative incoherences in the mythic story, without considering that many presumed irregularities can be explained perfectly well in terms of the 'Alexandrian' narrative technique adopted by Virgil (asymmetrical narration, non-uniform narrative time, erudite oscillation between mythological and geographical variants). Or else they try to demonstrate, on the basis of (admittedly real) similarities with certain passages in the *Aeneid*, that the Aristaeus epyllion was composed during work on the new poem, with hasty reuse of expressions already coined for episodes of the *Aeneid*. These are highly uncertain arguments, upon which a critical judgement cannot be based. But considerations of another sort preclude our dismissing as false the report of a revision. Above all, no one has yet explained who could have invented *ex nihilo* a notice of this sort, and why. It may be added that, even if the search for cases of narrative incoherence has turned out to be fruitless, there nonetheless exists an evident textual problem—of an unparalleled gravity in the manuscript tradition of the *Georgics*—in the brief passage which serves as an introduction to the theme of *bugonia* and to the aetiological narrative: vv. 290–3 are transmitted in a different order in each of the three most important manuscripts, and it has long since been noticed that these verses discuss Egypt, Gallus' province. At this point some scholars have tried to excogitate an intermediate solution, supposing for example that a *brief* mention of Gallus was hastily deleted and that the text still bears a trace of an imperfect readjustment. But this explanation, which does have some points in its favour, ends up forgetting the exact statement of Servius, our source, who speaks not of a deletion and a brief revision but of a massive substitution. A final *non liquet* leaves, as always, a sense of disappointment, but it should not preclude an attentive and objective evaluation of the Aristaeus epyllion, which remains the only secure terrain for critical analysis. An excellent discussion of the problems connected with Servius' notice and of the many solutions that have been proposed for this question can be found in Jocelyn (1981), but I believe that his own position is too extreme. I find very interesting and plausible the recent suggestion of Delvigo (1995) that there were two editions of the *Georgics*. See also below, n. 34.

addition.[8] In any case, even if the authenticity of Servius' notice and hence of the presumed revision could some day be demonstrated rigorously, this would in no way justify an interpretation which ignored the semantic coherence of the new text.

Let us proceed by looking for meanings in the story of Aristaeus and Orpheus which enter into free and complex interaction with the didactic part of book 4 and, more generally, with the economy of the whole poem. We shall try to show that there is a profound harmony between the meaning suggested by the final mythic narrative and the ideological construction of the *Georgics* as a whole. At the deepest level, the two discursive forms—the expository, didactic form and the mythic, narrative form—will turn out to be complementary, two different representations of the very same theme.

In the same way, Plato's dialogues often conclude the exposition of doctrine with a myth. It should suffice to recall the *Gorgias*, the *Phaedo*, and the *Republic*, but in almost every dialogue the reader encounters more or less extended mythic narratives. In these extended 'similes' (let us call them this to make the point clearer) Plato reflects upon his literary works: this is the case, for example, in the comparisons with the statues of Silenus in the *Symposium* and with the gardens of Adonis in the *Phaedrus*. They form part of that 'language by means of images' which characterizes Platonic discourse, and therefore should not be separated from the metaphors, similes, and easily understood examples with which at every step in his dialogues Plato vividly illustrates the matter under discussion.[9] These myths illustrate the Truth in a form accessible to intuition. The *mythos* completes the *logos*, but is not opposed to it: it completes it *per imaginem*. The didactic discourse, which proceeds by analysis and argumentation, and the mythic discourse, which proceeds in the condensed and paradigmatic form of narrative, are complementary.

---

[8] I omit here, as insufficiently methodical, attempts to connect the contents of the 'substituted' epyllion allegorically with Gallus' historical vicissitudes (I mean the suggestion that the epyllion refers in code to Cornelius Gallus, the governor of Egypt, rather than to the founder of the new love poetry): e.g. Coleman (1962).

[9] Gaiser (1984), 125–50, is fundamental; Arrighetti (1991) is also important. Both Gaiser and Arrighetti discuss well the function of the myth in the body of Platonic dialogues, but they also succeed in explaining persuasively the aversion Plato displays for the poets' myths, which he often rejects as false. See also Brisson (1982).

Both discourses approach the truth by different but equally legitimate paths: neither form can be substituted for the other. *Logos* has the advantage of exact thought and subtle distinctions, but it lacks the force to represent its contents with realistic vivacity— precisely what *mythos* can do, thanks to its symbols and concrete images. The truth will be found at the point where *mythos* and *logos* accord or converge.[10]

As we have said, Plato often uses a myth to provide the doctrinal exposition with a climax, a final suggestive frame in which he bids his reader farewell, the perceptible representation of a philosophical 'truth'. Thus the *Phaedo* closes with the 'myth of the souls after death' (107d–114c) and the *Gorgias* with an eschatological myth (523–7). Indeed, the words that introduce the myth in the latter dialogue are particularly significant (523a): 'Listen to a very fine story (Ἄκουε δή . . . μάλα καλοῦ λόγου); you will consider it a fable, I suppose (ὃν σὺ μὲν ἡγήσῃ μῦθον) but for me it is a story (ἐγὼ δὲ λόγον) since the content of what I am about to tell you is true, according to me.' This myth exhibits many elements drawn from the Greek literary tradition (Homer, Pindar, Aeschylus); but its function within the *Gorgias* is to convey a superior revelation, so that it becomes the only form of discourse to which Plato can entrust the loftiest, and for that very reason the most elusive, contents of the philosophy expounded in the preceding part of the dialogue.

In the same way, Plato's long and complex exposition of his ideal of society and the state in the ten books of the *Republic* is concluded by a grand illustrative epilogue, the myth of Er of Pamphylia. This is a structure which Cicero chose to emulate in his *De Republica* when he decided to represent the doctrinal content of his thought suggestively (*per imaginem*) and closed the dialogue with the *Somnium Scipionis*. Like Er's, Scipio's voyage too is a philosophical voyage, not only because the respective contexts are philosophical, but also because the narrative contents are strongly ideological.

The dream voyage is substantially a form of revelation. Here the addressee of the Ciceronian political project receives a moral lesson which is fully congruent with the political doctrine expounded and discussed in the *De Republica* as a whole. In the form of an intuitive and

---

[10] Cf. Gaiser (1984), 134.

almost initiatory vision, the narrative of the *Somnium*—a mythic excursus illustrating emblematically Cicero's political ideal—condenses and sublimates the dominant theme of the *De Republica*, that is, the *princeps*, the political figure to whom Cicero assigned the task of healing the wounds of the Roman republic. The other world Scipio dreams of is certainly the universe of Plato and Pythagoreanism (which we shall find once again, differently elaborated, in book 6 of the *Aeneid*), but it is also another world which is supposed to serve the *princeps* as a model to which he must conform. Scipio, the dreamer-voyager, is merely the prototype of the Ciceronian *princeps*.[11] We shall try to show that—analogously—Virgil's Aristaeus is the prototype of the perfect *agricola*, or rather, in other words, that the mythic narrative of Aristaeus and of what happens to him is a significant and paradigmatic illustration of the theme which underlies the whole of the *Georgics*.

By its very nature, didactic discourse cannot help but have a form which is, so to speak, 'static': it accumulates information and precepts, it instructs and admonishes. The proper form of the didactic mode is not the story but the description. Its fundamental stance is gnomic and could be summarized in the formula 'This is how things are; I teach you them and you learn them.' So too in the model text, Hesiod's *Works and Days*, the farmer's 'virtues' are expounded as incontestable truths, like entries in a catalogue: the *georgos*' stubborn effort, the value of human labour and justice, must be learned. The narrative discourse, on the other hand, has a 'dynamic' form: it flows in a succession of events and actions, and is constructed according to a line of development. An initial situation is followed by a new situation, and meanings result from the attitudes, actions, and reactions of the characters involved in the narrated events.

The only reason I am recalling these elementary differences between didactic and narrative forms is that I suspect that the disorientation of many interpreters of the story of Aristaeus arises in some way from a misunderstanding of this radical diversity. Just like Plato and Cicero, as indicated above, so too at the close of his own poem Virgil chooses to illustrate emblematically the fundamental theme of his teaching by permitting his poetic discourse to take on

[11] So excellently Stok (1993), 29.

temporarily the linear movement of a narrative. The poet changes discursive form and passes from the prescriptive-descriptive code to the epic-narrative code. The story he narrates 'deposits' at the end the very same moral message advocated throughout the poem. But it does so this time *sub specie mythica*.

Almost everyone who interprets the epyllion of Aristaeus and Orpheus as a narrative endowed with a meaning that in some way coheres with the general meaning of the poem starts out by acknowledging an opposition between the story of Aristaeus (the framing narrative) and the story of Orpheus (the inserted narrative). Above all one must recognize that this opposition corresponds to a significant contrast between two different types of content, that is, that it is a way to make a statement by dramatizing two opposed models of behaviour. The comparison demonstrates paradigmatically that behaving oneself in one way produces one outcome (and hence means one thing) while behaving oneself in the opposite way produces a different outcome (and hence signifies the opposite). But it is evident that, even if the narrative is articulated dialectically, its meaning is unified, that is, it arises as a *result* of the two components which are contextually opposed to one another.

It is no less evident that this opposition between Aristaeus and Orpheus, like any other opposition, must necessarily be based upon an analogy between the two heroes' constitutive features: only because these are shared can the two characters be compared and their significant differences emerge. I believe that, even when interpreters have recognized that the meaning of Virgil's poetic composition is based upon an organic conception of the story, nonetheless, when it has come to indicating the analogous elements, they have sometimes lacked the analytic rigour which alone permits the truly pertinent narrative features to be identified and set in significant relation to one another. What sense does it make, for example, to treat the contrast between the epyllion's two stories in terms as abstract as 'Death' and 'Life'?[12] Reducing the significant correspondences to an entirely general oppositional matrix—one valid for much poetry, for too much poetry—dilutes the epyllion's meaning almost to the vanishing point. At the most, one ends up saying with triumphant

---

[12] Klingner (1967), 326–63, in particular 359–63.

fervour that 'the myth of Aristaeus is the myth of resurrection and salvation, contrasted with the myth of Orpheus, which is the myth of death—and resurrection, naturally, conquers death'.[13]

On the other hand, the detailed correspondences between the two episodes which go to make up the epyllion have been studied with greater care:[14] this approach has revealed a minute system of connections and contrasts. Understanding this aspect of the epyllion has been helped by comparison with Catullus poem 64, which is unmistakably constructed as a story that has another story as a kind of inverted mirror image: the frame (the wedding of Peleus and Thetis) and, on its inside, the inserted episode (Ariadne abandoned).

In the story of Aristaeus and Orpheus too, the embedded structure is only an external feature of the narrative technique peculiar to epyllion. But it should be noted that an articulation of this sort is merely a *superficial* narrative mode, since it serves to transform the opposition between two mythical events into a continuous narrative, one which continues on the inside of another narrative. It is dangerous to assign to what is merely an external articulation of the narrative a meaning which goes beyond the superficial structure of the text. The technique of embedding has the function here of giving a hypotactic structure to a discourse whose content has in its substance a paratactic structure: the narration, in fact, defines two opposite attitudes, and it places them precisely in comparison with one another. In reality there is a parallelism between the stories of Orpheus and Aristaeus; the true relation between the two stories is one of comparison.

Even if, for reasons of narrative technique, the superficial structure has taken on the formulation 'Aristaeus because of Orpheus' (or even, if one wishes, 'Orpheus because of Aristaeus'), the logical structure of the discourse requires the formulation 'Aristaeus differently from Orpheus', 'Aristaeus as the opposite of Orpheus'. The external form of the discourse is causality (hypotactic), the internal form is opposition (paratactic). And it is precisely because

[13] La Penna in Canali (1983), 100.
[14] Otis (1963), 190–214; Pridik (1971), 220 ff.; Wilkinson (1969), 327–8. The best analysis among those which consider the episode in the tradition of the 'new' Alexandrian epyllion is given by Perutelli (1980). On the technique of the 'framed narrative' there are acute observations in Rosati (1981).

some scholars have failed to distinguish in their analysis the different levels of the text and have treated the merely external artifice of embedding as though it were in fact a substantial nexus linking cause and effect that they have even gone so far as to claim that Aristaeus derives from the story of Orpheus and his troubles, simply by listening to it, a lesson capable of overcoming death.[15] But there is not the slightest trace of this sort of *Bildungsroman* in Virgil's text.

The most promising line of interpretation, I believe, tries simultaneously both to analyse the details of the text (which are like the epidermal symptoms of larger meanings) and to reveal the skeleton of the epyllion (that is, the configuration which the story's fundamental points have taken on): in short, to look from afar in order to ascertain the general outline of the text's meaning, to look from close up because the discourse's very soul often manifests itself (or is condensed) in a detail. In practical terms, we should first try to identify clearly the constitutive elements of the two parts of the epyllion, those which by their very presence qualify each of the two characters and the events of the narrative, and then look for a confirmation of this qualification in the linguistic form in which the idea has found expression.

Let us begin by establishing that both episodes tell the story of a particularly excellent hero (*a*) stricken by an extremely painful privation (*b*): death deprives Aristaeus of his bees, the pride of his life, and Orpheus of his wife Eurydice, his deeply beloved companion. Both try to overcome their respective privations by means of an ordeal (*c*), of which the 'voyage to another realm' is an essential feature. The ordeal has different outcomes (*d*): Aristaeus is successful and transforms the death of the bees into life; Orpheus fails and adds his own death to Eurydice's. In this way the two heroes are linked in the end by a contextual opposition which conveys a profound significance.

But we shall deal later with this significant difference between Aristaeus and Orpheus; let us instead cast light now upon their analogies, the features which make it possible to assimilate them in

---

[15] Cf. especially Parry (1972) and Putnam (1979), 314 n. 61: 'Aristaeus ... absorbs, we presume, the lesson of Orpheus'.

some way, and hence to compare them. It is evident that Virgil decided to construct his narrative in such a way as to establish a comparison between his two parallel characters and that his inventiveness permitted him both to exploit certain pre-existing elements of comparability and also to introduce new ones.[16]

Outside Virgil's narrative too, the two heroes have a functional affinity, a series of significant features which qualify them both as *cultural heroes*: they are like two *protoi heuretai*, discoverers of two inventions devised for the benefit of mankind. The work of acculturation they perform is linked to two quite distinct domains. Aristaeus moves exclusively in the agricultural sphere and promotes civilizing activities like stock-breeding and apiculture; Orpheus is the inventor of music and poetry, and in this domain he too fosters the passage from the primitive to the civilized state. The one appears as the prototype of the farmer-shepherd, the other as that of the poet-musician.

Obviously, the mythic complexity of these two figures is not exhausted by this feature: this is merely the *facies* they present in Virgil's text for the purposes of the roles they are supposed to play in his narrative. Nor should it be forgotten that in ancient culture Orpheus' scope and importance were incomparably greater than Aristaeus': it is enough to think of Orphism and of Orpheus' literary and religious diffusion. Nonetheless many critics have tried to interpret Virgil's epyllion by functionalizing only one arbitrarily privileged set of Orpheus' mythic and historical characteristics, or even *the totality* of them—as though a customer in a good restaurant were not supposed to select certain dishes and wines from the ample menu of food and drink in order to have a decent meal but had to eat and drink everything available. This has led such critics to forget the salient feature of Virgil's technique, namely the *partiality* with which he read and used the myth of Orpheus, once he decided to make him a character in his poetry.

---

[16] At least since the magisterial analysis by Norden (1934), it has been an established fact that as a whole the epyllion is one of Virgil's most original creations. The sources do not connect Aristaeus with the *bugonia* nor with Proteus, and there is even less trace of any relation whatsoever between Aristaeus and Orpheus before Virgil. So too the story of the death of Eurydice, bitten by a snake while she tries to escape from Aristaeus, seems to be an original invention on the part of the Latin poet.

It goes without saying that every myth (with its variants) possesses a plurality of meanings which aggregate around a fundamental thematic function. But when a poet utilizes a myth or a mythic character, he operates by *selection*, re-orientating the story in the direction of his own text. If I may permit myself an example, I would refer to the most popular hero of the Greeks. Hercules is celebrated by the poets for innumerable exploits and for the most various characteristics. A civilizing hero, he frees the earth from dangerous wild animals and monstrous creatures; invincible for his physical force and an impeccable warrior, he is extraordinarily exuberant in sexual matters (to the point of becoming Omphale's slave) but he is also an insatiable eater and an intemperate drinker of wine; a tragic figure, he goes mad and kills his wife and children; the mythic progenitor of the Spartan kings, he is the founder of the Olympic games and also the protector of gymnasia and ephebes. In Roman culture, he becomes a divinity who protects both the fertility of the soil and also armies in the field, and (as though this were not enough) guarantees oaths in commercial transactions. I have presented this playful 'enumeratio chaotica' only in order to ask: would you have expected that the sophist Prodicus (as Xenophon reports in his *Memorabilia* 2.1.21–34) would one day invent a fable whose protagonist was Hercules, but this time as an exemplar of wisdom and self-control, a paradigm of moral virtue? Certainly Prodicus was able to do this, and perhaps Hercules' mythic tradition also contained elements which lent themselves to such a treatment; but it is self-evident that Prodicus must have decided to reject many fundamental features of the myth when he chose Hercules to be the protagonist of his story.

In short, I only wish to repeat that Virgil has necessarily reduced the significant features of the myth of Orpheus, or, rather, has activated some of them at the expense of others and has adapted them to his own text. For poets, myth is like a word contained in a dictionary: when it leaves the dictionary and enters their text, it retains only one of its possible meanings. Myth too, like a word, must be modified by 'declensions' and 'conjugations' in order to conform to the discourse's global meaning: its function is determined by its context.

Every Greek poet (and *a fortiori* every Latin poet, who inevitably found himself confronting a richly stratified set of variants and

adaptations) felt authorized to intervene in the tradition and
'conjugated' freely the mythic paradigm: in all probability Homer
already did this, certainly Hesiod did.[17] It is well known, if only to take
a single example, that in his Sixth Paean Pindar told the story of
the death of the hero Neoptolemus in a way completely different from
the Seventh Nemean (one time accusing him of villainy, the other
time treating him with honour and respect): the contexts
were different, and so too were the functions which the myth of
Neoptolemus fulfilled in the one text and the other.[18]

In terms which are typically idealistic but which we can nonetheless accept, Werner Jaeger recalled that 'myth is like an organism
whose soul is constantly being renewed and changed. The person
who produces such changes is the poet; but, in doing this, he does
not merely obey his own caprice. The poet is the creator of a new
norm of life for his age and he interprets the myth on the base of this
new norm [...] Myth can only stay alive thanks to the incessant
metamorphosis of its idea, but the new idea rests upon the secure
vehicle of myth.'[19]

In short, the text of Virgil's epyllion leaves out much of the myth of
Orpheus: Virgil's Orpheus is neither a seer nor a revealer of mysteries
nor a demiurge of human progress. And yet, as we shall see, the single
qualification that the poet chooses to render pertinent, at the expense
of all the others contemplated by the tradition, still grasps something
essential.

In Virgil's representation, Aristaeus is the most complete hero
of the georgic realm and possesses all the significant attributes of
the agricultural art.[20] His initial lament is filled with intertextual
references which recall the themes of the didactic part of the poem;
thus 4.326–8 *hunc ipsum vitae mortalis honorem | quem mihi vix
frugum et pecudum custodia sollers | omnia temptanti extuderat* refers
directly to the exposition of books 1 and 2 (*fruges*) and book 3
(*pecudum custodia*). An industrious experimenter, Aristaeus must

[17] Cf. March (1987).
[18] Cf. Most (1985) and Arrighetti (1987), 76–97. And naturally I am omitting the
version of the myth in Euripides' *Andromache*.
[19] Jaeger (1945), iii.172–3.
[20] Already the mythological tradition made Aristaeus the cultural hero of the
agricultural world: cf. Chuvin (1976), 91–2.

be considered a great benefactor of mankind and hence worthy of the
reverence which would belong to a god; Diodorus Siculus 4.81 says
that Aristaeus had received 'godlike honours' for his services as
'universal inventor' of the farmer's techniques. And note already
1.133 *ut varias usus meditando extunderet artis*, and 1.168 *divini
gloria ruris*.

But Virgil had already signalled Aristaeus' emblematic importance
as the heroic benefactor of the georgic life even more emphatically
when he had promoted him to become one of the tutelary divinities
of his incipient poem, innovating significantly with respect to the
model constituted by the prooemium of Varro, *De Re Rust.* 1.1.4–6.
And, even more importantly, Virgil had drawn the reader's attention
to Aristaeus by designating him with an erudite periphrasis of
Alexandrian taste: 1.14–15 *et cultor nemorum, cui pinguia Ceae* | *ter
centum nivei tondent dumeta iuvenci*.[21] By presenting him as the hero
of his georgic poem, Virgil makes Aristaeus an emblematic figure of
the farmer's culture and the prototype of the perfect *agricola*: 'Aristaeus, whom they say was the greatest farmer amongst the ancients'
(Ἀρισταῖον, ὅν φασι γεωργικώτατον εἶναι ἐπὶ τῶν ἀρχαίων, Ps.-Arist.
Mir. Ausc. 100.838b): an ancient definition which would serve well as
an epigraph for the Virgilian character.[22]

When Aristaeus is stricken by disaster and sees his bees die, he
searches for the reason for his misfortune and lets himself
be instructed so that he can find the remedy. With obedient trust
he will perform his ordeal. Once he has been warned (396–7
ut omnem | *expediat morbi causam eventusque secundet*), he finds in
'tenacity' the most effective means for success, and he will be able to
learn from Proteus the origin of his misfortunes and to receive from
his mother the divine injunction of a ritual he must perform without
deviating in the slightest detail. The two virtues required for his
venture are first tenacity, in order to know, then obedience, in
order to enact. The ordeal is difficult because Proteus refuses
to answer his questions, transforming himself and striking terror

---

[21] Cf. Thomas (1988*a*), 68 and 71. The procedure of periphrastic *griphos*, which
makes the reader curious and alert, is notoriously praised by Horace at *Ars*
143–4 ... *ex fumo dare lucem* | *cogitat, ut speciosa dehinc miracula promat*.

[22] Cf. my article 'Aristeo' (Conte 1984*b*).

into anyone who lacks the force to 'hold firm' (*tenere*) both the terrifyingly metamorphic, struggling prophet and his own heart, which would gladly surrender. *Vinclisque tenebis* (405)—his mother Cyrene tells him one time; and then she repeats again, *tu, nate, magis contende tenacia vincla* (412). *Tenacitas,* a humble but effective virtue, is exactly the same force as that of the farmer who combats the reluctance of the miserly earth. Aristaeus' mother Cyrene, warning her son of the ordeal that awaited him, had admonished him: *nam sine vi non ulla dabit praecepta, neque illum | orando flectes; vim duram et vincula capto | tende* (398–400).

Durus, another key word in these lines, indicates the other, complementary aspect of 'tenacity'. It often appears in the *Georgics* to signify the 'hard' reluctance of nature, which can only be overcome by toil: thus *labor omnia vicit | improbus et duris urgens in rebus egestas* (1.146); *durus uterque labor* (2.412); *ipse labore manum duro terat* (4.114); and in the end the farmers too must be 'hard' themselves, 'resistant to toil': *dicendum et quae sint duris agrestibus arma, | quis sine nec potuere seri nec surgere messes* (1.160–1). Resistance to toil, knowing how to persevere in an arduous task with faith and obstinacy—these are Roman virtues. They are ancient virtues, but always remain relevant, and it is these which obtain success for Aristaeus when they are wedded to scrupulous obedience to divine dictates.

Orpheus, on the other hand, fails. He fails because he contravenes the rigorous conditions imposed by the god of the dead: *rupta tyranni | foedera* (492–3). To respect the orders he has received would require tenacity and firmness, but Orpheus lacks these virtues because he is a lover. He is possessed by his love which makes him, so to speak, light-headed. He turns his eyes to look upon the object of his love, and thus violates the *lex* dictated by Proserpina (487). Love carries him away and makes a fool of him. He yields to love just as any lover can yield all too easily to the illusion that *omnia vincit amor* (*Buc.* 10.59)—as though this sentence could be truer than the one that says *labor omnia vicit* (*Georg.* 1.145), which contains a large part of the ideology of the *Georgics.*

Thus a slightly more systematic comparison between the two heroes obtains a first result. It seems clear to me that the parallelism between Orpheus and Aristaeus (obtained by means of the Alexandrian–Catullan expedient of embedding) has the function of indicating a pertinent opposition between two attitudes and two ways of life. On the one hand, the submissive and scrupulous *georgos*, the perfect paradigm of religious obedience; on the other, the lover, who, even if the force of his love can carry away and convulse other people, is nevertheless carried away himself by the very same *furor* (495) that animates him. Love is a powerful force, but it is *dementia* (488 *cum subita incautum dementia cepit amantem*). The madness of love deceives Orpheus: its prisoner, he does not preserve obedience to the will of the gods. The exemplary truth that the narration leaves behind—like a sediment which precipitates from the comparison between the two contrasting attitudes—is that only he who gives full recognition to the power and will of divinity wins. And this is in evident harmony with the general ideology and didactic economy of the *Georgics*.

We have spoken of the morphological parallelism between Orpheus and Aristaeus, indicating in this the essential procedure with which the two stories are set in significant relation to one another in Virgil's text. Each of the two narrative structures is made up of some corresponding elementary features, but (it is as well to remember) this is done in such a way that the constitutive elements of the one story are demarcated and orientated by those of the other story. That is, each story's narrative skeleton is similar enough to the other's, but neither story is conceived for its own sake. Each is modelled on the other, but the parallelism is adroitly veiled by the technical artifice of embedding one story within the other. Technique too calls for fantasy and expressive freedom.

The structural parallelism, in short, dialectically mediates the story's emblematic meaning; but the epyllion's poetic fascination can obviously not be reduced to this naked skeleton. Instead, the extraordinary artistry of Virgil's story consists precisely in the pathetic force with which each of the two stories (and in particular that of Orpheus) acquires expressive autonomy and is elaborated into a complex narrative. Perhaps no other Latin epyllion, not even Catullus' poem on the wedding of Peleus and Thetis, has attained a more complete artistic expression; probably there is no other Latin epyllion in which the art of the 'miniature epic' has reached such high levels of perfection.

A fairly good explanation which might be given is the following: in a certain sense, Virgil wished to leave unstressed the comparative (contrastive) project connecting the two parts of his epyllion. In short, he let his discourse's illustrative value be glimpsed as an ultimate content, but also made sure that his liberty of invention was not oppressed by its emblematic function. His capacity for poetic representation and his stylistic vigour superimposed themselves upon the ideological, programmatic scheme, and filled it with all the enchantment of a fable. And in point of fact the story has a strong sense of the tragic, the lightness of fables, and also the customary empathetic and sympathetic participation which is the true mark of Virgil's style.[23]

This might be a good explanation, but it would certainly omit something important. The extraordinary seduction that Virgil's myth of Orpheus exerts upon the reader is not an uncalculated result of the text, but is a significant effect which it exploits: I mean that this effect is an essential part of the idea that the poet wants to represent. The sympathy which the story of Orpheus receives in the text suggests to the reader how painful it is for the poet to permit his character's love to be condemned to failure. Let us put it like this for now; later we shall see the meaning of this idea more clearly.

We have said that the two stories are constructed according to a reciprocal and parallel determination of their elements. Both heroes lose their most precious possession: the farmer-breeder loses the object of his most lively care, the poet-lover the object of his passionate song. Aristaeus' offence belongs to the story's prehistory: rather than being an important element in the narrative, it is the indispensable premiss of the hero's loss, his search for the remedy for the loss he has sustained, and his final success—in fact, Aristaeus is

---

[23] These are strong signs of free poetic elaboration, which have misled some interpreters into analysing and appreciating the form of the expression in Virgil's discourse more than the structuring of the content, and hence into neglecting the correspondences between the two parts of the epyllion which are set in contrast with one another. Some critics had already got lost because of the impressionistic mode of reading that guided them. Thus La Penna goes so far as to assert: 'Aristeo [...] non è particolarmente attivo e industrioso perché possa servire da modello etico in nessun senso: nell'epillio di Aristeo a Virgilio interessavano il viaggio fiabesco nel mondo sotterraneo delle acque e il ricantamento con gusto alessandrino del mito di Proteo' (La Penna in Canali (1983), 101).

not only unaware of the fault he has committed but is also only involuntarily the cause of Eurydice's death. The other parallel and analogical element which links the two heroes is the difficult ordeal which unites them in a voyage of search and recovery: both must descend into another realm, the one performing a katabasis to the origin of the waters and the other a katabasis to the Underworld. Both enjoy success in this first phase of their exploits, but in the end one will succeed in his aim while the other will fail.

The difference in outcome, as I have said, corresponds to the difference in attitude maintained by the two heroes. Let us examine the matter in more detail. Aristaeus asks for help: his desperate lament corresponds in some way to the plaintive song of Orpheus, the lover-poet who sings of his pain. But the farmer hero *resolves to learn* from the very beginning: he does not go beyond the orders he has received and he makes himself the scrupulous performer of the divine dictate. The linguistic clue to this attitude is the presence in the text of an archaic and almost sacral style: 548 *haud mora, continuo matris praecepta facessit*. Here the formulaic structure reproduces— at the level of verbal expression—Aristaeus' prompt and respectful response to the ordinances which have been imparted to him and the rigorous precision of the liturgical procedure. The clausula *praecepta facessit* has an epic colouring,[24] but Mynors, comparing Ennius, *Ann.* 57 Sk. *dicta facessunt*, rightly notes in his commentary that 'both words seem to suggest active compliance'.[25]

Aristaeus' attitude is in perfect harmony with his passive appearance: the text leaves no room for his emotional reactions or development. He is simply an executor: obedience is his virtue. He opens himself up docilely to the revelation of a secret which will save him. In his role of pupil Aristaeus fully embodies the status of the *Georgics*' ideal recipient: the farmer who is master of techniques and

---

[24] Cf. *Aen.* 9.45 *praecepta facessunt*; 4.295 *iussa facessunt*. Cf. Biotti (1994), 412.

[25] Moreover, the fact that in vv. 548–53 many of the expressions that describe Aristaeus' miraculous actions are repeated from the instructions dictated by Cyrene (537–47) has a precedent in Homer, *Od.* 10.517–25 and 11.25–33 (the ritual prescriptions imparted by Circe to Odysseus for evoking the souls of the dead): cf. Biotti (1994), 412. When Aristaeus exactly repeats the religious ritual as it has been prescribed to him, he is fully exercising his farmer's *pietas*: still unaware of the miracle, he will be rewarded for his obedience and discipline.

is ready for *durus labor*, but who is above all strong in religious observance.

Beyond the parallelism of the two stories, Virgil's Orpheus has an additional feature which, precisely because it is so evident (the text insists upon it), seems to be strongly significant. Orpheus is not only an unfortunate lover: he is above all a *poet*, a passionate singer of his love. Does this marked characterization as poet have a meaning, a reason? Certainly, it might be sufficiently motivated by extratextual considerations: in the traditional paradigm of the myth Orpheus is the singer *par excellence*. But I want to emphasize now what I said earlier: in a literary work, certain values of a myth are activated at the expense of others; the meaning the myth acquires is determined by its representative function, the orientation the context impresses upon it. To repeat some of Jaeger's words I quoted earlier, 'The poet is the creator of a new norm of life for his age and he interprets the myth on the base of this new norm.' The myth is conjugated like a grammatical paradigm and permits new discourses when it enters into new contexts. And in the present case the fact that Orpheus is represented as a poet is significant: we shall see that this whole finale is dominated by poetry—or rather, by poetry as the problem of choice between different ways of writing poetry.

But then again, it is perhaps too general to call the Orpheus of Virgil's epyllion simply a poet. What type of poetry does this Orpheus sing? On the basis of the mythic background, we would expect a traditional Orphic song, one about cosmogony or nature. In Apollonius Rhodius' *Argonautica* (1.496–511), Orpheus allays a quarrel among his sailing companions by singing a scientific (Empedoclean) poem on the genesis of the cosmos; such an almost Lucretian mode would not be at all extraneous to a didactic, georgic poem like Virgil's. But instead this Orpheus sings of love, the pain of parting, the loss of the woman he loves. In short: this is poetry made up of personal vicissitudes, of unhappy passion.

In this way we have identified another reason for Orpheus' intrinsic weakness: he is not only a lover, he is a lover-poet, a character who turns love, or rather the suffering of love, into the exclusive object of his song. He is indeed a prototype of the poet-singer, but of the singer of an *erotikon pathema*, made up of heart-wrenchingly painful notes. It has been said that Orpheus' *labor* is spent in vain (491–2 *omnis* | *effusus labor*)²⁶ because his tactic is different from Aristaeus'. It is not that he evades the more difficult ordeal, for the risk he runs is in fact grander and more audacious than Aristaeus'. But he works *alone*, animated by the pain that fills him: 465 *te, dulcis coniunx, te solo in litore secum.* Isolated, he cannot help but turn to himself and dissolve everything into song; and the erotic *furor* which is the very source of his poetry (his song is nourished by the passion that blinds him) ends up destroying him.²⁷

The same paradox stands at the origin of much elegiac poetry. Poetry is born as a means of consolation, for overcoming the unhappiness of the passion of love: 464 *solans aegrum... amorem.* But in the final instance this same poetry has no choice but to become a *reflection* of the lover's suffering, for it cannot help but derive its theme from the very pain of the passion. And so Orpheus sings and weeps alone with himself: 509 *flesse sibi et gelidis haec evolvisse sub antris*—and in the comparison of vv. 511–15 *qualis... maerens philomela... flet... miserabile carmen* | *integrat... maestis... quaestibus implet.* How can an elegiac poet be defined exactly in a mordant epigram? Domitius Marsus (v. 9 Morel = fr. 7.3 Courtney) defines Tibullus as *elegis molles qui fleret amores*, a definition which could well be applied to elegy in general. In singing his *erotikon pathema*, Virgil's Orpheus sings in the mode of an elegiac poet, just like Gallus, the founder of Latin elegy, suffering from love in the Tenth Eclogue (vv. 14–15).²⁸

It did not escape Horace's notice that Virgil's Orpheus showed the unmistakable lineaments of the elegiac poet. In *Odes* 2.9 he turns to his dear poet friend Valgius Rufus with a smile of affectionate

---

²⁶ Thomas (1988*b*) notes in his comment on these verses (231): 'words crucial to the poem, and indicating one of the main connections between Orpheus and the participants of the agricultural *Georgics*; Orpheus, paradigm for the man who controls not only nature, but even the powers of the Underworld, finds his own *labor* destroyed by a momentary lapse—a lapse caused by *amor*, one of the very forces of nature which destroyed man's work in Book 3. Cf. 1.325–26 (of the storm) *sata laeta boumque labores* | *diluit*; 3.525 *quid labor aut benefacta iuvant?*'

²⁷ 494–5 *Illa: 'quis et me' inquit 'miseram et te perdidit, Orpheu,* | *quis tantus furor?...'*: in presenting love as a ruinous folly, Virgil's language resorts to elegiac accents, cf. Prop. 2.28a.7 *hoc perdit miseras, hoc perdidit ante puellas.*

²⁸ See Conte (1986*a*), 100–29. Cf. Prop. 1.18.27–9; 1.20.13–14; cf. also Barchiesi (1980), 130–1.

criticism: 'not always do the rain and wind rage, sometimes the bad weather too stops; but you on the contrary never stop lamenting your lost love and constantly compose tearful elegies': vv. 9–12 *tu semper urges flebilibus modis | Mysten ademptum, nec tibi Vespero | surgente decedunt amores, | nec rapidum fugiente solem.* Without bothering to conceal his cards, Horace designates Valgius' kind of sentimental elegy by alluding to the very same lines with which Virgil had represented Orpheus: 464–6 *ipse cava solans aegrum testudine amorem | te, dulcis coniunx, te solo in litore secum, | te veniente die, te decedente canebat.* Horace's ode offers a felicitous example of *urbanitas*, made up as it is of elegant irony and at the same time of affectionate seriousness: the poet makes a display of consoling his friend by reminding him of the virtue of moderation, but in fact he wishes to touch upon literary themes; he invites Valgius to commit himself to more serious literary themes but in fact asserts his distance from a type of love poetry enclosed in its obsessive repetitiveness.[29]

When poetry adheres totally to life (when the poet is also a lover and can only sing of his unhappy love), pain becomes its sole, indispensable nourishment, the substance of its contents.[30] Thus, in the end, only Orpheus' tongue and voice will remain, surviving as the minimal, indestructible residue, the very nucleus of Virgil's representation of Orpheus. At the end of the process of reduction (poetry =song of suffering, poet=afflicted voice), singing a love song will be nothing more than calling the beloved's name: 525–6 *Eurydicen vox ipsa et frigida lingua | a miseram Eurydicen! anima fugiente vocabat.* The residual lamenting voice, the quintessence of this way of composing poetry, is the seal that symbolizes the ultimate meaning of the elegiac Orpheus Virgil invented.

The poetry of love fails because it is constitutively divorced from action: it is entirely and merely egotistic. Its form of existence, at least insofar as it is opposed to the 'active' form, is so to speak 'contemplative'. Though endowed with immense force, it is only good for

---

[29] The date of composition of Horace's ode can be placed with some probability in 27 BC: there is an excellent treatment of the problem in Nisbet and Hubbard (1978), 137–8, but see also 135 and 145, where Horace's relation with the verses of Cinna's *Zmyrna* (fr. 6 Morel) is well discussed.
[30] See Conte (1994*b*), 37–43.

trying to console its singer (without, however, succeeding in this intent) and for sweeping its listener into an enchanted stupor.

In conclusion, the finale of the *Georgics* juxtaposes Aristaeus, the prototypical hero of the *pius agricola*'s toilsome life, and Orpheus, the mythical figure of the poet-singer, deprived of any feature irrelevant to this specific characteristic. What does the reader think at this point? Let us begin by noting that the epyllion's very position, so close to the poet's farewell, is the same as the location in the *Bucolics* occupied by the Tenth Eclogue, which sets the seal upon pastoral poetry by reflecting upon the borders of the bucolic genre and defining them in a direct comparison with the love elegy of Gallus, the character-protagonist of that Eclogue.

Is it legitimate to see in this similarity of contextual functions an indication suggesting that we consider Virgil's story of Orpheus as his reflection upon the function and modes of composing poetry? More precisely, I mean that the story of Orpheus' love song—his ordeal and his failure—becomes *indirectly* a discourse about the limits that this kind of poetry encounters when it tries to become a practical activity, to engage with 'reality'.

We have said that the two stories of Aristaeus and Orpheus are constructed in a system of reciprocal relations which coordinate them with one another. They have a rather limited number of shared or corresponding features (those entailed by the narrative model of an ordeal difficult to overcome) and they are opposed to one another above all in their final outcomes. This is the level of description which analysis must hold on to without getting lost in the superficial modalities of narrative: only in this way can we grasp the meaning of the comparison-opposition between the stories of the two prototypical heroes.

But in opposing the singer of love to the georgic hero I do not intend to introduce some form of allegorism. I firmly reject the familiar realistic allegorism of those critics who look for improbable historical personages behind the figures of Aristaeus and Orpheus (Aristaeus has even been seen as Augustus, or else as a prefiguration of Aeneas). Nor do I wish to claim that the epyllion's function is to 'stage' a genuine (self-reflective, metapoetic) literary-critical discourse which opposes two different forms of poetry, as though the *Georgics* intended in some way to allegorize its own genre—for then the only reason the epyllion stands in the poem would be to allow room for a treatise on poetics conducted in the form of a contrast.

Let me clarify. There is indeed an opposition between georgic poetry and love poetry arising from the opposition between a 'practical dimension' and a 'contemplative dimension', in which the latter turns out to be ineffective and is defeated. But the opposition that orientates the meaning of this text does not, properly speaking, set in contrast two forms of poetry in order to delimit their proper contents and language in terms of their differences, in the way that, as I have said, in the *Bucolics* the last Eclogue measures the boundaries between the elegiac and pastoral genres. Here the comparison is instead between two different dispositions which produce poetry, and it has the function of mediating symbolically the irreducible difference between two *ways of life*.

Aristaeus is the representation, *sub specie narrationis*, of the *georgos'* life. He identifies and embodies the fundamental theme of Virgil's work, namely the laborious victory obtained by the farmer, trusting in divine aid and with an obedience capable of redeeming his own errors, against the evils of history and of nature—different manifestations, at the end of the first and third books, of the same hostile disorder in the world. Aristaeus, as an agricultural hero, is the very model of the perfect farmer, the final representation of the instruction which the poet has dispensed throughout the four books of his poem; but he himself appears as a farmer who needs to be instructed so that—by learning, just like every addressee the poet's words contemplate—he can win his daily battle.

Aristaeus, the ideal model *who* receives and performs teaching, is at the same time the complete model *for whoever* is intended to receive and perform it. In short: he is a farmer in whom farmers can see their reflection. One could say, then, that the *fabula Aristaei* is simply the translation into a dynamic narrative form of the literary stance which underlies the entire poem and foresees its reception. In order to make this meaning stronger and more definite, the text evokes both the 'didactic' model represented by Aristaeus and another model—one which configures an entirely different relation between poetry and reality, indeed the most distant one possible. Orpheus provides a model mediated by the enchantment of a poetry which is heart-rending and passionate, but unproductive, unable to prevail in practice. Thus it has come about that a poetic discourse of a properly preceptive mode, namely the didactic form, has taken on the formulation and dynamic rhythm of a narrative, a sequence of events recounted so that an exemplary and instructive story can emerge from them.

Modelled by contrast upon Aristaeus, Orpheus, the character in the epyllion who embodies the other pole of the opposition, fails his ordeal because he does not know how to yield to obedience towards the will of the gods. His way of life is capable of extraordinary miracles, but (as I have said) it lacks practical effectiveness. The song of lament is the very substance of the life the love poet chooses, and it is also the necessary condition of his existence, since the poet's song can only exist by virtue of the suffering of love. So too for the elegiac poet, whose poetry is nourished by love and the sufferings deriving from it: without these, the elegiac poet would cease to be a poet. But this uncompromising loyalty to his own suffering cannot succeed where other forces, other spiritual dispositions, are required.

Solitude removes the love poet from the real world, commits him to himself, makes him egotistically indifferent to every external solicitation. Locked into this autonomy of his, he is not able (nor is he willing) to break the closed circle outside of which alone there can be salvation. This is the paradox of the elegiac poet, and it is the paradox of Orpheus, a powerful singer but a powerless agent.

On the other hand, the georgic song too is a way of composing poetry, but the life it promises is different. It communicates a secret of possible happiness to anyone willing to accept the tenacious *labor* of an existence controlled by simple and sacred rules, open to the teachings that can give it help. And in the end the force of this life, which is capable of overcoming the most difficult obstacles, will be revealed to be nothing else than the awareness of a bliss possessed unconsciously until now: 2.458–9 O *fortunatos nimium, sua si bona norint,* | *agricolas.* The farmer Aristaeus testifies to a choice of life. Upon this choice, the poet Virgil constructs the meaning of his own choice of poetry.

The difficult task to which Maecenas challenged Virgil (3.41 *tua, Maecenas, haud mollia iussa*) turned him into a 'poet-*vates*', a 'useful poet', one dedicated to a song which would be able to serve the collectivity, to instruct it and make it participate in positive suggestions and shared values. Lucretius' example carries Virgil towards poetry aspiring to the same seriousness as his Latin predecessor's but confronting him with material of an inferior level. A lesser *vates*, Virgil knows that Lucretius has gone beyond the Alexandrians' preciosity to refound the central intention of the didactic genre by charging it with passion and ardour.

This commitment he makes his own. In a certain sense he goes beyond Lucretius, at least by continuing his example in a different field, but at the same time he takes a step back because he offers knowledge which is less cosmic and more mundane. He accepts the responsibility of speaking to the conscience of his contemporaries and embraces an ambitious cultural programme. He seeks, and finds, Hesiod's grand distant voice, and chooses for himself the grand myth of the Italian countryside, the land of Saturn, inhabited by men whose hearts are simple and who love justice. In order to declare this vocation with even greater force, Virgil opposes his own poetic choice to the most fascinating poetry of his day, love elegy. On the one hand Virgil and the world of his Aristaeus, on the other an entirely private poetry which only obeys the law of *servitium amoris*, invents an enclosed and absolute 'form of the world', and in fact advocates a self-sufficient ideology indifferent to the values of the collectivity.

Certainly, in Virgil's text the opposition between didactic and elegiac is configured as a bitterly dramatic experience because its substance is made up of *renunciations*. I said earlier[31] that the sympathy which the story of Orpheus encounters in the text shows the reader how great a sacrifice it cost Virgil to permit dedication to love, that great force hidden in nature, to be condemned to failure. The love that holds Orpheus prisoner, the individualism that characterizes him and makes him behave in a way so different from Aristaeus, are not valueless. On the contrary, Virgil knows how to render homage to elegiac poetry as the poetic form best adapted to representing human weakness and capable of winning sympathy for the pain of anyone who suffers an existential failure. His is a grand

---

[31] Above, p. 139.

homage: he agrees to expose himself to the risk of that genre and succeeds perfectly in this test—perhaps he does so with the pride of a poet who thereby demonstrates what he could have achieved if only his choice had gone in that direction. But he has to renounce that possibility.

At the same time as he shows all the force and fascination of the poet Orpheus' destiny, Virgil denounces the costs of the 'weak' choice, that of elegy, and the bitter price of his own 'strong' choice, the mission of a didactic commitment which exalts the simple and solid values of the farmer's life. His *arator* is *durus*, and the virtues that guide him must be indifferent to the mournful complaint of the poor nightingale deprived of its nest; but this is the *dura* law of the world Jupiter willed for men, the world of *labor*.[32] Consider once again vv. 511–15 *qualis... maerens philomela... | amissos queritur fetus, quos durus arator | ... detraxit; at illa | flet noctem ramoque sedens miserabile carmen | integrat et maestis late loca questibus implet.* The nightingale sings and laments, just as the poet-lover Orpheus sings and laments: and the nightingale—at least since Catullus 65[33]—is the emblematic figure of the elegiac poet. *Durities* is a constitutive feature of the *arator*'s character, an indispensable aspect of that perseverance which will help him to pass the test: his choice of life does not know failure, but its price is high. This is the same price which the didactic poet Virgil must pay for his refusal of the poetry of love.[34]

---

[32] Important in this connection is the comparison with *Georg.* 2.207–11, where the farmer exercises his dominion upon nature by deforesting the land to free it from sloth and assign it to productivity; but the didactic poet views this violent action from the perspective of the birds that lived in the trees that are being cut down when they see their nest sacrificed to the farmer's hard necessities: ... *unde iratus silvam devexit arator | et nemora evertit multos ignava per annos, | antiquasque domos avium cum stirpibus imis | eruit; illae altum nidis petiere relictis.* The protagonist of the *Georgics*—the patient, tenacious *agricola*, able to crown his toil with success—is also a character not free of shadows, and he too requires victims.

[33] See the excellent article by Rosati (1996), who offers a full discussion and a rich bibliography (noteworthy is the comparison with Callimachus' epigram [*AP* 7.80 = 2 Pf.] in memory of his friend Heraclitus, an elegiac poet).

[34] Perhaps we may even understand Servius' notice about Gallus in this light. Glenn Most suggests to me that if, in Virgil's own lifetime, the Aristaeus epyllion was read in just this way, as a refusal to write poetry like Gallus' and as a counterpart to the end of the *Bucolics* (cf. n. 27 above), it might have been said that the end of the *Georgics* was 'really' about Gallus. At some later point, readers might have wondered why then he is not mentioned by name and the story could have been invented that

An aestheticizing criticism often leaves interpreters dissatisfied because it tends to turn every great poetic work into a wholly individual piece whose existence is placed miraculously outside of time and space. To be sure, literary historians always take care to react against this tendency by making an undeniable claim for the historicity of the poetic text; but often this only serves to demand that the meaning of the individual work be relocated within the opaque body of history.

The right way to consider a poetic work is not to dilute it *in history* but rather to see history flash like lightning *in it*. Incorporated in the text's final structure are a poet, a language and an imagination, meanings and addressees capable of receiving them: this is why in every work there is also, necessarily, history. Here too—in the *Georgics*, and in particular in the story of Aristaeus—there is history, and it has become part of Virgil's poetry: Maecenas and the programme of his circle, everyone's anxieties and hopes after the 'great fear', the dramatic commitment of a poet who becomes a *vates* in order to transmit strong values and ancient truths, the magnificent ambition of a grand new Latin literature which chooses to direct itself to the conscience of a national collectivity.[35]

an earlier version mentioning him had been suppressed. Thilo (1886), p. xxiv (cf. Delvigo (1995), 24 and 27), and Nisbet (1987), 189, had already put forward a similar suggestion.

[35] See the fine discussion in Griffin (1979), 174–80, with a good reconstruction of the ideological-cultural ambience which provides a background for the specific ideology of Virgil's poem and for the literary symbols which express it. Especially attractive is the correct way in which he studies the so-called 'Augustan ideology' not as an immediate and brutal reflection of the regime's politics and propaganda, but as a coherent discourse to which intellectuals (poets and writers in general) give expression. It is hard to believe that some interpreters of the literary texts of the period speak of 'Augustan ideology' and neglect the autonomous creativity of the great men of letters, who themselves were the creators of that ideology and not just its mouthpieces, interpreters perhaps, but original ones.

5

The Strategy of Contradiction: On the Dramatic Form of the *Aeneid*

Connecting the peaks of discourse one to another not by following a single path.

Empedocles fr. B24 Diels–Kranz

THE fact that things in this world and discourse about them contain contradictions is an outrage to common sense. Contradiction is regarded not as the inevitable nature of historical reality, but more like a weed that has invaded the garden of consensus. Critical dogmatism loves simplicity and maintains that whatever is univocal is good and true, whereas whatever appears ambiguous or contradictory seems to arise from the errors of interpreters who have 'strayed from the proper path'. I believe, on the contrary, that contradictions can prove extraordinarily fertile for critical thinking: they engage the interpreter and compel him or her to seek out a new order of understanding, a more complex and better articulated order. In short, far from constituting violations of meaning, contradictions are part of meaning; more than that, they are its living and growing part.

Literary criticism often commits the sin of reductionism. Precisely because it aims to redirect all the components of meaning into a univocal formulation, it ends by imposing a single direction on the twisting paths that have led to the formation of a poetic work. However, the reduction of the text to a simple entity does not cancel its inevitable internal contradictions: in reality, these move outside the text and take up residence in the critical debate, and there take the shape of the dissenting theses of interpreters who simply embrace one or other pole of the contradiction. This is why it is proper, if we are seeking the comprehensive meaning of a work, to keep an eye on the history of criticism, for this is where the internal contradictions of a text come into the open. Traversing the history of criticism is a good way of entering the text, an indirect way; we are not going through the main gate but by the service entrance (and the idea rather pleases me that the interpreter should show some modesty and enter by the back door).

The history of Virgilian criticism is one of the most ancient critical traditions, but we will not retrace it too far back in time. It will be enough to take into account the criticism of the last forty years or so: enough, since the judgements (and prejudices) of previous criticism often flow back into it with various modifications. We will talk of sins without naming the sinners; the key is to know which critical tendencies have developed in contradiction with one another rather than to blame or praise individual offenders. We will mention some emblematic name if it is really helpful; but it is not useful to follow the path of polemic. All the more so because in the last analysis we are not talking about real, proper sins; each of the interpreters has simply made absolute verities out of what were in each case only partial truths.

Moreover, those who have indeed detected contradiction in the *Aeneid* have generally regarded it only as an unresolved feature of the Virgilian text, the visible sign of a flaw to be remedied. Some scholars have even considered it as the irreducible residue of suppressed ideas that were trying to surface to confront others that dominated the text: in short, an excess or at least an imperfection. For my part, I believe that Virgil was aiming at contradiction, and doing this deliberately and programmatically, in order to make it the very essence of his discourse. This is a wound deliberately left gaping, so that it would not close. For Virgil, reason, and with it the language of justice and morality, was now divided, and could no longer voice simple univocal truths; they were compelled to speak in dualistic, contradictory terms. The text of the *Aeneid* had to open up to welcome antagonistic claims and forces: the meaning of the discourse would be enriched by it and so inevitably would become complex.

So the clashes, the incompatible situations, the dissonance of voices and points of view, correspond to a structural principle which radically renews the mode of epic. This is why contradiction in the *Aeneid* does not demand to be smoothed out. Through it the poet acquires the advantage of being able to say two things that are simultaneously contradictory and true, two things that are individually true but each incapable of being reduced to the other. It borrows its language from drama, from the experience of the great Greek tragedies. This is the conclusion to anticipate from now on: that Virgil strategically constructed his epic poem in the form of contradictions. The logic which he follows in the *Aeneid* is like the logic of the emotions, and so it allows him to handle ideas, persons, events, and states of mind in a way that enables opposites to coexist legitimately (if also dramatically). It is the reader's job to face this dualism and to experience to the utmost, within his or her own conscience, the painful anxiety of doubt.

We have mentioned the disagreement among interpreters, who have projected outside the text—polarizing into two opposing factions—that ideological dualism which is really wholly within the poetic form of the *Aeneid*. For some time now it has been the practice to distinguish two approaches in Virgilian criticism, an 'optimistic' and a 'pessimistic' tendency, but these are labels that seem increasingly more inadequate.[1] In recent times the boundaries have become much less clear between the two schools (one improperly called 'European' and the other just as improperly 'Harvard School'):[2] each of the two has included something from the other; the 'Europeans' have incorporated pessimistic elements into their optimistic vision, and conversely the 'Harvard critics' have also welcomed positive elements into their own pessimism. But the opposition, however unfounded, still persists, if only from academic inertia.

For all that they diverge, the two schools have used a similar interpretative procedure. Each one has emphasized only one aspect of the Virgilian contradiction, and has then made this aspect absolute, making it the single principle of construction of the entire text of the *Aeneid*. In this way, for the 'Europeans' every negative has in the end been reabsorbed into the positivity of the celebratory

[1] For a survey of 20th-cent. views see Harrison (1990), 1–20.

[2] On the dubious nature of the term 'Harvard School' see W. V. Clausen, 'The Harvard School', in Horsfall (1995), 313–14.

vision, and on the contrary, for the 'Harvard critics' every apparent positive element has been eclipsed in the face of the radically negative conception they see as predominating in the text. There have even been some critics who, trying to mediate between the two hostile positions, have sought a way out in psychological explanation. So for one group the authentic Virgil would be the poet who celebrates the glorious story of heroic men engaged in creating a new world order, even if here and there suppressed doubts beset him *à contre cœur*, doubts likely to trouble his optimism. For the other group, Virgil, a poet obsessed with the suffering of every innocent victim, wrote his poem as a desolate lament on the human condition; neither the edifying epic historical picture offered by the *Aeneid*, nor the providentiality of Rome's destiny, nor the positivity of Aeneas' hero-ism would be sufficient to mask his profound pessimism: they are all merely superficial correctives, ideological disguises superimposed on the text.

What matters, however, is that both interpretations, although they arrive at opposite verdicts by opposing paths, are looking at the Virgilian poem as a univocal structure; for the critics of one school the final optimism cancels out all negative doubt; for those of the other, pessimism pre-emptively invalidates any possible positive vision. Neither group recognizes the dualism that divides Virgilian poetry; they do not follow the poet in his choice of making himself the mouthpiece of antagonistic notions, that is, of mutually contra-dictory ideas that stand alongside each other in the text without one being subordinated to the other. In short, we are concerned with the form of the discourse itself, not the unconscious mind of the author.

Thus the psychological acrobatics of the critics do not work, as they undermine the celebratory edifice of the Roman national epic, seeking to bring into the open the unexpressed anxieties of the poet; it is their conviction that behind these anxieties are hidden more authentic truths, resurfacing despite every ideological layer that covers them. But the poet's truths in the *Aeneid*, whether positive or negative, all find more or less open expression in the text; these truths are equally possible and equally valid, and they are placed next to each other in a kind of logical parataxis. The reader who accepts the double proposition of the poet cannot be content with superfi-cially harmonizing the contradictions, but must accept the negative without separating it from the positive and seek out a new order of thinking. It is the same textual strategy, I would say the same form of composition, which every genuinely dramatic work offers its spectator, who is forced to face the dualism of contradictory principles. In fact in drama the meaning of the whole results from a complex system of different truths, a system within which opposing claims enter into reciprocal tension.

I think it will be instructive to start from the most heavily studied passages of the *Aeneid*, crucial moments in the text which have already attracted the attention of critics. But we need to reconsider them in a new perspective. In the middle of the poem Aeneas goes down to the world of the dead to meet his father Anchises and be instructed in the destiny that awaits him. Of the many teachings that Anchises will dispense to his son the most important, indeed the most comprehensive, is *parcere subiectis et debellare superbos* (6.863): a simple formula that condenses the ethics necessary for the government of the world. It is to receive this teaching that Aeneas goes down to the Underworld. But in the epilogue of the poem, when Turnus, now defeated, is kneeling at his feet, Aeneas disregards his father's teaching and kills his enemy. And yet Turnus, to try to save his life, even recalls Anchises to memory, and shows himself *subiectus* (*Aen.* 12.930 *ille humilis supplex oculos dextramque precantem | protendens*). Two principles oppose each other in the text: on the one side the duty of vengeance, on the other the necessity of forgiveness. Aeneas hesitates. The reader who has benefited from Anchises' instruction will hesitate even more, but immediately the gesture of Aeneas makes him change belief, and forces him to seek out a new and more problematic criterion of truth.

Here the *pius* Aeneas seems to betray his mission; he almost takes on the appearance of the terrible Achilles who killed Hector in vengeance towards the end of the *Iliad* (and do not forget that the Homeric poem ends, instead, with an Achilles who found himself akin to Priam in grief and was able to show him compassion). But the resemblance with Achilles is only apparent. In reality the gesture with which Aeneas kills Turnus is a kind of religious act, as his own words reveal: *Pallas te hoc vulnere Pallas | immolat et poenam scelerato ex sanguine sumit* (12.948–9). The meaning of the verb *immolat* is strongly marked and very specific: it means that Aeneas 'offers Turnus as a sacrificial victim, and kills him like the priest who carries out a sacrificial ritual'. Employing the terminology peculiar to sacrifice to indicate death inflicted as a just act of punishment on the guilty is frequent in the tragic language of Aeschylus, Sophocles, and even more of Euripides; this was shown some time ago by both Burkert and Zeitlin.[3] So, for example in Euripides' *Medea*, the killings of her children become 'sacrifices' (1054 *thumasin*); in *Electra* 774–843 Orestes kills Aegisthus with the sacrificial knife; at Aesch. *Agam.* 1118 the killing of Agamemnon which Clytemnestra is about to commit is called a 'sacrifice' (*thumatos*) because it is vengeance for the killing of Iphigenia: the motif, which is obsessive in *Agamemnon*, is less powerful in *Choephoroe*, but returns with renewed dominating force in *Eumenides*.

Immolare is exactly *thuein*: essentially Aeneas in the last scene of the poem is a *thuter*, a sacrificing priest. Thus Turnus' blood becomes blood consecrated to Pallas.[4] A serious crime has been committed (cf. *scelerato ex sanguine*) and so an expiation is necessary, necessary, that is, on *religious* grounds, to restore and cleanse the violated order. Virgil wants his readers to confront a difficult choice and face the torment of a dramatic truth, that is, a truth divided between two contradictory claims. Turnus is not an ignoble hero, but he has not shown restraint or respect towards a weaker fighter; Aeneas knows the teaching of forgiveness, but he is also responsible for an entire nation that has been entrusted to him and for Pallas in particular (his *pietas*, which can be well enough translated as 'sense of responsibility', is a lay virtue, even if it finds warrant in a religious basis).

Respect for one value can have as its price the negation of another: this is the harsh teaching left to Virgil by the great tragic theatre of Greece.[5] Virgil asks his readers to acknowledge the fatal necessity of victory, but also to evaluate how problematically close the boundaries are between justice and injustice. The victor, Aeneas, does not emerge unsullied from the final ordeal. Epic glory is thus halved,

---

[3] Burkert (1966) and Zeitlin (1965).

[4] For recent discussions of the end of the *Aeneid* in terms of sacrifice see Hardie (1993), 33–4 and Dyson (2001).

[5] See further Hardie (1997).

because it is divided between two truths that are simultaneously valid: it is contradicted by doubt and anxiety, two traits that constitute the very essence of the dramatic genre. Virgil's new narrative technique comes from a grafting operation which makes the bitter branches of tragic ambiguity spring from the ancient trunk of epic. It is in this way that the divided language of tragedy invades the epic narrative. The text is opened up to contain opposing truths and points of view: the reader is asked to reflect.

Yet, from the very moment when the reader realizes that Aeneas' final action is a religious act that satisfies the divine will, the reader also remembers that this same divine will, on the night of Troy's destruction, was turned against an innocent people. Here is another contradiction which compromises the ideological coherence of the text and troubles the reader's understanding. How can the gods be guarantors of justice and at the same time responsible for injustice? If *pietas* is collaboration in the divine ordering of the world—if it is human justice that makes itself the interpreter of divine justice—how can the gods violate their *fides* and repay devout men so savagely? This is all the more so since the bond of *pietas* is a kind of reciprocal bond: as men are bound to feel obligation towards the gods, so the gods are bound to reward the pious man with acts of justice and compassion, or to punish the *impii*; this is the same 'circle of *pietas*' defined by Karl Kerényi.[6] Indeed it is precisely in the *Aeneid*—the poem that sets *pietas* at the heart of an entire value system—that this idea finds its most explicit realization: it is enough to recall the heartfelt words with which Priam, amid the slaughter of Troy, curses Pyrrhus, demanding that the gods punish him: 2.536 *si qua est caelo pietas quae talia curet.*

The bond of *pietas*, in short, ought also to condition the behaviour of the gods towards men; yet on the same cruel last night of Troy (again in the second book) they allow the just Ripheus to be killed: 426–8 *cadit et Ripheus, iustissimus unus | qui fuit in Teucris et servantissimus aequi | (dis aliter visum).* Virgil is not afraid to force himself almost to the point of sacrilege; Aeneas' anguished doubt is dangerously near to blasphemy (near enough to worry Servius, who tries in his commentary to justify the pious hero in whatever way he can).

<hr />

[6] Kerényi (1951), 85.

The contradiction is dramatic in type; it resembles the contradictions that underlie Athenian tragedy. On one side is the divine will of fate, *Weltwille*, both supreme and blind; on the other, the search for justice by individuals who find no response: two differing perspectives, both simultaneously true, without one being able to claim more truth than the other.

The parenthesis *dis aliter visum* seems to recall a Homeric formula, νῦν δ' ἑτέρως ἐβόλοντο θεοί (*Od.* 1.234), but the distance from the model is enormous. In this passage of the *Odyssey* Telemachus is remembering the father of whose whereabouts he knows nothing, once the happy sovereign of Ithaca. 'But now the gods who devise misfortunes have decided otherwise and have made him into the least known of all men on earth.' In these words of Telemachus there is no charge against the gods: what has happened to Odysseus is in his son's eyes simply a reversal of fortune, an event which can obviously strike humans. The death of Ripheus, on the other hand, seems an inexplicable betrayal by the gods, given that Ripheus should have earned their protection by his own just and virtuous life. This undeserved death throws the fundamental value system of the text into crisis, introducing a sharp contradiction into it (in fact the parenthesis *dis aliter visum* is strongly adversative). Between the Homeric and the Virgilian text the experience of the great tragic poets has intervened. Virgil has learnt how to take on the burden of their sorrowful meditation and has transplanted it into his poem. In fact the conflict that opens up in the *Aeneid* between the innocence of the victim and the indifference of the gods is tragic in kind: at the end there are only questions; there are no answers to appease the anguish of doubt.

Virgil's *pietas*, as Alfonso Traina maintains in his exemplary entry in the *Enciclopedia Virgiliana*,[7] is brought to a halt before the mystery of providence, which sacrifices the happiness of individuals to the general good. But there is something more we can add. Virgil is not inclined to deny the existence or value of any of the victims; his strategy is to present the reader with a contradictory response, one composed of two antagonistic truths, difficult to believe simultaneously, but nonetheless inseparable. In Virgil contradiction does not

---

[7] Traina (1988).

ask to be resolved, but only to be accepted for what it is, as double and irreducibly double.

If fate will not make room for Dido, Dido herself is not subservient to fate: she is *fati nescia* (*Aeneid* 1.299). She does not recognize fate but she knows her own personal rights and reasons. As in the genre of tragedy, so in the *Aeneid* different claims oppose each other and each one receives a hearing. In many respects Dido is a character very close to Sophocles' Ajax. A strong awareness of their own merits makes each of them proud; a deep sense of shame at their own mistakes drives them mad; both are victims of *hamartia,* an 'error of fact' which, without being a true offence, is still a sufficient cause of tragic downfall. Wounded honour imposes the choice of death on both of them as a necessary redemption.

It has long been established that when Dido meets Aeneas in the world of the dead in the sixth book and turns her back on him, she is repeating the same gesture with which Ajax had shown his contempt for his rival Odysseus in the Homeric *Nekyia*. But even when he alludes precisely to this episode of the *Odyssey,* Virgil wants to suggest to his reader that his Dido is a tragic character more closely similar to the maddened Ajax, as he was put on stage by Sophocles: a grandiose model of offended dignity.

It is less well established that there are three powerful motifs in the dramatic construction of Sophocles' *Ajax,* and that all three return significantly in the tragic history of Dido as it was conceived by Virgil. Here is the first strong analogy: once she has decided on suicide, the Virgilian queen, like the Sophoclean hero, speaks a *Trugrede,* a deceptive speech which conceals beneath a surface of calm resignation the fixed resolve to embrace death alone. Ajax's words are designed to deceive his wife Tecmessa (*Ajax* 646–92), those of Dido are addressed to her sister Anna: *Aen.* 4.476–7 *et maestam dictis adgressa sororem | consilium vultu tegit ac spem fronte serenat.* Then there is the second strong analogy: just as Ajax uses the sword given by Hector to kill himself, so Dido employs the sword given to her by Aeneas: 4.646–7 *ensemque recludit | Dardanium, non hos quaesitum munus in usus.* The apposition *non hos… in usus* adds to the epic narrative a note of empathy loaded with tragic irony: Dido reflects bitterly just as the Sophoclean Ajax had previously done in vv. 815 ff. 'Here is the murderous sword… If I can allow myself time to reflect, this sword is the gift of Hector, the most hated among my guest-friends.' The third and highly significant analogy, which confirms definitively the forceful degree of suggestion exercised on Virgil by the model of Sophocles' Ajax, is to be found in the final monologue which both Ajax and Dido deliver before their respective suicides. In his monologue (vv. 837–47) Ajax invokes the Furies and the all-seeing Sun to curse the sons of Atreus at his death ('I call on . . . the holy, long-footed Erinyes . . . and you, who drive your chariot across the steep heaven, Sun'); closely parallel is Dido's invocation of the same powers to introduce her dying curse on Aeneas (4.607–12):

> Sol, qui terrarum flammis opera omnia lustras,
> tuque harum interpres curarum et conscia Iuno,
> nocturnisque Hecate triuiis ululata per urbes
> et Dirae ultrices et di morientis Elissae,
> accipite haec, meritumque malis aduertite numen
> et nostras audite preces.

Certainly Sophocles' tragedy in its entirety is one of the works which most strongly marked the pathos of Virgil's imagination.[8] The action of the *Ajax* is constructed around the idea, so dear to Virgil, that the destiny of a tragic protagonist is inscribed in his own character, as Ajax in fact says to his wife Tecmessa; 'I think you are deluded if you expect to educate my character at this time' (594–5). When, towards the end of the poem, Virgil aims to condense the dramatic nucleus of Sophocles' tragedy, he will treat it as concentrated in the words with which Ajax had said farewell to his son before killing himself (550–1): 'my son, be more fortunate than your father but like him in all else, and you will not be worthless'. This is a tragic reaffirmation of heroic valour betrayed by a calamitous destiny. In fact it has been noticed that the memory of these words returns in the analogous scene where Aeneas bids farewell to his son before going to his final combat with Turnus: *disce, puer, virtutem ex me, verumque laborem,* | *fortunam ex aliis* (12.435–6). As is well known,[9] Virgil filtered the text of Sophocles through the version of Accius in the *Armorum iudicium* (fr. 171 Dangel): *virtute sis par, dispar fortunis*

---

[8] Cf. Lyne (1987), 9–12, 113–14.   [9] Cf. Lyne (1987), 9.

patris. The reader hears echoing in the words of Aeneas the voice of Ajax, a brave and deserving hero, but one condemned to defeat. The epic poet has appropriated the tragic contradiction and has mirrored in it the destiny of Aeneas, a virtuous hero undeservedly condemned to suffering. The antithesis of *virtus* and *fortuna* is rooted in the bitter earth of Sophocles.

In the dualistic strategy of the tragic form contradictions can also coexist without one right prevailing decisively over the other; or at least, there is in the wrong a residue of right which cannot be cancelled out: hence the torment of doubt which characterizes late Euripides above all—we can in fact wonder, without ever receiving a definite answer, which is the secret face of truth in *Bacchae*. Where is truth concealed, in the madness of Dionysus or in the rationality of Pentheus? And which madness is true madness? That of Dionysus and the Bacchae, or the feigned madness of Teiresias? And again, does the final meaning of the tragedy exalt the power of the supernatural or does it rather denounce its complete absurdity? The antagonism of truths—one set alongside the other—seems to leave everything in mystery and to ask the spectators not to solve the riddle, but to accept it in its contradictions, that is to think that contradictions are the essence that cannot be eliminated from truth.

At other times the dramatic contrast between opposing claims is less ambiguous, but is still sufficiently marked to constitute the structural principle that controls every tragedy. In *Supplices* (in that of Aeschylus as well as Euripides) and in *Heracleidae* too, the clash is between the obligation to receive suppliants and the obligation not to damage one's own city. In Euripides' *Electra* Orestes is the character who incarnates the conflict between the obligation of avenging his father and the revulsion at being obliged to kill his mother: the insolubility of this conflict is sanctioned by the intervention of the *dei ex machina*, the Dioscuri. Castor indeed says (1244–7) 'Clytemnestra has had justice done to her, but you are not the one to carry out justice. And Apollo, Apollo—but he is my lord and I am silent: he is wise but has not given a wise oracle. In any case it is necessary to accept these events.' In *Phoenissae* the conflict is between the duty of defending one's country (and maintaining power within the city) and the obligation of *philia* towards a brother-enemy. In *Iphigenia in Tauris*, it is between the obligation to commit human sacrifice and that of *philia* towards (unrecognized) kinsmen; there is the same kind of dramatic conflict in *Medea*, and in *Hippolytus*, in which Theseus is obliged to avenge the supposed violation of his wife's chastity and does not hesitate to curse his son. But if an explicit formulation is needed to mark a conflict without solution it is enough to recall line 460 of *Choephoroe*, 'Ares will struggle with Ares and justice with justice'.

Sometimes there is open contradiction between the obedience owed to the gods and the obedience owed to human authority. So in Sophocles' *Antigone* the protagonist is divided between respect for the law that rules the city and obligations towards the gods and the dead: 'it is not Zeus who sent out this edict, nor was it Justice who lives together with the gods of the underworld who established these laws for mortals' (450–3). And a few lines later Haemon in the dialogue with his father Creon will say 'I cannot and will not admit that you are wrong; and yet others too can have right on their side' (685–7). Sometimes in Euripides the contradiction is so unbearable that it unleashes a veritable theological crisis; it is enough to remember the case of the *Trojan Women* in which the obligation to honour and pray to the gods is in irremediable conflict with the tremendous suffering which those same gods have inflicted on Troy: 'O Troy, which once breathed grandeur among the barbarians, soon you will be deprived of your glorious name. They are burning you and carrying us away from the land as slaves. Ye gods! But why do I call on the gods? Even before they did not heed us, however often they were called upon' (1277–81).

For Virgil, therefore, destabilizing the meaning of his text by fuelling it with internal contradictions is a genuine strategy of composition, a strategy by which the 'ambiguous' manner of Greek tragedy infects the language of epic. Dramatic dualism redoubles the poet's possibilities; indeed it multiplies these possibilities beyond all measure, like a yeast which enters the mind of the reader and ferments it, so that it swells into new ways of thinking. For some time now Virgilian criticism has agreed to define certain characters of the *Aeneid* as tragic, especially Dido and Turnus, but the definition seems to refer only to the unhappy outcome of their individual histories; and for this very reason the label, valid in its own right, seems too vague. It would be more fruitful to show that

these characters are constructed in the dualistic form proper to the
characters of tragedy, that they are conceived on the dramatic model,
that is, in essentially contradictory terms. Or, to put it more precisely,
the response imposed by the poet on his readers is analogous in
certain respects to that required of the tragic spectator, who should
not look for a univocal meaning when faced with the fortunes of
characters, and should not confine them to a simple verdict of
acquittal or condemnation.

The case of Turnus is emblematic. He has appeared to many critics
a tragic figure, since he is a hero condemned to clash with the
invincibility of Fate. The model of anti-Stoic individualism, he is
almost the antitype of Aeneas and of his modern and thoughtful
heroism; dominated by *superbia* and *violentia*, Turnus is the victim of
furor, like so many characters of tragedy. But if, as we proposed, we
use the history of Virgilian criticism as a privileged field of observation, we realize that the contradictions within the make-up of the
hero have been projected outside the text to become simply the
differing voices of interpreters who contradict each other. And
so we discover that there is a complete spectrum of judgements
pronounced on Turnus, from absolute aversion to the most open
encomium. At one extreme he is barbarous and uncivilized, an
enemy of the state, a daemonic dark character: at the other he is
the innocent victim of Fate, champion of liberty (this is the choice of
the so-called 'Harvard critics', led by Michael Putnam; and the
'Europeans' have not failed to react polemically).[10]

But to express evaluations of sympathy or condemnation for
Turnus does not help to resolve the question, even if similar evaluations are to some extent legitimate, since they are motivated by
readers' reactions. An effective criterion of analysis should instead try
to determine the structural features of the character, that is, to define
the form of its construction. It leads us to see the form of Turnus as
tragic, because it is intrinsically contradictory. He is, though at
different times, both an Achilles and a Hector, both the proud and
pitiless warrior and the heroic defender of his invaded land. This is a
contradiction that the poet has strategically programmed to leave the
reader a choice that cannot be univocal; the reader's response must

---

[10] For a useful overview of critical views on Turnus see Schenk (1984), 7–24.

necessarily be double and ambiguous, because the truth itself is no longer single but divided. Contradiction imposes the search for a new order of judgement, one which is more complex and problematic.

When the Sibyl prophesies war in Latium to Aeneas, Turnus is described as the new Achilles whom the Trojan hero must face: 6.89 *alius Latio iam partus Achilles*. And in fact Turnus, by his inclinations and actions, will at many moments of the poem faithfully conform to this model. But it will be the antithetical model of Hector (though deprived of the bitter foresight which characterizes the defender of Troy) that dominates the final combat between Turnus and Aeneas; like Hector, Turnus will abase himself to supplicate his conqueror and, like Hector, will find no response. Rather than the synthesis of two antagonistic types of hero, Turnus is an original invention of a poet who wants to suggest to his reader a tragic knowledge: that right is not easily separable from wrong, that opposites can coexist, one alongside the other, in the same person.

In the *Aeneid* the strategy of contradiction disconcerts the reader, who is thus forced to broaden his/her ideological horizon; the reader is thus exposed to a crisis of doubt, engaged in difficult choices, and obliged to accept even what would appear in itself unacceptable. If an extreme case will help us, we have only to observe Mezentius.[11] The configuration of this character, before his entry into the action, could not be more negative. Merciless and bloodthirsty tyrant, savage torturer, outrageous despiser of the gods—in every regard, he is entirely like a wild beast. We could simply say he is a pre-Homeric character, without the slightest glimmer of humanity. He is the antitype of Aeneas and the incarnation of all the negative values which the *Aeneid* rejects. And yet the *Aeneid* opens its arms to embrace him. It does not need much; it is enough to add to all these negative features one positive aspect—his love for his son Lausus—and immediately the image of Mezentius becomes contradictory; it is no longer univocal. The reader of the *Aeneid* knows very well what extraordinary importance is given in the value system of the text to the theme of love binding fathers and

---

[11] On modern views of Mezentius see the convenient bibliography given by Harrison (1991), 236.

children together: Anchises and Aeneas, Aeneas and Iulus, Priam and Polites, Evander and Pallas, Metabus and Camilla are all examples of a single ideal paradigm. At the very moment when Mezentius and Lausus enter this series, the father acquires a new attribute which surprisingly obscures all negative aspects.

So Mezentius—that repulsive example of barbarous bestiality, but at the same time a positive example of paternal love—lives out the same contradictory role which many dramatic characters must live. Criticism has even thought of juxtaposing his figure with that of Sophocles' Creon, whose son Haemon kills himself over the body of Antigone, his betrothed, condemned to death for disobeying the tyrant's decrees.[12] Yet the comparison is hardly pertinent and actually deadens the boldness of Virgil's creation: indeed it can only be seen as partially valid, that is for the remorse (*metanoia*) which seizes both fathers after the deaths of their sons. The situation which sees a tyrant cruelly overwhelmed by the death of a loved son is certainly tragic in origin, but although Creon is an odious figure of tyranny, he is not characterized by such strongly negative traits that he can be compared with Mezentius. In fact in *Antigone* Creon seems guilty of having exaggerated out of blind arrogance claims that in themselves would not be unworthy; in contrast Mezentius is an utterly abominable character, a monster invented solely to arouse loathing and disgust. In short, Virgil pushes his provocation to the extreme: he exaggerates the negative traits of his character to the utmost and then dares to redeem him on account of one sole positive aspect, yet one that is enough to transform someone 'other' into a person 'like us'. He challenges readers to follow him in his contradictory strategy: they must accept the positive without being able to separate it from the negative, and then they will understand that grief is a primary value, sufficient to redeem any degree of guilt.

We have already said that Mezentius is a pre-Homeric character. In fact, in some respects his world could be that of the mythical Gigantomachies; it makes the inhumanity of the character, his complete alienation from the values of civilization, even more remarkable. When Mezentius advances to clash with Aeneas in battle, he is compared to the hunter Orion, so immense that his head touches

[12] See Harrison (1991), 272.

the clouds while his feet touch the earth (*Aen.* 10.763 ff.). One critic has suggested that the simile offers the impious Orion as a parallel in order to mark even more heavily the impiety of Mezentius,[13] but this is only partly true and does not grasp the specific function performed by the simile in the construction of the episode. In fact it is immaterial that Orion is impious (as indeed is Mezentius); it matters more that he is a giant. An earlier simile offers clear proof of this, when (10.565) Aeneas himself raging in battle is compared to the giant Aegaeon, the hundred-hander who fought against the Titans in their assault on Olympus. In the intention of the epic text Mezentius must be one of the race of the giants, and the combat he will have with Aeneas should present itself as a Gigantomachy, so it is necessary that in parallel fashion Aeneas too be compared to a giant. In short the reader should consider the duel as an episode of pre-Homeric epic, and think that Mezentius does not belong to the world of men, but to an anterior, pre-human world. Mezentius cannot know or accept the values which inspire the *Aeneid*, but the *Aeneid* can accept even him: in him too the poet recognizes the right to human suffering. The strategy of contradiction opens up new, far wider horizons for Virgilian humanity.

So it comes to pass that the reader addressed by the Virgilian text, presented with these contradictory situations and moral demands, ends by resembling the addressee of a tragic text: in fact the *Aeneid*, rather than abandoning itself to a Homeric 'Lust zum Fabulieren', mere storytelling, rather than offering a glorifying and celebratory narrative, drives its readers to face questions and doubts, to become spectators and judges of dramatic contradictions. In this respect it is evident that Virgil has derived from tragic models not only a collection of themes and arguments, but above all the very form of divided truth. What I am interested in highlighting in the Virgilian text is not the living memory of exemplary tragic figures (Medea, Alcestis, Andromache) or the recurrence of motifs from a tragic source, still less the strict intertextuality that binds passages of the *Aeneid* to passages from individual tragedies. These things are familiar to those who consult Virgilian commentaries, where borrowings and reminiscences have long been abundantly recorded; to make it clear,

---

[13] See La Penna (1980) and Williams (1983), 180.

this is exactly what Macrobius meant when he commented: *est enim ingens ei* [sc. *Virgilio*] *cum Graecarum tragediarum scriptoribus familiaritas* (5.18.2). What I want to point to is the way in which Virgil constructs his legendary narrative of the Roman people by opening it up to the form of interrogation and doubt, the form which inevitably carries readers towards a sympathetic reflection, towards tragic *eleos* or pity. Conceived in this way, the text of the *Aeneid* does not dispense rewards, but anxieties and problems. In short the epic narrative finally takes on the pattern of drama, by proposing not an entrenched truth, but the search for truth: it no longer aims only to catechize and edify its readers, it wants to distress them, to agitate them, perhaps even transform them, by associating the positive with the negative, certainties with doubts. This is a strategy, therefore, very close to that set in motion by tragic poetry. Flavian classicism guessed as much when it felt obliged a century later to define the poet of the *Aeneid* with the words of Martial (5.5.58 and 7.63.5) as *Maro cothurnatus*: this means a poet of strong tragic vocation, comparable to Aeschylus, Sophocles, and Euripides.

We can conclude that the complexity of the *Aeneid* is the product of the competition between conflicting claims and ideas—the strategy of a text which searches for contradictions in order to expand the overall significance of the work dialectically, by multiplying its implications and perspectives. But before we conclude, we must inevitably turn our attention to another contradictory feature of the *Aeneid*, a feature with an analogous formal function and derived from this same dualistic strategy. This is the aspect of doubleness (but we could perhaps say contradiction in this case too) which comes from the ambiguous nature of the *Aeneid*, and its ambition to be simultaneously both mythical and historical epic. We cannot eliminate the difficulty, as much twentieth-century criticism has done, by making the simplistic claim that there is no essential conflict between the legendary nature of myth and the political and ideological nature of history, that there is even a natural continuity between myth and history, that myth is only the archaeology of history, that Roman culture would not be alert to the distinction. The path Virgil follows is utterly different from (even if it might appear similar to) that travelled by the historical epic of Naevius (and

of Ennius in its wake): there the record of historical events in the
form of a chronicle could absorb into itself a mythical retrospective, a
legendary prehistory which gave a Homeric colour to the events
narrated. This was a rhetorical and artistic procedure, then, through
which the *Bellum Poenicum* aimed to 'distance historical events from
contemporary actuality'[14] and bring them close to the fabulous
grandeur of myth.

Virgil, on the other hand, immerses himself totally in myth, but he
considers the myth with the eyes of the contemporary world: he
redirects it towards the present and immerses it in history. The
prophetic intrusions in books 1 (from the mouth of Jupiter himself),
6 (spoken by Anchises), and 8 (through the representations on the
shield of Aeneas) all validate and give authenticity to the myth,
linking it to the real events of history. The reader is caught up in a
dizzying switch of perspectives, a movement alternating between two
temporal extremes: the result is not just (as is obvious) that the
present is history and the past is myth, but also (as is less obvious)
that myth becomes a reflection of the present and history becomes a
new myth. The text swings between two perspectives which by their
nature are in opposition; on one side the time of real events (history)
and on the other the time of legend (myth).

In appearance Virgil simply wanted to revive myth and follow in
Homer's footsteps, but in substance his gesture of submission to his
model also contained a gesture of challenge: he put Homer on display
in order to make his differences from Homer more conspicuous.
Subordination to the dominant model of mythical antiquity masked
the ambition of the modern descendant of Homer, who wanted
nothing less than to reinvent the very genre of epic, and recreate it
ab integro. And it was precisely the common space shared by the two
texts that made possible the comparison between the old and new
epic; this is why the path of modernity, in order to measure its
enormous distance from Homer, paradoxically took its point of
departure from Homer himself (see Chapter 2 above).

It must certainly appear a paradox to us—a real contradiction of
terms—that Virgil bound himself to Homer with the intention
of giving voice to his own modernity: even if the idea of myth

[14] Norden (1954), 15.

might still appear the same, the idea of heroism was now essentially different. To take the myth of the Homeric heroes and submit it to the filter of the tragic poets' meditation and of post-Socratic ethical speculation, this was the path which was available for the new Virgilian epic; in the end his readers would find themselves facing a completely discordant image of heroism. The new hero, Aeneas, would experience a thoughtfulness completely alien to Achilles, to Hector and Odysseus, so that the distant world of these heroes would from now on seem too simple and too primitive.

Of course modern epic would also feel an invincible nostalgia for these representations of a life so close to nature, through the plethora and vitality of the characters, and the grandeur of the actions narrated in the *Iliad* and *Odyssey*: this nostalgia would have been openly demonstrated in Virgil's effort to provide himself with the guarantee of the entire Homeric apparatus: type-scenes, narrative structures, thematic sequences, stylistic patterns, in short whatever could be retrieved from the great model. But even more than nostalgia, Virgil was moved by the longing to accommodate to epic the proper ideals of a modern sensibility. If he wanted to imbue his readers with new hopes of social order and humane rationality, he was obliged to drop whatever elements of his great model now appeared unacceptable.

This is why it was necessary to reconceive the very idea of heroism, basing it on values that had ripened outside the universe of Homer: values such as *humanitas, pietas, ratio, clementia*. This was a new culture with its roots in the reflections of the philosophers and tragic poets, a culture that believed in the individual conscience, in compassion, in responsibility, and which made doubt into the chief instrument of an indulgent enlightenment. Virgil had perforce to believe in a transcendental order capable of motivating the epic celebration of Rome's destiny, the historical victory of *ratio* over *furor*. This too had been anticipated by the speculation of many ethical and political thinkers, inspired by Panaetius and Poseidonius or more specifically by Cicero: for Virgil too the new history of Rome had to be one of civil order and harmony, a *cosmos* able to guarantee the good government of the world.[15]

---

[15] Obviously I am thinking here of the work of Hardie (1986), one of the most significant studies produced by the 'European' school.

As celebratory epic, the *Aeneid* is fully aware that myth (represented by Homer) and the new concept of heroism (embodied in Aeneas) are to some extent mutually incompatible, that the perspective of mythical epos contradicts in some ways that of historical epos. But for all that, it does not renounce either of its two components, however discordant they may be; it sets them down alongside each other, leaving to its readers the task of shifting between the two, indeed forcing them to accept both together. From their conflict arises a new function for epic, an artistically and culturally complex meaning. In this, too, Virgil's undertaking is configured as a system shot through with tensions, a system within which greater and lesser contradictions oppose each other and, through their development, dynamically determine the meaning of the whole.

However provisionally, we might state the following conclusion, that perhaps the 'European' and 'Harvard' schools can now conclude an honourable peace, each group declaring themselves satisfied with the contribution that each for its own part has made to the understanding of the *Aeneid*—satisfied, above all, that through their critical opposition they have brought to light some contradictory aspects of the text. I hope to have proved that these contradictions do indeed exist, but that they are internal to the text and form part of an artistic strategy. The reader is called upon to confront and allow him/herself to be disturbed by them. From them s/he should derive doubts and questions but also productive fermentation and stimulus; above all s/he should learn that not only the heart but also thought can follow indirect paths on the road to truth. And perhaps s/he will discover in the end that truth does not have a single face, that contraries can legitimately stand together, and that the claims of celebration coexist on equal terms with the claims of doubt and denial.

6

Defensor Vergilii: Richard Heinze on Virgil's Epic Technique

'THERE is a sense in which Roman literature was born dead': With this verdict B. G. Niebuhr in about 1810 gave a definitive form to the Romantic prejudice.[1] How could it be otherwise? The generation reared on Herder, passionately focused on the primitive and fascinated by everything that seemed closest to origins and to nature, prone to feel poetry as a product of spontaneous energy and so mistrustful of every form of derivative (*abgeleitete*) or merely conditioned (*bedingte*) culture, could neither understand nor love the Virgil who was a 'derivative' of Homer. The same fervent enthusiasm for the recently rediscovered Homeric epic which had inflamed Winckelmann or Herder[2] contributed to making the poetry of Virgil feel more alien. It was the same for Wilhelm von Humboldt, who saw history as decadence and loss of the perfection achieved by the Greeks, the same for the German romantic poets (especially Schiller), and the

I am most grateful to my friend M. Martina for some valuable references. The remarkable quality of his Italian translation to which this piece originally formed an introduction, Heinze (1996), which is precise and rigorous but also elegant, bears witness to the translator's admirable intimacy with the text of Virgil, and demonstrates a profound knowledge of the cultural milieu in which *Virgil's epische Technik* was created a century ago.

  [1] Niebuhr (1842), 403. Here I am freely adapting some of my comments in Conte (1966c).

  [2] The hatred of the Enlightenment for tyranny led Herder, one of the patriarchs of German romanticism, to interpret (in *Ideen zur philosophie der Geschichte der Menschheit*) the entire historical development as an affirmation of might and conquest, which stifled and destroyed 'the pure energy of coming into being/becoming' everywhere. And Virgil, reduced to the greatest glorifier of this process, could not escape this condemnation.

same again for a philologist as distinguished as Friedrich August Wolf: indeed, before his *Prolegomena ad Homerum* (1795) Wolf had written a brief *Geschichte der römischen Literatur*,[3] an opening, one might almost say an official, step in the period of devaluation which awaited Latin literature in Germany, and affected Virgil in particular.

If Latin culture subsequently, in the post-Romantic era, found a conspicuous position, even to the point of appearing suddenly exemplary, this did not happen without misunderstandings. In fact the discovery of the originality of Roman culture was only prompted from one direction; it was simply another way of exalting the ethical and political values on which the social structure of Rome was based. The young German nation wanted to derive its own principles of ethical and political formation from this Roman model. In short, the culture of Rome was indeed original, but only because it was a great culture of law, of political institutions, and of civil and military discipline; the most accomplished expression of this belief, and also the strongest thrust in this direction would be provided by the extraordinary learning of Mommsen.

Thus, alongside the ideal of a Greece that created absolute and exemplary art, was set the complementary ideal of a Rome that had expressed the highest forms of nationhood. Behind this alleged specialization of Latin culture the old romantic prejudice still persisted: it was precisely this notion, that made poetry the spontaneous energy of uninhibited creators, which denied any value to Latin literature, as a 'derivative' product lacking in originality. For a different view it would be necessary to wait for a new generation of critics, or rather one with a new conception of poetry and of literary activity. Critics would have to understand that real originality is not something which is like nothing else, but something that surpasses resemblances, and is both guaranteed and authorized by them. Once this understanding was reached, it became easier to take the road that led to the revaluation of Latin literature.

Enfin Malherbe vint.[4] But unlike Malherbe, when Heinze came he did not come alone. He had another great interpreter of Virgil

---

[3] Wolf (1787).

[4] 'At last came Malherbe' from Boileau's 1674 *Art Poètique* (1.131) marks what the French 17th cent. saw as the moment of maturity in national literature.

at his side, Eduard Norden, who was preparing his monumental commentary on the sixth book of the *Aeneid* in the same period. Although Norden differed from Heinze in his interests and was less concerned with the vindication of Virgil's originality, he was still a powerful ally in his struggle.

In the year before the publication of *Virgils epische Technik*, a long article[5] by Norden had appeared, which towards the end voiced a condemnation of the critical attitude of German studies to Virgil and opened up new perspectives of evaluation:

To admit the purpose, both national and universal, of the *Aeneid*, means doing it justice as a poetical work. This certainly was not possible in an age when, after Pope and Wood, it became usual to judge every epic poem by taking the Homeric epic as the absolute norm, and stigmatize every deviation from it as a fault. These were times in which the 'original genius' of Homer was opposed to the 'courtier's mentality of Virgil' as Lessing defined it: after Herder it was Lessing who contributed most to transplanting into Germany the aesthetic of these two Englishmen. We owe it to the respect shown towards the great men of letters of the eighteenth century that even today this way of seeing things, despite some intermittent dissent, continues to dominate. And yet our own era, thanks to its capacity for a vision of history, to which even aesthetics must submit, has succeeded in overcoming the judgment of these great men.

In actual fact Friedrich Leo, one of the most powerful intellects that German scholarship ever produced, had inaugurated a process of reaction against eighteenth-century critical prejudices more than a decade earlier, and thanks to him, much of archaic Latin literature was acquiring a new profile and validation. His judgement on Virgil, too, shown in a few casual, short but pithy comments in *Plautinische Forschungen*,[6] showed signs of the new thinking.

But on Virgil the predominant, even official position was that represented by Paul Jahn and Wilhelm Kroll.[7] A model representative

---

[5] Norden (1901). [6] Leo (1895), 23–4.

[7] One should also mention, as an authoritative example, the article on Virgil published in 1852 by W. S. Teuffel in Pauly's *Real-encyclopädie* (vi pp. 2644–62, especially 2650–1) or the verdict expressed again by Teuffel in his literary history of Latin (Teuffel (1870), 391): it was always the same accusation, that Virgil was not a 'natural' poet, but a talented writer, a bookish man of letters. Compare the preface of A. Wlosok to the English translation (Heinze (1993), x–xiv).

of 'source criticism', Jahn suffered from a learned myopia that led him to reduce the *Aeneid* to an inert compilation of borrowings, sure evidence of Virgil's dependence. He was not content to write a series of heavily positivistic articles which treated Virgil as a 'craftsman' without creativity (he gave them the title 'From Virgil's Workshop');[8] he also felt obliged to welcome Heinze's book with a malicious and even bitter review.

Kroll, an authoritative critic of Latin poetry to whom we are indebted for some important scholarly papers,[9] approached Virgil with so many strong prejudices that he could believe that the Latin poet was unable to recognize lacunas, contradictions, and doublets in his own work, just because he was always constrained in his work of imitative adaptation to the limited space of single passages and episodes which he would assemble from one moment to the next— that is, that Virgil was incapable of anything but the fragmented vision of someone composing in isolated excerpts without a broad context.[10]

This was the critical horizon peculiar to Virgilian studies in Germany when Heinze's book appeared. The situation was very different in England, where the work of William Sellar had taught students to appreciate the difficult art of Virgil,[11] or in France, where the influence of a great critic like Sainte-Beuve, 'Virgil's high priest', was still effective.[12] It was just the merit which Kroll denied to Virgil that the French critic had recognized in him without reservation: 'unity of tone and colour, of harmony and the agreement of parts with each other, and of proportion, of that sustained tastefulness which is one of the marks of genius, because it reaches the depths, the kernel of the soul, something I might be allowed to call a supreme delicacy'.[13] In addition, a

---

[8] Jahn (1904) and (1905).

[9] Kroll (1924) may suffer in some respects from a rather mechanical positivism and critical schematicism, but should be considered as among the most intelligent contributions of German philology.

[10] See Perutelli (1973).   [11] Sellar (1876).   [12] Sainte-Beuve (1857).

[13] Sainte-Beuve (1857), 89: 'L'unité de ton et de couleur, de l'harmonie et de la convenance des parties entre elles, de la proportion, de ce goût soutenu, qui est ici un des signes de génie, parce qu'il tient au fond comme à la fleur de l'âme, et qu'on me laissera appeler une suprême delicatesse.'

certain nationalistic and anti-French spirit probably contributed to conditioning the attitudes and judgements of many German scholars at that time.

As we said, Heinze was not alone. Leo had already prompted the new direction and from now on Latin literature gradually achieved reassessment. Anyone who agreed to interpret Latin texts in discriminating terms came to recognize its *Eigentum*, its original features and distinctive qualities. But Virgil still required greater critical attention, and so to some extent did Horace: Catullus was less in need, although Mommsen had recognized the 'natural' force of his originality: still thinking like a romantic and without being willing to see all his sophisticated literary quality, Mommsen took pleasure in calling this 'Das Demonische'. And it was on Virgil that Norden was to concentrate all his energies.

There was a kind of division of responsibilities between the two scholars. Heinze kept for himself the treatment of *inventio* and *dispositio* and left *elocutio* to Norden; he acted as herald to his friend's commentary on book 6, which would appear some months later. The brotherhood between Virgil's two rescuers went back to the years in Bonn where they were student contemporaries (Heinze was a year older, being born in 1867) and followed the courses of Bücheler and Usener.[14] In short, Heinze had allies. Not only was there a fellow soldier beside him as valuable as Norden, but Leo, a scholar of the highest authority, entered the fray on his side, defining *Virgils epische Technik* in an immediate review as 'the most important work ever written on Virgil'.[15] In Germany the new Virgilian criticism, indeed the new criticism of Latin literature, was now a concrete reality.

Years later, when Friedrich Klingner, Heinze's successor in the chair at Leipzig, was paying homage to his predecessor just after his death, he accurately identified in him and his work the fundamental prerequisite (*Vorraussetzung*) for the renewal of Latin studies in Germany.[16] This was the path on which to continue. It would be

[14] Of the two great teachers in the Bonn faculty Heinze preferred Usener, a philologist interested in ancient religion and philosophical thought; the stamp of his teaching can easily be recognized in his doctoral dissertation, *De Horatio Bionis imitatore* (1899), halfway between literature and philosophy.

[15] Leo (1903), 594.   [16] Klingner (1930).

Klingner, again, who declared twelve years later that a long historic period of negative evaluation had been finally ended. For almost a century and a half German culture had been prevented from understanding and appreciating the poetry of Horace, and even more that of Virgil: if a different method of judgement was now possible for the new generation of philologists, this was due above all to Heinze's book; this was where the 'rediscovery' of Virgil had begun. In fact 'rediscovery of a poet' was the title that Klingner gave to his piece on this topic.[17]

Sometimes it happens that discoveries (and of course rediscoveries) have a forerunner. This obviously will happen when the time is ripe. So it was that Heinze had a brilliant and shrewd forerunner, Hans Theodor Plüss, a professor at the University of Basel who had published about twenty years earlier a volume entitled *Vergil und die epische Kunst*.[18] There are many admirable things in this book: its method of facing problems, its plain but incisive style of argumentation, a lively sensibility to Virgil's poetic language. Plüss has a true critical spirit, he knows how to think for himself, and he does not tremble when he has to refute an interpretation that has been declared as a verdict and acquired canonical status.

But Plüss is not always right. This does not prevent the reader, even today, from feeling a measure of sympathy with his way of seeing things. There is real vitality in his critical approach, some real bursts of humour and apostrophes to enliven the text, and he shows a kind of empathy in interpretation. One can see in him the effort (which will be systematized in Heinze) to put himself in the author's position, to reanimate and foster the artistic experience of the poet in the process of criticism. Above all there is already the germ of the idea that a poet's creativity does not exist outside his own culture: he is completely saturated with it. Virgil's creativity consisted in giving new meaning and function to Homeric motifs and themes—and even giving them a new form. Homer himself had worked on inherited materials. Not even he was a 'naive' poet: as a poet he too was 'sentimental'.[19]

Both Norden and Heinze agreed in constantly giving credit to Plüss. Even Heinze's title is simply a refinement of Plüss: *Technik*

---

[17] Klingner (1942).   [18] Plüss (1884).   [19] Plüss (1884), 345.

is not very different from his predecessor's *Kunst*. The particular attention given by Heinze to composition, an idea of structure which is articulated but organic to the text, with autonomous parts arranged so as to be harmonized in a unitary whole, might be seen as echoing Plüss, who had searched repeatedly in his reading of the *Aeneid* for the *Kompositionszweck*, the purpose behind the composition of the poetic text. To be sure Plüss was no Heinze; his work was fragmentary and discontinuous, without the same breadth, the same critical maturity, or the same philological learning.

And yet, reading some of his formulations, one can sometimes have the sensation of reading Heinze; for instance when he writes 'to judge Virgil's form of representation correctly and to appreciate him in terms of his own poetic values, we must be clear about the aims of his representation'.[20] If we pass over the value judgement (which Heinze is not explicitly concerned with, but which remains implicit in his analysis), this principle that one cannot judge without first understanding what the poet intended to do is precisely what guides Heinze. The idea is that criticism should be inspired by sympathy, should be an act of understanding; that the real objective is to recognize the historical preconditions that have determined different poetic works. Relying on this principle, Plüss asked himself what was Virgil's intention, or better, what it was that Virgil could not help doing. At least in this respect Heinze found the way prepared.

This is criticism as the art of understanding, where understanding means entering the text to retrace the same path as the author. Understanding and interpretation become virtually a single process. Or better 'understanding and interpreting differ only as the interior discourse differs from what is spoken aloud', following the imaginative formulation of Schleiermacher.[21] As translator and exegete of Plato, Schleiermacher (alone among the Romantics) had defined

---

[20] Plüss (1884), 84: 'Um die Darstellungsform des Dichters richtig zu beurteilen und in ihrem poetischen Werte zu würdigen, müssen wir über den Darstellungszweck uns klar sein.'

[21] Schleiermacher (1835), 382: 'Das Auslegen unterscheidet sich von dem Verstehen durchaus nur wie das laute Reden von dem innern reden.' The same awareness that every work is generated from the interior act of a poet with his own tastes and culture, led him to believe that the critic and interpreter should observe every artistic work in its own right, seeking to recognize its specific 'intentions': cf. Oderbrecht (1931), 87: 'Jedes Kunstwerk muss absolut für sich betrachtet werden, also seinen absoluten Wert haben.'

poetry as sentiment, as a conscious state of mind, and not as a phenomenon of Nature, a spontaneous creation in which Nature herself found a voice. For him 'understanding'—the real task of the critic—was equivalent to 'intuiting' the mind of the author.

His approach had been revived by Dilthey, whose hermeneutic historicism, in the last decades of the eighteenth century, was concerned to validate the peculiar methods of philology against those of the positive sciences. No doubt Heinze had responded to the thought and critical model of Dilthey; the influence of this philosopher on all literary studies in the Germany of those years was truly immense. But it was not so much Dilthey as theorist of literary creativity (the author of works dedicated to the *Einbildungskraft und Erlebnis*, the imaginative power and experience of poets) nor Dilthey as philosopher of history (the inventor of *Zeitgeist* and individuality of signification); both those aspects will meet a particular reception in the twenties and thirties of our century and will be the foundation of literary studies of *Geistesgeschichte*.[22]

Instead, Heinze's rigorously philological training, his interest as an interpreter of texts, drove him to view Dilthey as a theoretician of literary criticism (not very different, in the last analysis, from Croce in Italy). As theoretician Dilthey took as his fundamental presupposition a substantial identity between the author's spirit, its expression in the text, and the reaction of the reader and interpreter. In virtue of this identity, the work of the critic became simply a *Nacherleben*, understanding and reliving the author's artistic experience. And it is of *Nachschaffen*, re-creating, that Heinze talks. For him too the interpreter, following the traces of the author, actually reproduces his act of creation. It would be worth while, had we time and space, to reflect on an interesting difference between these influences; where the objective idealism of Dilthey favoured philology in Germany, though assigning it to the sole service of lofty *Geistesgeschichte*, in Italy the ideas of Croce contributed to mortifying, or at least devaluing, philological studies. The cultural substratum was different in the two countries, just as their experience of positivism had different roots.

---

[22] Even Heinze's successor Klingner will feel this (I am referring above all to the papers gathered in Klingner (1961); cf. Conte (1966c), 486).

The idea of *Nacherleben* (re-living) worked productively on Heinze in one respect in particular: it led him to escape from the trap of value judgement and transfer critical discourse to the level of 'understanding'.[23] The very first words of his preamble are absolutely radical: 'this book does not want to express value judgements, but to determine historical facts.' Heinze then continued programmatically by denying that his goal had been to ask himself what Virgil should have done (as had been done up to then): 'My goal is to understand the creation of the *Aeneid*, within the limits in which such creation can be referred to a conscious artistic effort by the poet, guided by precise purposes.' What has come from reading Dilthey is quite obvious.

On the other hand what is peculiar to Heinze, or at least belongs within the horizon of his contemporary philological experience, is the strong awareness that culture is nothing but the transformation and continuation of elements that have entered the tradition, that creation itself is based on experiences, structures, and forms of language that have been assimilated and modified. 'I have tried to verify what the poet found in his sources and what he borrowed from his models, and therefore to explore his work of re-elaboration and transformation'.[24] Dilthey had taught that comprehension of literary creations must necessarily base itself on historical relativism (every epoch reveals its own precise *Zeitgeist*: 'even the perfect form will be historically relative').[25] But he had never developed[26] the idea that

---

[23] Perhaps Heinze followed in this refusal to be concerned with absolute value judgements the example of Heinrich Wölfflin, a great critic of figurative art, who exercised equally great influence over him. If the influence of his father, a great scholar of philosophy, enabled Heinze to appreciate the study of ancient thought, and to have a strong theoretical consciousness of his critical principles, his mother, a refined connoisseur of art, familiarized him with figurative culture (cf. the obituary by Norden (1930)). But beyond doubt Heinze admired Wölfflin's work without reservation; how could he not feel unanimity with a man who declared that one must not observe the baroque with the eyes of a renaissance man, and vice versa, one must not look at renaissance art from a baroque perspective? In his essay on Livy (in Heinze (1930), 102) Heinze defined Wölfflin's famous essay *Die Klassische Kunst* as 'a marvellous book from which I have learned much more, for the purposes of literary research than from any philological offering'. Indeed with due consideration I believe that in *Virgils epische Technik* we can recognize traces of critical terminology influenced by Wölfflin.

[24] Heinze (1902), viii.

[25] Dilthey (1985) [German original 1887], 170.

[26] Actually in his later reflections, when historicism and emotional psychologism have already gone into crisis, Dilthey suggests a more concrete method of reading literary works.

making a historical reconstruction of the emotions and psychological experiences of poets required the historical study of meanings and the structures that supported them.

But Heinze for his part knew how to do this, and do it systematically. He defended Virgil and revalued him, but without diminishing Homer in any way. Homer was superlative in breadth of fantasy and imaginative power;[27] but according to Heinze Virgil possesses other qualities, and it is a blunder to confuse the absence of *Phantasie* with the lack of *Gefühl*.[28] The first virtue of Virgilian poetry is precisely its 'sentiment', the sentiment which touches things and gives shape to discourse; one can recognize in this the core of the poetics which Dilthey had worked out in the last decades of the century in a wide series of studies of the great German poets.

For Heinze, Virgil's genius—his poetic vocation or *Kunstwollen*— is to rationalize, select, condense, and arrange the materials offered by great Greek poetry, in order to impart depth of sentiment. The poet's entire creative energy is concentrated on this effort, which is also a drive towards the intensification and interiorization of ideas. Care and tact in the choice or words, their effective and harmonious arrangement, their perspicuity and precision, their exhaustive fullness and simultaneously their astringency of expression: this is for Heinze the essence of Virgilian style. Yet it seemed to him that this style was defined above all as a highly disciplined movement between liberty and constraint (*Freiheit und Gebundheit*), between the invention of a new epic language and the acceptance of a consecrated code.

Better still, Virgilian invention, *Erfindung*, seemed to Heinze not very different from the *inventio* of classical rhetoric. He considered it as the appropriation of authoritative structures, of canonical themes, and exemplary stylizations—all elements of the tradition to be transformed so that they would emerge recognizable but essentially different. The respectful observance of the epic archetype helped Virgil to give prestige to the new discourse. This ancient formal

---

[27] In fact Heinze was not slow to distinguish between different 'Homers', that is, he showed himself aware of the differences of conception and style which could be distinguished in different songs of the Homeric poems.

[28] Heinze (1902), 253.

system guaranteed a profound *ordo* to Virgilian narrative, a frame of reference rich in aesthetic values; yet it was also an articulated language, a paradigm to be inflected, which could accordingly generate new combinations and discourses, and could fill itself with new meanings. Above all it was no longer the language of some other poet, but it had become the actual language of great literature, the qualified idiom of every high poetic imagination. Thus Homer was the guarantee of the epic Virgil: sought out and displayed, not just experienced. This was a guarantee, no longer a burden.

Heinze understood that Virgil had chosen to compose a Homeric epic not out of weakness but from pride, a choice of liberty even if it was a controlled liberty. He had to pass through the strict rules of his great model in order to reach the autonomy of a new epic discourse, to make differences and originality leap out in contrast.[29] On these lines, more than sixty years after Heinze, Friedrich Klingner taught the young students of his seminar on the *Aeneid* to recognize carefully in Virgil's 'epic technique' the combination of traditional and of strongly innovative elements, elements of order and of disorder; a most original strategy which works by arousing Homeric expectations and then deviating from them, in a dialectic of fidelity and emulation. Klingner liked to repeat that the style of Virgil was 'maximum freedom in maximum order': he said it as if the distillation of his long and intense experience lay behind this precept. Nor can I forget the many concrete proofs and examples drawn from the text with which he convinced and enchanted us, in the Munich of the 1960s.

Above all Heinze understood that Virgil's narrative 'technique' was utterly different from that of Homer.[30] He concentrated its essence in

[29] However, Heinze actually remained to some extent conditioned by the debate of anti-Virgilian romantic criticism and did not conceive the Virgilian creative act in synthetic terms. Even he did not escape a schism between style and *Handlung* in one of the concluding pages of *Technik* he declares that the essential of Virgilian *Erfindung* does not lie in the act but the speeches and sentiments. This affirmation was sufficiently generic to be applied by Eduard Fraenkel to the case of Plautus, 'incapable of inventing a dramatic action for himself' even on a small scale, but an author original in style; the quotation from Heinze is in Fraenkel (1960), 441–2.

[30] Cf. Otis (1964), 14. This study by Otis is certainly the work that reflects most strongly a reading of Heinze: in a sense it renewed and confirmed his proposition. This is probably its greatest service.

a psychological and dramatic construction of the narrative, in a 'suggestive' colouring of representation.

This was a determining factor through the effects it produced. Affective pathos seeped into the text. Thus while the *Aeneid* reports occasions and personalities, it also allows the emotional commitment of the author to play a part in the events that are narrated (Heinze called this *Subjectivität*). This was not all: the emotional disposition of the characters insinuated itself into the form of the narrative, penetrating it thoroughly (Heinze called this *Empfindung*). Thus Virgil's epic representation, by allowing itself to be saturated with the emotions of the characters, and modelling itself on their way of seeing and feeling, is indivisibly a representation of both circumstances and emotions. This is no longer the Homeric imagination of things, detached and as it were objective; instead it is a partisan imagination, open to distortions, as if it were refracted through the prism of feeling.[31]

This is how Heinze came to discover the secret of a new and original way of composing epic poetry. With the term 'epic technique' he wanted to show modestly and empirically the complex of operations effected by Virgil on the traditional texts, his selection of themes, transformation of models, condensation or expansion of material, superimposition or inversion of structures, grafting of episodes, and insertions of monologues and speeches. But by studying attentively these procedures, the procedures of a literary laboratory which looked to Homer but had different poetic ambitions, Heinze succeeded in finding the quintessential ingredients of the Virgilian epic method: dramatization and pathetic subjectivization of the narrative. He reached the heart of the poet's artistic originality, but he reached it with modesty, and the laborious precision of a clear and precise analysis, made by means of comparison and differentiation. This is why his results are still presented to us, still valid and to a great extent irreplaceable.

---

[31] These two factors of Virgilian style, *Subjectivität* and *Empfindung*, are treated by Heinze as two versions of the same expressive action. They are certainly two complementary aspects (generated by the same case of dramatic patheticization of the narrative) but I believe I have shown that they operate on two different levels of the text and produce functionally different effects; see Conte (1986*a*), 167–75 and Ch. 2 above.

I do not want to insist on the idea that everything in *Virgils epische Technik* should still be accepted today. Indeed, there are quite a number of matters on which the critical labours of recent years have contributed corrections and modifications. It had to be so: over a century has passed, a century full of methodological and critical upheavals. Even the scholars who have followed in Heinze's footsteps have been able from time to time to criticize some aspects of his work;[32] the same scholars, while continuing and developing his fundamental theses, have suggested important corrections.[33] But the substance of Heinze's work still remains. It is not just the methodological example of impassioned but unprejudiced criticism; above all, his view still stands firm that Virgil's great innovation, even with respect to his Hellenistic predecessors, his true originality, is to have introduced the notion of 'dramatic style' into epic narrative. Heinze understood that the *Aeneid* is many things at the same time: it is a narrative of myth and history, it is the sacred book of a community, it is the nostalgic representation of exemplary values offered to a modern society anxiously preoccupied with its original identity, but above all it is the impassioned representation of emotions and of grief, such that the reader must, as in the Aristotelian ideal of tragedy, feel 'pity and fear'.

I first read Heinze more than thirty years ago. I have re-read this or that part of his book many times, and each time I have been impressed by the lucidity of his pages. But I only came to digest this reading with the passage of time, and then to translate it into a new drive towards interpretation. I remember one day while lecturing, I happened to read a line of the *Aeneid* and suddenly intuit the mechanism of composition that had produced it. At that moment I felt I understood much more about Virgil, and equally, much more about Heinze, who had trained me to interpret 'Virgil's epic technique'. Since then, whenever I needed to demonstrate how Virgil

[32] The works of Klingner, Pöschl, and Büchner in Germany, as well as the book of Otis (and I would add my own work) have been largely dependent on Heinze; the studies by Buchheit and Binder are more like the descendants of Norden. See Wlosok (1973) and Serpa (1987).

[33] What has met the most serious objections is the idea that Aeneas' personality is based on the model of the Stoic *proficiens*: see on this topic the excellent discussion by Hardie (1995), with which I largely agree.

worked according to Heinze, I repeated this example as if I had found it in his book. I shall repeat it here.[34]

The line belongs to the narrative of the last night of Troy, at the climax of Pyrrhus' slaughter: *quinquaginta illi thalami, spes tanta nepotum (Aen.* 2.503). It is obviously a reminiscence of a Homeric hexameter: *Iliad* 6.244 πεντήκοντ' ἔνεσαν θάλαμοι ξεστοῖο λίθοιο. Virgilian adaptation achieves the virtual transliteration of the Homeric hemistich, as each letter coincides in Greek and in Latin; πεντήκοντ' ἔνεσαν θάλαμοι = *quinquaginta illi thalami,* those bridal chambers of Priam's sons described by Homer when they were still a safe refuge and Hector visited them. But Homer had completed the line with the clausula ξεστοῖο λίθοιο 'of well-polished stone'. The descriptive objectivity of this Homeric model is overlaid—with a strong shift—by Virgil's sympathetic and thoughtful intrusion: *spes tanta nepotum.* The intimate contact with the model (in the first half of the verse as far as the penthemimeral caesura the sounds and rhythms are unchanged, as if it were produced in the same language) is a sufficient instance to show the extremely difficult and original balance Virgil has attempted. He faced a challenge. The more the new text, imbued with subjective pathos, clings to the old 'impersonal and objective' model, the more one hears the new voice, modern and sentimental. The closeness is impressive, and clearly displayed, but the distance is enormous. The interaction of two different literary codes establishes a new configuration for epic language.

Homer could not be more actively present, but Virgil's modern and sentimental poetics displays only longing for an unbridgeable distance, perhaps even the obsolescence of poetics. For Virgil, to rediscover Homer and his distant poetry meant rediscovering the authentic epic code; but his ambition was not to imitate Homer in the sense of copying him and producing a duplicate. Virgil wanted to create a modern work that would take the place of Homeric epic. Heinze understood that the intertextuality which bound the *Aeneid* to the Homeric poems was constitutive, essential, inscribed within the matrix of his composition. He understood Virgil's idea, and he defended it.

---

[34] See Ch. 2 above, pp. 27–9.

7

Towards a New Exegesis of Virgil: Reconsiderations and Proposals

A FIRST glance back at the many vicissitudes in the history of Virgilian commentary will generate a slight sense of dizziness for any new commentator, a sense which quickly translates itself into a series of practical dilemmas. Above all, we ask ourselves how and to what extent it is possible to describe the history of each problem. Faced by such an expansive and complex vulgate tradition, will it ever be possible to be sure of the original paternity of a given solution, or of a particular interpretative contribution?

I begin with this question because it is, when all is said and done, the problem which is most superficially obvious. Well, the first impression is discouraging; it is only with difficulty that our efforts will be able to retie all the broken threads, overcoming the indifference shown by the great commentators of the nineteenth and twentieth century towards a systematic individual appreciation of their predecessors. If it is true that any Virgilian commentary should ideally be entitled *cum notis variorum*, there is still the regret that we cannot always precisely acknowledge our own debts to the past. Let a small example suffice (on the erratic and intermittent progress of Virgilian exegesis from the sixteenth to the twentieth

These pages were originally delivered as a lecture at the *None Giornate Filologiche Genovesi* (23–24 February 1981) honouring the bimillenary of Virgil's death; hence their conversational tone (bibliographical notes have been added by the translator and editor). The *desiderata* I indicated here were amply fulfilled in the following years by the commentaries of Harrison (1991) on *Aeneid* 10 and Hardie (1994) on *Aeneid* 11.

century, I can only refer in general to the fundamental research of G. N. Knauer).[1]

In his commentary on *Aeneid* 8,[2] Warde Fowler notes that the patronymic *Anchisiades* is not solely ornamental in character; Virgil tended to call Aeneas 'son of Anchises' only in contexts in which this information can have implicit relevance: where the theme is in some way about fathers and sons or paternal love. He adds 'I can never forget the thrill that went through me when the meaning of *Anchisiades* was first made plain to me by my tutor, H. Nettleship'.[3] At this point we already feel ourselves to be in the climate of symbolist exegesis; it is no accident that such interpretations have asserted themselves more recently, with the work of Viktor Pöschl,[4] a scholar profoundly attentive to symbolic implications, who 'hears' Virgil with an ear trained on modern poetry. It is a fairly direct form of confirmation that this type of exegesis, which concentrates on the connotative margins of the text, was already practised by Pascoli. Faced by the periphrasis *ductor Rhoeteius*, applied to Aeneas in a bloody scene of battle (12.456), Pascoli as commentator noted that 'the epithet *Rhoeteius* with its designation of a remote place covered with tombs, is not casual, and is in fact unique'.[5] There has been the temptation to stop at that point and conclude that the tendency to find evocative values in epic periphrases is both typical of *fin de siècle* criticism and an index of recent sensibility. But a retrospective check immediately gives us the lie; that *Anchisiades* was not just an ornamental epithet was already the view of la Cerda,[6] in a very short note in his commentary; this little critical discovery can thus be dated back to the first decade of the seventeenth century.

In other cases, when the problems at issue are ultra-familiar, a historical check produces a curious sense of arrested progress. You will remember the age-old problem of the invocation to Erato in the seventh book of the *Aeneid*: we are still asking ourselves whether the

---

[1] Knauer (1964) and (1980).   [2] Warde Fowler (1917), 86–8, quotation from 88 n. 1.

[3] Henry Nettleship (1839–93), co-editor of Conington and Nettleship (1858–71).

[4] Pöschl (1950) and (1977).   [5] Pascoli (1911), xx.

[6] Juan Luis de la Cerda (1560–1643) in la Cerda (1612–19); for an account of Cerda's work see Laird (2002).

choice of this muse is simply a tribute to Apollonius Rhodius,[7] or if there is some motivation in the Virgilian context. One attempt at explanation, repeated many times even recently, is that the war announced in this proem will concern a rivalry in love, the disputed marriage with Lavinia; hence the choice of Erato. An ingenious explanation, but not beyond doubt; certainly nothing better has been proposed. But this *status quaestionis* goes back to a note of Germanus[8] in 1575, and yet I am sure there are very few modern commentaries which cite the gallant bishop of Orleans for this insight.

On the other hand, it is even more cause for concern that significant contributions have simply been lost from sight, instead of being preserved under the aegis of a more recent (and false) paternity. It is worth while insisting on this point because the better commentaries of the nineteenth century, the ones we resort to as a basis for our research, show a great lack of confidence in their predecessors. It is clear that they were conducting a justified campaign of resistance against the uncritical accumulation of material, and the result was a very severe degree of selection. For example, Conington[9] accused la Cerda of a passion for irrelevant parallel passages; indeed this programmatic declaration is not mistaken, but we can ask ourselves whether the modern commentator, keeping this verdict in mind, has really evaluated all the material offered by la Cerda, or is merely content, as is only human, with an intermittent and hesitant use of his work. Contrariwise, anyone working less selectively has only (sadly) won the lasting reputation of a compiler; this is the unlucky case of the useful and obscure toil of a man like Forbiger.[10]

There have been many times in the history of Virgilian exegesis when scholars cultivated the image of an irreparable rupture with the past, of (as it were) an epistemological divide. A few years after the death of Conington, his continuator Nettleship distanced himself from his predecessor, acknowledging his great gifts as a literary critic,

---

[7] *Argonautica* 3.1, where Erato is invoked to tell of the love of Medea.
[8] Germanus (1575), *ad loc.*
[9] Conington (1858–69) [1858], i. xiv, n. 3.
[10] Albert Forbiger (1798–1878), author of Forbiger (1852).

but making it understood that by his own time the conditions of scholarly work had reached the maturity of a more philological and scientific approach in accordance with the developments of German *Altertumswissenschaft*.[11] The period since then has seen the perfection of the image of the modern philological commentator, embodied in Eduard Norden in the first years of the twentieth century.[12] It is easy for us to forget a whole previous stage of development in which even the physical format of the commentary was very different.

It has long seemed obvious that the commentary should lay out parallel with its object text the series of literary models which facilitate its understanding. For Virgil, the great series including Ursinus,[13] la Cerda, the miscellaneous commentaries of the eighteenth century, and Heyne has worked to this effect. But it is interesting to remember that the parallels between Homer and Virgil, now laboriously articulated and reassembled by Knauer, have long had a separate fate. From the sixteenth to the nineteenth centuries the location assigned to these parallels has been that of pure and simple collections of similar passages without comment, often presented like anthologies of famous sayings, indirect heirs of a well-known Alexandrian-Roman tradition, which could very well carry the title *furta Vergilii*.[14] Even at the end of the nineteenth century the Virgilian commentary of Sabbadini[15] (intended for schools but a work of the highest level in the context of Italian publications of that time) excluded the Homeric models from the exegetical notes, and only listed some of them at the end of individual volumes. It is just as remarkable that these comparisons seemed to be of far more interest to scholars of Homer, Hellenists like Hartung or Samuel Clarke,[16] who in the eighteenth century displayed an important array of Virgilian parallels in the margin of his edition of Homer; with this

---

[11] Conington–Nettleship (1858–71) [1858], I. vii.

[12] Eduard Norden (1868–1941), author of Norden (1902).

[13] Ursinus (1568).

[14] The 'plagiarisms of Virgil' collected by near-contemporary pedagogues according to Suetonius' life of the poet, many of which are reproduced in Macrobius' *Saturnalia* 5 and 6.

[15] Sabbadini (1888).

[16] J. J. Hartung, whose annotations appeared in Fabricius' 1551 edition of Virgil; Samuel Clarke (1675–1729), author of Clarke (1729–32).

we have arrived at a vision of the literary tradition that I would call a mirror image of our own.

Obviously, in surveying this tradition we are seeking anxiously for the most conspicuous points of modernity, ignoring the tenacity with which some prejudices adhere to the practice of commentary-writing. Let us note with admiration that in 1575 Germanus found the comparison between Virgil and Homer intrinsically interesting, and declared himself indifferent to the problem of competition between the two: this was a courageous decision in the face of that real and genuine *certamen Homeri et Vergilii* which was the contemporary *Poetice* of Scaliger.[17] The rejection of competition will only become fully operative two centuries later, and the evaluatory approach imposed by *synkrisis*[18] has (at least in my opinion) left persistent traces even after that. Another fine lesson, ahead of its own times, is hidden in Heyne's preface; there we read that the time has come to study poetic imitations not as isolated episodes, but in relation to the *summa carminis et partium concentus*—an excellent programme precisely for the commentator, the person who, as if following the institutional tradition, must fragment the text into its minimal parts.[19]

But I would like to make a preliminary objection that it is not fair to go back to old commentaries only in order to seek out prefigurations of modern thinking. The point is that ideas quite different from our own, indeed unacceptable to us, long had a dynamic function and momentum. I have already hinted at the importance, which holds good today, of the seventeenth-century commentary of Juan Luis de la Cerda;[20] well, this Spanish Jesuit gives a place of honour in his commentary to a collection of *elogia Vergilii* which proclaim his own fundamental motivation—to demonstrate the superiority of Virgil over any other poet. This is a compilation of judgements under the headings: *Vergilius maior Homero*; *maior reliquis graecis poetis*; *maior Latinis poetis*; *maximus poetarum* (admittedly there is also a section *Vergilius proximus vel par Homero,*

---

[17] J. C. Scaliger (1561).

[18] The ancient technique of criticism through comparison.

[19] See Heyne (1803), i–lvi for the complete and interesting prefaces to all three of his editions.

[20] See now Laird (2002).

but la Cerda notes with a charming partiality that all the verdicts assembled in this section are false and baseless). The index of the commentary gathers abundant material under the headings *Homeri vitium, Homeri frigus, Homerum superat Vergilius,* and even *Homero Statius praefertur.* However, it is just this questionable agonistic vision of the literary tradition that has served as an impulse for research; it has driven scholars to go beyond the simple accumulation of erudite information and scrutinize the secrets of poetic technique, giving value to the differences between texts; this is the aim of commentaries and treatises of the sixteenth century, like the *Poetice* of Scaliger mentioned above.

Slow-moving, conservative, always lagging behind the developments of research, the commentary will pay dearly for this failure to keep up: both in public esteem and even in the self-esteem of its authors. Forbiger in his preface declines any grateful recognition; he hopes to be remembered not for his shrewdness but for his industry; and Conington, strange to recall, believed he had produced a useful work for advanced school and university students. Admittedly, in the long run the situation has reversed itself; in fact the 'inferior' practice of the commentary has outlived the evolution of ideas, passing unharmed through the revolutions of taste and scientific method. It is precisely the commentary's apparent independence of the times, its impersonality, that has preserved it in general use.[21] The scholar who practises this kind of research has no inclination to theorize, and the resulting work tends to present an air of naturalness and simplicity. Conington writes: 'my custom has been to take each line as it came before me, and ask myself whether I thoroughly understood it; and this process has often led me to entertain difficulties which had not previously made themselves felt'.[22] Indeed the portrait of him traced by his successor Henry Nettleship is equally simple: 'He knew a few authors, notably Virgil, Horace, Aeschylus and Sophocles, almost by heart, and poetical instinct led him to pore continually over their diction and to analyse the connections of their ideas'.[23]

---

[21] See now Most (1999) and Gibson and Kraus (2002).
[22] Conington–Nettleship (1858–71), I. xii.
[23] Conington–Nettleship (1858–71), III. v.

It would be wearisome to retrieve from every Virgilian commentary what each author denies us, the model of the poetic text which operates implicitly throughout the entire analysis and determines (even subconsciously) the choice of a particular 'style of work', the choice, that is, of information relevant to the kind of understanding the commentator wanted to achieve. (As is obvious, I exclude *a priori* the idea that a commentary is simply a collection of information brought up to date; in this case, naturally, the idea of a new commentary would be justified by itself as if by inertia; think what linguistics and textual criticism, historical and antiquarian expertise, have become today, in contrast with Conington's epoch.) The existence of this kind of implied model, at least in the most significant instances, seems axiomatic to us. In some cases there are connections of thought that speak for themselves. We understand Heyne's activity as a scholar of Virgil more fully when we think of the whole complex of his scholarship: he was an initiator of the scientific study of mythology, and one of the very few philologists, to my knowledge, who worked on editions of Homer and of Virgil at the same time, so he was the right man to proclaim the necessity of an organic comparison between the literary texts.

This kind of 'retroactive' request might risk carrying us away too far. What we want to retain from this very short exploration is a current necessity: the need to confront an age-old institution, the commentary, with our present understanding of literary facts. Even an abbreviated summary has already shown that this institution has its own fluidity; indeed, it is our own daily experience with these working tools that teaches us that they cannot respond to requests and curiosities for which they were not originally designed. In the second part of this piece I shall try to set out the questions which we feel to be most urgent and least satisfied by the commentaries of the past. There is no need on our part to reassert our own continuity with this tradition; on the contrary, to remain faithful to it, we too cannot but seek to translate our own culture into a new interpretation.

In recent years, criticism, as we all know, has formulated a new concept of the literary text; I might indeed express this better if I said that a large part of the debate on literary theory and critical method can be summarized as the acquisition of a new concept of the text.

The underlying idea is not new, in fact: that the literary text is constructed as a system of relationships. Even if the act of producing the text is a unitary act, analysis can consider its various levels individually, as autonomous frameworks—the grammatical, stylistic, narrative, thematic, ideological and other levels. But the interpreter's real task is to bring together the structural relationships between the various levels of literary construction, levels which, taken one at a time, have been well studied or at least roughly defined. For example, the study of characters can no longer take its point of origin from a 'realistic' hypothesis based on nineteenth-century experience of fictional narrative, which is no longer convincing even in that field: instead, it must accept the idea that a character is nothing but an *effet du réel* created by (*a*) language, (*b*) certain presuppositions, that is ways of reading natural to the epic, and (*c*) thematization. Hence the necessity to apply linguistic exegesis functionally, and correspondingly to limit psychological constructions. In other words it is precisely the commentator who has a starting advantage in this respect, being always constrained to make concrete applications in analysis; so it is precisely the commentator who should not throw away the effect constructed in the context in the name of psychological generalizations.

If I had to say now in what respects the new commentary will (or should) emerge as distinct from its predecessors, I would first and foremost refer to our present-day conception of the narrative text. It is almost automatic that this new model of the text produces new demands on the interpreter. To answer a potential accusation of ideologizing, I would recall that commentators on Virgil have always (more or less consciously) devised their own model of the text; some have made this explicit, but others have not, and when this has been openly declared, the act of declaration has been an advantage to them. The success of Heyne's commentary, so rich in specific and concrete advances, cannot be separated from a fundamental idea, openly acknowledged and even proclaimed (it is less important that this is not an isolated discovery of Heyne). This is an uncompromising invitation to abandon the practice of accumulating *synkriseis* of isolated phrases, to put an end to the tradition of *furta Vergilii*, because any imitation can only be evaluated in relation to the *summa totius carminis et partium concentus*; this, as can be seen, is still the battle to be fought by Klingner a century and a half later—*das Ganze, das Gefüge,* 'the whole, the framework'.[24]

In other words, the fact that even in making a commentary we see only what we are looking for, is no reason to panic; furthermore, the very concreteness unavoidable in exegetical work will regularly serve to refute or validate (or at least put to the test) the underlying critical approach.

From here derive, as we were saying, the new questions we must apply to the text. The most radical—on which many lesser questions depend—coincides completely with the problem of narrativity in Virgilian epic. To set this issue forcefully at the centre of our task as commentators is not just a terminological gain. Think now, abandoning for a moment the field of actual formal exegesis, what it meant for Heinze[25] to establish an intermediate area between (let us say) aesthetic criticism and formal philology. Heinze had the shrewdness to call it 'technique', thus escaping a defensive discussion of the originality and poetry of Virgil, and legitimizing a typological and systematic analysis of Virgil's narrative procedures. These advances, it goes without saying, have long been part of the common inheritance of Virgilian scholarship; but the commentator's clock moves more slowly and is always a little behind the times. Indeed, I do not think this attention to the structured character of Virgilian narration has been fully understood in the fashions of reading practised by commentators. Heinze's concept of 'epic technique' (considering the inevitable diversity of cultural climate) is pretty directly associated with our image of narrativity: that is, of a level of the text which requires an independent level of description. The first characteristic that the commentator comes to perceive in an epic narrative is the presence of some significant repetitions, which just because they recur at regular intervals in the epic text seem like structural features, like the stereotypes that constitute epic discourse.

Here the modern commentator can usefully continue along the lines of Heinze's clinical observation, highlighting recurrent narrative structures, the use of type-scenes, modes of description, the handling

---

[24] Klingner (1967). The Latin of Heyne and German of Klingner coincide in making the criterion the total effect of the entire poem, and the harmony of its parts.
[25] For Heinze see Ch. 6 above.

of narrative time and the like, but with an alertness that constitutes our necessary contribution if we are to go beyond Heinze. What we call typology, employing the point of view of the critic, takes on an important function, considered from the point of view of the addressee (that is, considered in terms of the relation between text and reader which it prefigures). What we call typology can be defined from the addressee's point of view as convention.

For the reader, what is involved is a series of constants in the narration, which organize the text according to a system of expectations: through this conventional framework, the narrative text operates like a programmed structure, something which is even more obvious in the epic text, which shows more respect for the rules of construction. Then it becomes the locus of a strategy between author and reader, a strategy whose effect turns the predictability of the discourse into the basis on which to build communication. Such conventions are not easily or instantly recognized like thematic parallels or allusions, and the commentator may be tempted to assign them less importance, assigning them to other types of reading and other interpreters. But if this occurs, the commentator often renounces something precious: indeed, the person who deciphers the conventions of reading will also know how to say, through a typological competence, when it is time to react to a divergence, that is, to a violation of the conventional expectations which the text has set out in order to generate meaning. In such cases it is easy to understand how a typological study of epic narration does not distract from the comprehension of individual phenomena, far from it, indeed, since here the abstract level is an indispensable device for comprehending the concrete, for explaining a particular effect of reading (otherwise only implied).

Here is an example, straightforward, I hope. Many commentators (and for that matter, just as many general readers) have felt that the scene of Mezentius' death at the end of *Aeneid* 10 is something exceptional, a passage of poetry where a quite particular interest is expressed in the heroic individuality of the defeated: it has often been noticed how Mezentius' values, imbued as they are with violent negativity, dominate the scene, while Aeneas, the protagonist, is left in the background. But no one adds that this exceptional effect can also be explained in relation to a precise epic convention. In the epic

duel, when two heroes meet and one addresses the other, the rule
holds good that whoever emerges victorious in the encounter is
either the only one to speak, or the last speaker. To put it in another
way, the loser (or the one destined to lose) does not speak last in this
kind of scene. In surviving Graeco-Roman epic, this rule is followed
in some thirty cases (they mostly belong to the two Homeric poems
and the *Aeneid*) and breached in only one case known to me, in the
representation of the death of Mezentius. After the exchange of
challenges and provocations (Mezentius shouts, summoning Aeneas
to the encounter; Aeneas hastens and utters a few words, which
Mezentius proudly rejects), Mezentius is laid low and Aeneas taunts
him, according to the code for the victor, before administering the
fatal blow. But, against the rule, the text allows Mezentius to speak
again: he himself claims not to fear death, and even confirms that
killing in battle is just and proper. And from the whole final scene the
reader now realizes something already suspected from the preceding
passage; in a sense Mezentius desires death, to free himself from his
grief at the loss of his son Lausus. It is not really Aeneas who kills
him: Mezentius already knew (and now knows beyond doubt) that
he is going to be killed, and welcomes his own death (*haud inscius
accipit ensem*).[26] This is how the narrative strategy designed by the
text has operated here. Epic narrative has its own rhetoric, which has
established certain conventions: when conventional expectations are
violated, the reader's discovery of the divergence leads directly to the
meaning of the text.

Let us linger another moment in analysing the death of Mezentius,
and exploit this episode for another example and another general
consideration. Up to now we have examined the episode in contrast
with the epic model, in (so to speak) a vertical, diachronic view of the
text, but we should take care not to make this reference categorical
(even if it is only human for the commentator to become fond of
some small discoveries as a reward for toil). On other occasions when
I happened to be preoccupied with Mezentius, I noticed how his
coldness in exposing himself to death, in becoming the agent of his
own slaughter (*iuguloque haud inscius accipit ensem*) was completely
complementary to the system of values which first drove him to kill

26 *Aen.* 10.907; see now Harrison (1991), 283.

with equal coldness. In fact, the text has been programmed here according to a code of behaviour that does not seem reducible to the heroic model of the Homeric epic: Mezentius is practising a technique of dying, an *ars moriendi*, not a stylized heroism but an expertise in dying that is 'pragmatic and professional', in which the Romans must have recognized a precise cultural model. Here is how Cicero in *Tusculans* 2.41 illustrates the valour of good gladiators: *gladiatores, aut perditi homines aut barbari, quas plagas perferunt! quo modo illi, qui bene instituti sunt, accipere plagam malunt quam turpiter vitare... Quis mediocris gladiator ingemuit, quis vultum mutavit umquam? quis non modo stetit, verum etiam decubuit turpiter? quid cum decubuisset, ferrum recipere iussus collum contraxit?* We must thank Taubmann in the seventeenth century[27] for this appropriate comparison (linking *accipit ensem* in Virgil with *accipere plagas* and *recipere ferrum* in Cicero), but let us stress immediately that the Ciceronian precedent does not guarantee an immediate dependence between the two texts, nor even an exclusively linguistic clarification. Here too the commentator should pass through various levels of the text; after having found a linguistic code behind *accipit ensem*, attention should be drawn to the fact that in a correct reading of the text this linguistic cliché (so to speak) brings in its wake the cultural model which generated it. Thus the task of the commentator rises above the mania for comparison so as to rediscover from the individual linguistic choices the scenario which they presuppose. The construction of the last part of the episode is marked by a submerged cultural model which does not enter into the spirit of the epic-heroic tradition. The warrior is seen as a kind of gladiator, a 'technician' of killing and being killed: this is the effect designed by the text, the effect around which the scene is built.[28]

I said before that in making a commentary much depends on the new questions that are asked of the text. But it is obvious that the commentator's own idea of literary creation as such counts for much more. I believe that we have today a quite different conception of classical literary praxis, and above all we are focusing on a more systematic vision of the process of formation of poetic texts. I mean that the traditional demands of *imitatio* and (its opposite) creativity,

[27] Taubmann (1618), *ad loc.*   [28] See now Harrison (1991), 283.

with the compromise solution of *aemulatio*, no longer seem adequate. And yet they are very valuable criteria. They are the criteria that have allowed us to accumulate our inheritance of *loci similes* (debts and borrowings, comparisons and parallels) which remains one of the reliable tools used by the exemplary methodical rigour of classical philology. And in general the commentary is the place appointed to welcome them and make them instantly evident and functional for exegesis.

But there is a fundamental ambiguity in their use.[29] It arises from the lack of depth in the notion of 'model' in which there is actually an oscillation between two different ways of conceiving what the object of imitation can be. In the traditional sense of classical philology there is the idea of the model, which we might designate as 'copy-model'; this carries the notion of copying and a judgement on the lower status of the imitator, who is left little space for self-redemption. But there is also another conception of the model which takes more precise account of the actual procedure of the formation of the text: and this is the conception of 'code-model', the model understood as a code or literary institution that allows one to produce more or less complete renderings, a system of conscious and deliberate elements through which the author acknowledges the identity of the work and the plan according to which the text being constructed will be deciphered. In the first idea of the model (which I have designated as copy-model) there is no other reality than that of imitation, that is the borrowing which constitutes the *furtum* (plagiarism), or (at the most) than that of *aemulatio*, which is a mode of copying which involves entering into competition with the model (the intention of the imitator—since we must necessarily argue in terms of intentionality—is to outdo the model copied). In short, the production of the text is reduced at most to an emulatory impulse, an occasional and minute gesture of emulation.

Thus the whole formation of the text is left to a relationship between two subjectivities, with the inevitable implications of intentionalism: these are often inadequate to give an idea of the literary process, and in any case are always out of place, because they centre on

[29] Here and on the following page I summarize what I wrote (more diffusely on this specific issue) in Conte (1981).

the personalities of the authors compared, and not on the structural reality of the texts. If, instead, the place of the notion of intersubjectivity is taken by that of intertextuality, then every literary text takes its shape from the absorption and transformation of other texts. In fact a work can be read only in connection with other texts or opposed to them: these provide a network through which it is perceived according to expectations that equip the reader to take in the most significant traits and organize them into a structure of complex meaning.

The addressee who approaches the text (reader or imitator, which is one kind of reader) consists already of a plurality of other texts. Intertextuality, far from being a curious echo effect, defines the very condition of literary legibility. In fact the meaning and structure of a work cannot be comprehended except in relation to models, themselves retrieved from a long series of texts, in which they are in some way the constant elements. In respect of these fundamental models the literary work is always entering into a relationship of representation, of transformation or transgression. It is difficult to conceive a poetic work outside this system: its fruition presupposes a competence in deciphering the literary language, which has as a precondition the practical knowledge of a multitude of texts. In philological research it will on occasion be difficult to distinguish the rule that defines the separate modes of literary imitation, but it will still be fruitful to consider the relationships of texts to each other as relations of transformation. Substantial assistance will come from traditional 'source criticism' (provided it is not reduced to what I jokingly call the mania for comparison). But where idealistic and positivistic criticism (assuming differing ideologies of the literary construct) saw only 'influences' and 'sources' (aquatic and fluid metaphors), we would need to force ourselves to seek out texts and their constructions.

If going beyond the criteria of literary emulation means going beyond the inevitable limits of psychologizing criticism connected with these criteria, not to mention intentionalism in conceiving the production of literary texts, we will also have to face anew the whole problem of intertextual relationships between Virgil and Homer and adopt a new way of looking at Homer. Thus, for example, just to take Virgilian *imitatio*, Homer is often, very often indeed, not only the copy-model of Virgil (along with Apollonius Rhodius, obviously, and Naevius and Ennius, the Greek and Roman tragic writers, and quite a few other authors) but he is also—and constantly—the code-model. In short, while Homer operates by refracting himself through a series of concrete imitations and stratified comments, he also represents the institution of epic *tout court*: he embodies and guarantees in an exemplary fashion the ideological and literary functions of epic poetry itself. Thus Virgil can filter the model through the continuum of tradition, or restore a direct and unmediated contact with it.

To place the stress on the text rather than the author, on intertextuality rather than imitation, helps us to avoid another risk, that is, a critical attitude exactly opposed to what I call the mania for comparison. I mean that if the commentator must absolutely avoid delegating problems to inert comparisons, s/he must also beware of seeing in every similarity or difference the intentional work of a subjectivity. It seems to me that in our studies, a methodology is emerging which perhaps originates in the experience of Alexandrian literature. The critical recipe that I am thinking of is rather simple. First one isolates some specific type of resemblance between two texts, then one attributes to this resemblance an intentional character, and thirdly (here the philologist sharpens the scalpel), one decides on the psychological content of the allusive intent. Is it to be a compliment? Or a veiled criticism? Or a parody, or a retort? Or an improvement which implies emulation?

Precisely because I have written an essay on *arte allusiva*,[30] I am driven to criticize the unwarranted extension of the concept of allusion. The hypothesis that any allusion whatever must have a metaliterary character does not even deserve to be debated. As far as I am concerned, working on the notion of 'literary system' and on the analogy with rhetoric, I have been trying precisely to purify the concept of *arte allusiva* of any intentionalism. Now I would like to confirm the obvious truth that a text can resemble another without direct derivation, but because both, since they are communications,

[30] See Conte (1986a), 32–9. *Arte allusiva* ('the art of allusion') was defined and made famous by Pasquali (1942).

can refer back independently to a single code-model: and that even when the resemblance between two texts does not seem casual, the allusion will be described as a mode of functioning of the literary text that interests us in its own right, not as a sample of a mental impulse that we cannot recover. Then even the question of the author's consciousness will have only a rather marginal role for us. Gianfranco Contini[31] has written with justice that cultural reflexes in poets' minds may have been swift and unconscious, rather like those of car drivers: this does not make them less important, inasmuch as they are objectively there to be encountered in the text, and they do not derive their legitimacy from a more or less 'solar' artistic consciousness.

The need to avoid these deformations generates an important programme of work for the commentator; one might say that the necessity of correct evaluation of literary parallels counterbalances in a negative way the increased ease of access to every verbal coincidence nowadays, thanks to the quality of current tools of research.

Yet there is still a major problem for the would-be commentator; the specific quality of the model to be reconstructed. When I use the term 'Homer' (I have just tried to make this understood in theory, and hope now to prove it in practice), this designation is inherently problematic; the numerous (and differing) functions which the use of Homer as a model can assume in the formation of the Virgilian text can leave the exegete undecided. In fact, as I have said, in some cases 'Homer' stands for the epic code, the grammar of epic discourse which can generate new epics, in other cases 'Homer' can mean a less abstract model, it can simply indicate the Homeric manner (such as, for example a textual structure by which Virgil reproduces the generic features of Homeric language; it could be an example of a typical expression); in short, to limit the array of instances, 'Homer' can even mean translation of a single verse of Homer, the coincidental echo of an isolated combination, of a single linguistic item. A critical awareness that the relations of intertextuality between Homer and Virgil are variable and correspond to various possibilities in the model puts the scholar in the best condition to provide the correct interpretative solution.

---

[31] Contini (1970).

An instance from the tenth book of the *Aeneid* offers an example. When Aeneas is struck with grief for the death of Pallas and begins his pitiless slaughter, one of the first to fall at his hand is the priest Haemonides (10.540–2):

> quem congressus agit campo, lapsumque superstans
> immolat, ingentique umbra tegit, arma Serestus
> lecta refert umeris tibi, rex Gradive, tropaeum.

The explanatory problem here is embodied in the combination *ingenti... umbra tegit.* Servius reports two distinct interpretations; *aut magnitudine corporis sui aut clipei obumbrat eius cadaver aut 'ingenti umbra', id est morte tegit.* But for almost all commentators there are no doubts: *ingenti umbra* stands for death (not only Forbiger, Nettleship, but before that Wagner[32] and earlier still, J. C. Scaliger, Ursinus, and la Cerda). All of these scholars based their argument on comparison with the Homeric formula τὸν δὲ σκότος ὄσσε κάλυψεν ('and darkness covered his eyes', *Iliad* 4.461 etc.). Only Heyne (but Wagner criticizes him for it, though at times his editorial additions to Heyne are clearly changes for the worse) offers the first Servian interpretation: for him Aeneas stands over the defeated man and in killing him (and stripping off his armour) covers him with the great shadow of his own body (sc. *super astans et inclinans se, ut spolia legat. ordo verborum simplicior erat: lapsum immolat, superstansque ingenti umbra tegit. ita accipio nec aliter accipi posse puto...*). And he takes issue with Scaliger, Ursinus, and la Cerda who adduce the Homeric death-formula. Indeed the formula (so Heyne says) is that 'night and shadow cover his eyes'; as if one could tolerate 'covering someone with shadow' (to kill him) and then the combination *ingenti umbra* (and not, for example *tristi—letali—mortifera umbra*)? Personally I would tend towards Heyne's explanation (even if I have some unresolved doubts); the expression *lapsum... superstans* inclines me towards it, because it makes one think of a warrior's great torso, terrible as he stands over his enemy in the act of slaying him like a sacrificial victim (this is *immolat*).[33] And I would add to this the Virgilian tendency to use *ingens* to express sheer physical size.

---

[32] Wagner (1833), *ad loc.*   [33] See now similarly Harrison (1991), 208.

But it is not this aspect of the problem that I would like to set before you as a more general example of what is involved in the correct use of exegetical criteria. La Cerda probably did not feel entirely satisfied with the parallel drawn by Scaliger and Ursinus with the Homeric phrase; perhaps he had also realized that the Homeric formula entailed along with the shadow (σκότος) the eyes (ὄσσε) as a normal complement, and he reinforced this exegesis with another parallel which should have been decisive: *et adhuc ego firmo Homerica elocutione. Nam 13 Iliad. dicitur* [13.425] *Idomeneus ea fuisse virtute ut cuperet vel alium interficere, vel ipse cadere, ac illud primum ita effertur:* ἠέ τινα Τρώων ἐρεβεννῇ νυκτὶ καλύψαι. *Aut aliquem Troianorum obscura nocte tegere. Id est, interficere.* And with this parallel he convinced Nettleship, for example, who cites this in his note to support this explanation. Here is the point. Apart from any other contextual consideration that could (as I said) perhaps recommend Heyne's interpretation, I ask myself: is it methodologically correct to maintain the exegesis of an expression like that which here signifies dealing death to the enemy in single combat (a gesture, agreed, as thoroughly codified as any other in epic language), and to determine one's reading by a locution that appears only once in the *Iliad*, that is, has neither the function nor value of a formula (quite different from the stereotypical locution τὸν δὲ σκότος ὄσσε κάλυψεν, which is inadequate but otherwise not methodologically unsuitable as a model)? Then, note that this unique Homeric instance of ἐρεβεννῇ νυκτὶ καλύψαι is clear in its context; black night, the colour of Erebus, is clearly death; here, on the contrary, *umbra* does not seem to cover all the same semantic functions that are needed for this meaning. The problem could also, indeed, be formulated like this: in cases like these, does intertextuality between Homer and Virgil lie in the typology of the expression, or is it enough for the commentator to retrace, even with some distortion, due, shall we say, to the Virgilian adaptation, an incidental Homeric locution, a linguistic item, on condition that it is present in the Homeric text? Even if the problem sounds as if it is put in theoretical terms, it has serious consequences (as we have seen, and other cases could be found) for the practical level of concrete exegesis.

I have alluded to the great discoverers of Homer, the great philologists who established and to a large extent solved the problem of the relation of the *Aeneid* with the Homeric model: J. C. Scaliger, Ursinus, la Cerda. But every pioneer of a discovery always bears the obvious corresponding blame inseparably connected with his great achievement; and even these men can be ultimately accused of overestimating the resemblance between Homer and Virgil, with the consequences that Homer has always necessarily been seen as the copy-model of Virgil, and that this has often resulted in reading Homer (even if not Homer in general, then the Homer useful for explaining Virgil) as if he were the very same as the Virgilian text; as a result the distance between the two texts has been reduced. Often the habit of giving a reference to its Homeric antecedent for a Virgilian episode becomes a mode of avoiding the problem. The sense of imitation is subordinated to the comprehension of the model. But even so, imitation and model can come to be merged in the mind of the commentator, and their significant differences are lost.

The scene in which Hercules weeps because he cannot prevent the death of his protégé Pallas will surely come to mind here (*Aeneid* 10.464–5).[34] The Homeric model (*Iliad* 16.459 ff.) has been known since antiquity, and that is why Nettleship is content to say that 'The scene is of course suggested by the celebrated passage *Il.* 16.459 foll., where Zeus weeps tears of blood for his son, Sarpedon' (this 'of course' is precisely the most treacherous concept for a commentator).[35] For the person who reads Homer only through Virgil, everything fits: Hercules' tears reproduce the tears of Zeus. But Homer does not in fact present Zeus as weeping: 'Zeus shed bloody drops upon the earth' means, within the Homeric code, a rain of blood, a portentous manifestation of divine power. Instead, the idea of Zeus weeping arose in the cultural space between Homer and Virgil; it is a product of philosophical and exegetical meditation on the text of Homer, a particular reading of the model, which the commentator will have to distinguish and relate to other texts. And this is just what Alessandro Barchiesi has done, in reconstructing the journey which leads to Virgil's reading of the Homeric model in his piece 'Le molte voci di Omero',[36] a work I have many reasons to think truly

---

[34] See now Harrison (1991), 191.
[35] Conington–Nettleship (1858–71), III. 278.
[36] Now in Barchiesi (1984), 11–54.

important. In short, such cases generate the need to go beyond the tradition of *synkrisis*, beyond isolated and timeless juxtaposition of the two exemplary epic texts.

Indeed, in general many of these distortions and errors of evaluation contained in commentaries arise from the practice of *synkrisis*, that is the tradition which has roots in the exegesis of antiquity and dominates throughout the Renaissance; then the modern commentary originates from it. This method of proceeding sets up a sort of competition which puts two distinct literary entities face to face, without considering that they are immersed in a unitary but differentiated cultural flow, without considering that there are intermediaries which continually transform their meaning (that is, make them change position in the literary system, in the spectrum of cultural values). And all this obviously has an evaluative goal: to measure Virgil against Homer.

If the most productive way of approaching Virgil for commentators has been at times to be themselves, as I said a while ago, to be people of their own epoch who accept its cultural demands (and the very history of Virgilian exegesis confirms this truth), it is left to us to make the best use of a distinctive feature of our contemporary culture: the weakening and fading of the very concept of the perceiving and thinking subject. Then we will have to sacrifice much of that emulatory and agonistic character which has always marked the romantic conception of the relationship between Homer and Virgil: and we will find considerable profit in submerging the production of meaning belonging to the *Aeneid* in a continuum of other productions of meaning, examples of reading and writing in continuous transformation. Expressed like this, the matter may seem obvious, indeed it surely is, but it has seldom been realized: that is, this consideration has seldom operated by selecting from the panoply of notes the comparisons which serve to orientate reading and exegesis correctly.

I mean, if it will help make my argument clearer, that the Virgilian act of writing—the formation of the new text—is incorporated horizontally in the cultural spectrum, in the system of demands which a given culture makes upon the texts of the past, precisely within the boundaries of its own current needs. Clearly this involves a recodification of the past text according to the categories and requirements of a new cultural epoch. But one may well ask what concretely guarantees us access to the ways in which Virgil read his Homer. Above all, it is the great harvest of ancient exegesis which orientated our interpretation and imposed a new physiognomy on the Homeric text; just think of how the Homeric text penetrated everything, from school instruction to linguistic and grammatical culture, to the debate on morals and politics, to rhetoric and the theories of taste and literary elegance. If I had to point to the first of the cultural categories that work to transform Homer, I could not avoid picking out the rise of verisimilitude, that treacherous way of reading which pervades the Homeric text and makes it like the present. A simple glance at the Homeric scholia shows how the questions asked of the text are parallel and coherent with the manner of Virgilian writing,[37] that is, the way Virgil uses the Homeric model to create epic poetry. What is needed from Homer is a perfectly coherent text, rich in psychological plausibility, linked without lacunas—in a word, fully motivated; all of which, of course, has really nothing to do with the genuine and original demands of this poetry, and fails to recognize its distant conventions of language, forms, structures, and behaviour. The new epic text will be forced to move along these lines and conform and give full satisfaction to these cultural requirements. When Virgil, as happens so many times, changes the model in order to impose *decorum* (Greek *prepon*) upon it, we should not talk any longer about Virgil correcting Homer, as if everything took place in the context of a contest between literary entities, a competitive match. Instead, what will interest us in interpreting is to reconstruct, where possible, the system of reading and writing within which the modes of reading and writing are inextricably fused. The relevance of individual exegetical comparisons will often emerge from this corrected and restored to equilibrium. Indeed the comparison will find a new and fuller relevance to its intended meaning, and will send the commentator in the right direction.

I have spoken about the problem that a new conception of narrative imposes on the critic, and accordingly of the new questions that the commentator should direct to the text. Alongside the new

[37] On this relationship see Schlunk (1974).

(or at least renewed) awareness of narrative artifice, exegesis should pay particular attention to something which has long been seen as a primary factor for the production of meaning in studies of narrative: point of view. I don't wish to discuss here the problem of point of view in the text, understood as the relationship between narrator and narration; in other words, I don't wish to consider the position assumed by the narrator, the perspective from which the narrative is presented: this is one major problem which has preoccupied me among others, and this does not seem the right time to reconsider it, all the more because it does not hold great practical importance for the work of the exegete. Instead I want to direct my argument to a feature strictly of Virgilian style, rather than of Virgilian epic poetry. This is point of view as an element of Virgil's distinctive 'parole'. In fact, to make things clear, the problem of point of view for the Virgilian critic can also be treated as the outcome, in a refined contemporary form, of the critical attention that Heinze was beginning to focus on the interpenetration between the parole of the narrator and the character: he spoke of *Empfindung* to designate the *empatheia* of a narrative style suffused with the emotions of the different characters in action, that is the refraction of the narrative through the perspective of the characters represented (and the studies of Otis,[38] despite some defects which need not be discussed here, have achieved quite a few advances in the analysis of the text).

The most conspicuous effects of this element in Virgilian expression are to be found not only on the surface of the text but in the actual emotional construction of the narrative. The point of view of the narrative in the *Aeneid* seems to us the very quality that things, objects, and actions assume when viewed relatively or at different times. This means that in the Virgilian poetic discourse, linguistic expansions, epithets, and verbal modes (certain adjectives, or free indirect speech) become signs of perception, marking the relative aspect, the particular form in which things are perceived by each character: the narration has been saturated with relative subjectivity. This distortion of epic objectivity, this disturbance of the detached

---

[38] Otis (1964), following Heinze's stress on Virgil's technique of internalizing emotion, distinguished between *sympatheia* (objective compassion) and *empatheia* (entering the subjective emotion of each role)—see Chapters 2 and 6 above.

register proper to Homeric narration, constitutes a large part of Virgil's poetic originality: to analyse it with proper attention can only bring precious rewards for hard-working commentators. One of my pupils, Marzia Bonfante, has written a book on the point of view of a character as a technique of literary meaning in the *Aeneid*.[39] Bonfanti has recognized in the technique that tends to use perspective as a means to construct the discourse of epic an important instrument of Virgilian communication: what is the situation in which the point of view is generated? Who is granted its use, and who is denied it? How does it operate in the production of meaning?

Scholars have not failed to note the expressive importance in Virgil (this is the general verdict of commentators alert to the phenomenon) of sound-play, repeated consonants and vowels, in the texture of the verse, more perhaps than in other authors, thanks above all to Norden's keen stylistic attention, continued in the subsequent Oxford commentaries of Austin and Williams. This is a remarkably useful tendency for commentators, but we can also derive comfort from the growing trend of studying figures of sound either as simple reinforcement of meaning, or—better—as factors actively participating in the whole structure of textual significance. We can be sure that Jakobson's studies of phonic repetition in poetic discourse now justifiably form part of the philological tool-box:[40] in Italy, too, in his orthodox way, Traina is contributing significantly to the appreciation of this aspect of poetic language.[41] However, I still have a justified suspicion that a certain hedonistic tendency to find symbols in sound is not yet exhausted, and is present in our studies and perpetuated by school pedagogy.

Here it is probably worth while to be pedantic ourselves, even at the risk of appearing obvious. In *Aeneid* 2, as is well known, the priest Laocoon must prove an essential truth to his fellow citizens: 'don't believe that the gifts of the Greeks are what they seem.' In Virgil this runs *aut ulla putatis | DONa carere DOlis DaNaum* (2.43–4). A normally developed sensibility would immediately recognize the triple repetition; the identical opening syllable yokes *dona* to *dolis*, the relationship between *dona* and *Danaum* is stretched to the limit of paronomasia, and the alliteration of *d* naturally binds the whole

[39] Bonfanti (1985).　　　　[40] Cf. e.g. Jakobson (1987).　　　　[41] Traina (1977).

sequence. So the result is that gifts and deceits, that is 'deceitful gifts', become the very basis of the name *Danai*, and its secret essence is established. So some lines later, in his final sentence, the phrase *timeo DANaos et DONa ferentes* (2.49) has been able to achieve the status of a powerful apophthegm, compact and dense with meaning, because the reader comes to it prepared to decipher this repetition, in which both the explicit and implicit elements are felt. The pairing *Danaos–dona* of the final phrase invokes by phonetic resemblance the *doli*, the deceits that are the chief preoccupation of Laocoon. Thus the celebrated phrase has at its semantic centre a sort of ominous absence, and the simple repetition of a phonic figure almost assumes the demonstrative force of a syllogism. Nevertheless, I am convinced that for many exegetes the essential problem will still appear to be considering the potential that all these alliterations of *d* have for depicting one emotion rather than another. Whereas if you are willing to see the value of paying equal attention to the element of repetition of sounds in literary texts, you will necessarily believe that the function of such figures of sound is to give motivation to linguistic signs, that is, to fix an almost natural (and contextually obligatory) link between the form of words that constitute the phrase and the sense that the linguistic system associates with them.

Speaking of repetition, as of other matters, I realize I have so far followed a more or less univocal line, and not by chance. It is typical of the commentator to see the text as a 'rich' entity, a practically inexhaustible store of meanings, which constantly calls new techniques and new scientific interrogatives into play. Whether this image of literature is a self-interested projection or not is another topic. But I would not want to give the impression of legitimizing a foolish quest for hidden and inappropriate meanings, departing *ad libitum* from the context we have received, just as, for example I find it strange that even the most cautious philologists—I am thinking of a work as impeccable in so many ways as the commentary of Nisbet and Hubbard on Horace[42]—can grant so much space to polysemy in the actual process of interpretation: faced by contradictory interpretations, it would be better in my opinion for the commentator to

---

[42] Nisbet and Hubbard (1970) and (1978).

make a choice, after having supplied all the alternative elements that can lead the reader to other interpretative decisions. I would like to suggest a more cautious stance in connection with certain interpretations of textual repetition; and I would prefer in these cases to be disappointing rather than overloaded. I am thinking of the phenomenon of repetition which is usually designated 'the inner ear': frequently a commentator observes stylistic parallels between one context and another in Virgil's work. How are we to employ these juxtapositions? A well-received American study of the *Aeneid*, Michael Putnam's *The Poetry of the Aeneid*,[43] extensively employs the assumption that repetition at a distance is an intentional phenomenon. Thus each verbal recurrence would serve to project the light of the previous context on to the new one.

You will remember perhaps that, on the basis of stylistic parallels, Putnam manages to read the duel between Aeneas and Turnus as a projection of the battle between the bulls in the *Georgics* (a particularly strange idea, because it goes so far as to presume the absolute organic unity no longer of a single text but of the entire work of a given author). It would really be useful to work in an open and descriptive fashion, evaluating case by case the relevance of verbal echoes. Let me cite just one more small example instead of further discussion. We read that when Mezentius falls to the ground and approaches death, he rallies and ... *auras | suspiciens hausit caelum* (10.898–9). I have always been struck by the violent stylistic leap in this description, 'to gaze at the air and breathe in the sky' (technically this is both a double enallage and a double instance of synaesthesis). Well, some help in understanding this passage came to me from a verbal parallel in the *Georgics*. There Virgil describes a calf that *caelum | suspiciens patulis captavit naribus auras* (*Georg.* 1.375–6). It is clear that the leap—appropriate to the high stylistic level of the *Aeneid*—comes from a manipulation of the standard expression offered by the *Georgics*: *caelum | suspiciens captavit auras* is the model which is transformed into *auras | suspiciens hausit caelum*. As we see, the verbal echo is relevant to the exegesis, whereas it has no relevance, I would say, to the meaning; the two contexts remain unrelated, even if I shudder at the idea that someone, in the wake of Putnam's method mentioned above, might set up a complete parallelism between Mezentius and the little calf of the *Georgics*. I might end here, and the partial nature of the problematic spectrum which I have tried to mark out would already be in evidence. To insist on the themes and problems that are most familiar to me has been a way of confirming implicitly the inevitable partiality of every commentary. I do not believe that the Virgilian commentator should be an encyclopaedic author; and whoever gears up for a task of this kind cannot forget the weight of previous interests and experiences. Nonetheless, there is an aspect of the Virgilian text that should at least be mentioned here; it is a field of studies in which our century has seen significant progress. Any commentator (even if not conducting original research in this area), should refer to it in order to keep the enterprise up to date. I am talking of the historical background of the *Aeneid*—not, of course, the historical period in which it was created. The issue of Augustanism would need a whole additional discussion, which will be conducted sooner or later and will contribute to making the current bimillenary very different from that of 1930.[44] I mean the historical background which Virgil has created *for* his work by manipulating traditional information. In this area thousands of questions crowd in, historical, geographical, antiquarian, archaeological, and so on: disciplines in which research has made great progress since the time of the great nineteenth-century commentators. Above all, there is the problem of gathering and appraising the material, but we must note with interest that these problems are losing their separate and specialist character, above all because now they are the concern of scholars with a literary education and sensibility, who are able to look at the way in which individual data are organized within the spatial and temporal co-ordinates of the narrative work. Here too, in short, the complexity of levels of the text demands an exegesis of a depth which is sufficient (as I was saying) to connect the various levels with each other.

Once, if you will permit me to repeat myself, I defined a commentary as a net cast over the text, which lets certain things pass but

---

[44] The bimillenary of Virgil's birth in 70 BC, celebrated by Mussolini's fascist regime in 1930, made much of presenting Augustus as the Duce's immediate predecessor as (re)founder of the Roman Empire: cf. e.g. Stone (1999).

retains the others.[45] Obviously I was aware that not every approach is valid, just as all nets are not the same in size. The divergences between different methods of approaching the text depend on the tendency to privilege one aspect of it or another; and I don't believe that these divergences are to be discouraged, because this sheer variety of exegetical methods is the foundation of our hope of tackling (according to our individual capacities) the greatest number of particular aspects of the text. It can never be repeated often enough that the distinctive character of a literary text is the complexity of elaboration, the plurality of levels of meaning, which are interwoven in its production. But if the plurality of levels of composition entails a corresponding plurality of exegetical levels, we must not forget that exegesis is necessarily a unitary process, because the meaning of the text itself is unified. There is a risk lying in wait for the work of the commentator, a risk inherent in the actual form of commentary—the dissolution of the text. The necessary dissection of the poetic discourse into syntagms for analysis and comment must be treated as a calculated risk. There must be a corrective ready at hand to reduce the hazard, all the more so because the risk of dissolution is real for a narrative text, especially a continuous one—linear and winding but continuous—like the *Aeneid*.

Anyone who admires the extraordinary accuracy and precise analysis which Nisbet and Hubbard have achieved in their exegesis of Horatian lyric poetry cannot suppress some disappointment in contemplating the dissolution which the texts of the *Odes* suffer in their commentary. To these students of the great analytic philology of Eduard Fraenkel one can also direct the criticism that Klingner addressed to Fraenkel's *Horace*: what is lacking is real attention to the whole framework, the *Gefüge*. Here the great teaching of Klingner the Virgilian scholar comes to mind; attention should be directed not just to the elements of expression that blossom to form the poetic discourse, but to their convergence in a unity of purpose, a true structure of meaning, organic and compact in the interaction of its parts. *Summa totius carminis et partium concentus* was the programme proposed by Heyne at the start of his Virgilian commentary, as I noted above. His recommendation, made more immediate

---

[45] In Conte (1974*a*).

by the interest taken by modern philologists in the structure of poetic discourse, is still valid and indispensable. The attention which I believe should be paid by the Virgilian exegete to textual strategies, to the point of view that directs the narrative, to repetition of sound and language, will be the best corrective s/he can seek out. In fact a model that is still valid today is offered by the commentary of Heyne, with the large scope of its notes, which did not shun the individual difficulties of a dense and complex form of expression, but knew how to make room for the interpretation of more expansive features of composition.[46]

---

[46] For more recent discussion of the classical commentary form see the works cited in n. 21 above.

8

The Meeting of Stylistics and Textual Criticism

In the part of his *Institutiones* which deals with verbs and their change of voice (the possible absolute or intransitive use of verbs that properly have an active force) Priscian notes (8.26) *similiter 'inundo' modo absolutam, modo activam habere significationem invenitur, ut Virgilius in XI 'dum distinet hostes agger murorum nec inundant sanguine fossas.' Invenitur tamen in quibusdam codicibus 'dum distinet hostes agger murorum nec inundant sanguine fossae.'*

However, all the witnesses to our direct tradition for this line (*Aen.* 11.382) agree on the single reading *fossae*. And the structure of the context leaves no doubt that this is the correct reading. Turnus, who is retorting to the demagogic accusations of Drances, answers that it is too easy to be swollen with eloquence while out of danger: 'while the defensive walls are keeping the enemy at a distance, and the ditches are not overflowing with blood'.

The line recurs in practically identical form at *Aeneid* 10.24. In the council of the gods, Venus denounces to Jupiter the bloodthirsty aggression of the Rutuli and Turnus against the Trojan encampment (the previous book has just closed with this scene of slaughter)—10.22–4:

> ... non clausa tegunt iam moenia Teucros;
> quin intra portas atque ipsis proelia miscent
> aggeribus moerorum et inundant sanguine fossas.

This is the reading most recently of Geymonat,[1] who writes in his apparatus: fossas PRVaberu *γ: Tib., Serv., qui ita interpretatur:*

[1] Geymonat (1973), 534.

'inundant *implent et inundare faciunt*', Ribbeck; fossae M ω, *Sabbadini et Mynors, e Aen. 11,382.*' For clarity I reproduce his apparatus as the most complete and reliable in this case: the reading of the 'Romanus' (R) is in fact *fossas*, not *fossae* as is reported by Ribbeck, whose error seems to be followed by Hirzel, Sabbadini, Mynors, and all the subsequent editors who base their text on any of these four editions.[2]

It is not important or useful to determine the history of the choices which each editor felt obliged to make between the two readings. Before Burman, preference went to *inundant... fossae* (as N. Heinsius bore witness); but though Burman decided for *fossas*, the preference returned with Heyne to *fossae*. This wavering was caused by the lack of strong arguments in favour of one of the two readings, as is proved in a curious way by the oscillation of Jahn, who read *fossae* in the passage in question, but on 11.382 declared that the reading that should be preferred at 10.24 was in fact *fossas*. Ribbeck read *fossas*, but with Janell (a revised Ribbeck for the Teubner series) the text returned to *fossae*. Hirzel supported *fossas*; Sabbadini and then Castiglioni wanted *fossae*. It will be enough to mention that most recently Mynors has chosen *fossae*; Geymonat, as we saw, prefers *fossas*. Thus the picture derived from the history of scholarship is a nicely balanced one.[3]

The arguments for *fossas*, sometimes explicit but more often implicit, can be reduced essentially to two: (*a*) the harshness of the unprecedented intransitive use of *inundant*, where the construction with accusative *fossas* would complete a linear and coordinate sequence: (*Rutuli) proelia miscent... et inundant sanguine fossas*: (*b*) *fossae* would be an interpolation from a distant parallel passage, something not rare in the text of Virgil,[4] reproducing at 10.24 the (guaranteed) *inundant sanguine fossae* of 11.382. The weakness of this last argument—dictated more by suspiciousness than by mere caution—is quite obvious. Not even Sabbadini paid any attention to it, although he was the most vigorous defender of the excellent criterion

[2] Henry had already noticed this inaccuracy in Ribbeck's apparatus (Henry (1889), 10). I thank Monsignor J. Ruysschaert, who kindly examined the manuscript for me and communicated the exact reading.

[3] In addition Ladewig–Schafer–Deuticke, Peerlkamp, Forbiger, Mackail, Williams, and Harrison are for *fossae*, Conington–Nettleship, Durand, and Perret for *fossas*.

[4] See e.g. Courtney (1981).

'*poeta variat, libri iterant*', which he enunciated epigrammatically in a note to his apparatus to *Georg.* 4.173.[5]

It seems to me, rather, that there are good reasons to prefer the reading *fossae*.[6] *Fossas* seems to have arisen from the motive of fitting *inundant* and *miscent* into a single syntactic movement, constructed from a parallel pair of cola. Thus *inundant* was dislodged from its absolute usage (the one attested beyond doubt in the hemistich 'the ditches overflow with blood' at 11.382) and reduced to its ordinary usage (Servius; *implent et inundare faciunt*).[7] This normalization reduced the stylistic leap—with innovative effect—activated by Virgil's expression.

But *inundare* with a switch to intransitive mode is the analogue of the more common *abundare* and *exundare*, which are normally so used intransitively. Generated on this model, implicitly related to *abundare* and *exundare*, which strictly denote the overflowing of limits or excavations by a stream of water pouring out of its bed,[8] *inundare* expresses in this case the specific sense of a receptacle that

[5] A suggestion to this effect also came to him from the judgement of Probus (preserved by Servius Dan. *ad Aen.* 9.814): '*fessos quatit aeger anhelitus artus*' Probus *ait* '*commodius hic est aeger quam in qunito* (432) "*vastos quatit aeger anhelitus artus*": *quamvis consuetudo sit Vergilio ista mutandi. Quidam acer legunt et volunt in quinto aeger aptius dictum de sene, hic de iuvene acer melius convenire.*' Following this Sabbadini added in the apparatus; 'quod de Vergilii consuetudine mutandi acri iudicio Probus animadvertit, aut prorsus ignorant aut neglegunt librarii, qui ex locis similibus ea perperam iterant quae Vergilius maximo labore et acumine variavit.'

[6] See further Harrison (1991), 65.

[7] On the indirect tradition of this passage, see Unterharnschneidt (1911), 54; Courtney (1981), 24.

[8] Cf. Sen. *Ag.* 222 (with hyperbole) *alto sanguine exundans solum*. The intransitive use of *inundare* with the special significance that it has in this line of the *Aeneid* was favoured by Virgil with the absolute use—in a metaphorical sense—of the same verb, as appears in *Aen.* 12.280 *hinc densi rursus inundant* | *Troes Agyllinique et pictis Arcades armis*. In this case the image was prepared by the Homeric model of *Il.* 11.724 τὰ δ' ἐπέρρεον ἔθνεα πεζῶν; cf. Erbse (1974), 269, Eustathii *Commentarii ad Hom. Il. pert.* 881, 2–6 [Van der Valk ii, pp. 313–14]. The Homeric precedent is recalled as a model by Ar. *Ach.* 26 ἀθρόοι καταρρέοντες in *Scholia in Aristoph. ad l.* (cf. *Suidae Lex. A* 762 s.v.); cf. also Plato, *Phaedr.* 229d καὶ ἐπιρρεῖ δὲ ὄχλος τοιούτων Γοργόνων καὶ Πηγάσων; Theocr. 15.59 ὄχλος πολὺς ἄμμιν ἐπιρρει. In short, in Virgil's *inundant fossae* we have a convergence of the example provided by analogous verbs like *abundare* / *exundare* and of a technical use of *inundare* (with absolute force) as conveying 'pouring itself over, creating floods', cf. besides the Virgilian example 12.280 cited above (with a metaphorical extension), Livy 22.2.2 *qua fluvius Arnus… inundaverat*, Obsequens 179.3 *Padus inundavit*, Sen. *NQ* 4.2.9.

receives a liquid until it is full and eventually brims over. As for the form of the phrase, *inundant sanguine fossae* is to be taken in the last analysis as an enallage, the syntactic and semantic figure given to an exchange of functions between one part of the discourse and another: the matrix is almost always that of the more general figure of inversion (peculiar to the 'difficult' and strained elevated style) in which the relation between syntactical and semantic terms is inverted.[9]

But it is not just the criterion of *lectio difficilior*, or in this case the defence of a rarer and more expressive construction which leads me to prefer the reading *fossae*. I believe that in *et inundant sanguine fossae* one can recognize the analogue of a Homeric formula: ῥέε δ᾽ αἵματι γαῖα (*Iliad* 4.451=8.65).[10] It is one of those typical additions in the form of a clausula, which puts a seal on the sentence in which Homer's narrative movement concludes. These are narrative-descriptive appendices, codas that close off the action narrated (or the scene described): their function in this respect is accessory and sometimes complementary; they often indicate simultaneity or sequentiality. To provide an example I might recall the formula 16.743 λίπε δ᾽ ὀστέα θυμός which represents a concluding addition introduced in parataxis; thus in *Il.* 16.740–3: the sharp stone struck him on the brow... his eyes fell to the ground... he dived out of the chariot... λίπε δ᾽ ὀστέα θυμός (16.743) 'life left his bones' (structurally identical to the other instance of the phrase at *Iliad* 12.386). Perhaps even more representative of the category is the formula ἀράβησε δὲ τεύχε᾽ ἐπ᾽ αὐτῷ. (*Iliad* 4.504 etc.), one of the most frequent formulas to close a scene of combat or death: the combatant, who may be wounded in various ways, collapses dead on the ground 'and his weapons clashed over him'. The narrative coda is added by combination, with syntactic and rhythmic autonomy; there is a new movement with a new subject, after the caesura before which the primary narrative sequence exhausts itself. We could continue by quoting many other analogous cases. Let one do duty for all: the

---

[9] For a detailed study of Virgilian enallage see Ch. 2 above.

[10] The comparison had already occurred to the excellent J. L. de la Cerda (above all for reasons of content; in fact he cites it along with other cases in which the Homeric text makes more general reference to 'the blood of heroes which soaks the earth') and this is how it entered the lists of comparisons drawn up by Knauer (1964), 413.

famous τὸν δὲ σκότος ὄσσε κάλυψεν (*Iliad* 4.461 etc.), 'and darkness covered his eyes'. It is the usual system: the addition is in parataxis, since the new movement is shaped as a formal equivalent to what precedes, whereas in fact it is interdependent (hence the phraseology possesses it own syntactic autonomy as an accessory unit, guaranteed by the change in grammatical subject). The same construction and function in relation to the context characterize other combinations which signify simultaneity or sequentiality; thus *Iliad* 14.60 αὔτη δ' οὐρανὸν ἵκει or 2.810 (etc.) πολὺς δ' ὀρυμαγδὸς ὀρώρει.

In short we are dealing with syntactical and rhythmic microstructures (which can also give rise by expansion to more extensive elements of the narrative movement). Their function is to seal a sequence of the narrative, in the manner of a concluding appendix. Such phrases, generated as formulae that can be repeated with variations (whether fixed or open to a certain flexibility), correspond in the Homeric text to the requirements of oral composition.[11] But for Virgil (as previously for Apollonius Rhodius) segmental formularity is essentially something to be avoided.[12] Once the 'economic' reasons

---

[11] We do not need here to make more than a generic reference to the great blossoming of works produced at the beginning of the 1970s by the rediscovery of the work of Adam Parry: it is not just that there is no longer a real genuine Parryan orthodoxy, but the countless heresies document a turmoil and critical debate that has generated significant distinctions. I believe the positions represented by scholars like Hoekstra, Kirk, Dihle, etc. (with their other diachronic interests) deserve great respect, or at least attention, from anyone who is trying to construct the cultural system to which the Homeric poems belong (one should read the carefully weighed papers). But I believe that even a predominantly synchronic analysis of Homeric text like that conducted by J. B. Hainsworth or the American M. Nagler offers very useful materials for anyone who wants to improve his/her acquaintance with Homeric expression: for them it is a matter of reconstructing a genuine 'generative grammar' of formular diction, describing the rules of production and transformation of Homeric formulae. In this line of research I find particularly stimulating the study by Kiparsky (1976); in the same volume one should read Russo (1976).

[12] It is well known that in the *Argonautica* in comparison with archaic epic, segmental formularity is perceptibly reduced; indeed the repetition of even moderately long phrases is essentially avoided, while that of entire lines is avoided completely. Alexandrian epic is careful to realize a balanced contamination of preserving and varying formulae. Naturally the tendency of an epic discourse that is not bound by formular economy is quite different (for Apollonius as for Virgil); it seeks to take shape according to recurrent 'empty' paradigms, generative cells of rhythmic and syntactic structure, which can be variously 'filled' or aggregated—recurrences that together constitute both limitation and assistance in composition.

for formular repetition are lost, the formula can now be accepted only with an 'aesthetic' function, either enriched with a specific contextual motivation,[13] or surviving as a index of style, as a marked feature of the Homeric manner.[14]

Virgil thus inherited these ready-made formulaic codas with precisely this epic function; they denote specific events concluding or resulting from the narrated action, and together they connote Homer and his exemplary status. Sometimes one of these structures is repeated itself with the function of a quasi-formular stereotype;[15] but more often the occurrences are unique; what marks them out is the syntactic and rhythmic form, along with the function of concluding appendix. This is the pattern in 10.488, *sonitum super arma dedere* (of obvious Homeric stamp), serving as seal to a broad movement in which the wounding and death of a warrior are reported. The assaults and encounter between two heroes has as a coda in 12.724 *ingens fragor aethera complet.* The stylistic expressive matrix will be the same if (for example) there are two enraged bulls confronting each other (12.722): *gemitu nemus omne remugit.* If this occurs more than once, the formular paradigm can also be varied, but the contextual function and the structure (with a change of subject and parataxis) will be the same: 9.636 *Teucri clamore secuntur* and 10.799 *socii magno clamore secuntur.* Often coordination is asyndetic (9.666–7 *sternitur omne solum telis; tum scuta cavaeque | dant sonitum flictu galeae: pugna aspera surgit;* cf. 11.635), but at other times the coda is joined by an explicit grammatical connective (11.609 ff. *subito erumpunt clamore, furentisque | exhortantur equos, fundunt simul undique tela | crebra nivis ritu, caelumque obtexitur umbra*).

These examples could (and should) be multiplied to achieve a systematic analysis; this is something that really needs to be

---

[13] Cf. e.g. Conte (1986*a*), 47–52.

[14] A problem still left unsolved (one certainly of great interest for all studies of Greek poetry, but particularly experienced by those who want to reconstruct the consciousness of *aemulatio Homerica* in Latin literature; and the *Aeneid* is in this case the privileged field of research), is to understand the nature of their sensibility to what we call formula, what sensibility Greek and Latin poets of different periods had for the formular structures which are distinctive features of Homer (there are good comments in Rossi (1978)).

[15] Sparrow (1931), Moskalew (1982).

done, because this is also the way to achieve a structural stylistics of Virgilian verse; we must find the compositional matrices that generate the form of Virgilian expression, and then typologies based on metre, syntax, and phraseology will emerge, with their implicit rules of construction, expansion, and condensation of the discourse.

This, in conclusion, is the typology of Virgilian paraformulaic codas, regulated by their Homeric model; a syntactical and rhythmic structure circumscribed and easy to isolate, localized in the second half of the hexameter, linked paratactically to the context, marked by a change of subject and hence made autonomous, characterized by a complementary or supplementary content in relation to the narrative content of the phrase (or phrases) which precede it. These are just the structural features which qualify the phrase *et inundant sanguine fossae* ~ ῥέε δ' αἵματι γαῖα.

One last consideration, which is perhaps a preliminary to research on a more coherent level. From the current tendencies of oralist studies of Homer we can take up a challenge: for some time now these studies have been working on the recognition of repetitive matrices that are more abstract and general than formulae, but which are in a sense no less real than a formular repetition when it is separately analysed, matrices capable of showing more precisely the concrete functioning of the Homeric text and its self-construction. Thus I believe the study of the relationship between Homer and Virgil will need always to scrutinize certain 'imitative matrices' in Virgilian phraseology, which embrace countless possibilities of individual realization. The question is whether these matrices are only textual (within the text of Virgil) and not also to some degree intertextual; that is, we need to recognize in them, when they arise, genuine functional analogues in relation to specific marked structures in the Homeric text.[16]

---

[16] I have previously hinted at some general ideas elsewhere—see Conte (1981), 152–5.

9

Proems in the Middle

How to begin a poem forms an established part of rhetorical theory. But in practice poets know that the solemn celebration of a beginning is something that far transcends rhetoric: the exordium is an inauguration, almost a liturgy which mediates the text's passage and thereby permits it to escape from silence and to enter into the literary universe. At the border between fully poetic speech and speech still outside of poetry, the proem—the preliminary announcement of a poem which follows—is already song and is not yet song. When the poet invokes the Muse to inspire him (or in hymns invokes the divinity to whom the hymn is addressed), he imposes a precise delimitation upon the 'contents' of his poem. By indicating its essential themes (this or that story—or part of a story) he outlines the limits of a discourse which was undefined as long as it was merely virtual. In his discussion of the proem, Aristotle defines it in this way: δεῖγμά ἐστιν τοῦ λόγου, ἵνα προειδῶσι περὶ οὗ [ἦ] ὁ λόγος καὶ μὴ κρέμηται ἡ διάνοια· ('the proem provides a sample of the subject, in order that the hearers may know beforehand what it is about, and that the mind may not be kept in suspense', *Rhet.* 3, 1415ᵃ12 f.).

If the inauguration of poetic discourse is an act regulated by a literary ceremony, the empirical function which this act at the same time fulfils is to inform the public of the song's object, its *quid*, by serving as a periphrastic substitute for the title itself, or a plot-summary of the contents. Among its various possible functions, and aside from many others which could be added, this is the most characteristic function of the proem, the only necessary and constant one. Indeed (if I may be permitted to oversimplify for a moment) this is in substance the structural defining feature of almost all

proems found in Greek literature until the fourth century BC,
the indisputable sign of an immediate and as yet unproblematized
relation between poet and public. The community recognizes in the
speech of its poets its own literature, and not only do the poets
recognize in this community a unanimous and homogeneous public,
but, what is more, it does not even occur to them to doubt the nature
and modes of their own poetic production. From time to time, in
different ways, these poets will have a more or less clear sense of
the dignity which belongs to their function; but all of them, in
substantially the same way, know how poetry is produced.

But the political and social upheavals of the Hellenistic age created
a markedly different cultural system in the course of a very short
time: the ecumenical community of this new world shared a cultural
horizon which was likewise ecumenical (an indication of this, and to
a certain extent a condition for it, is the diffusion of the book as the
medium which most directly answers to the changed requirements
of cultural communication). Within this horizon, the position of
literature takes on a new configuration; the relation between poet
and public changes, for the very destination of poetry changes. And if
the poet no longer addresses himself to that community within
which he was directly integrated (his existential space now takes on
the shape of the court, of the libraries, and of the schools), the
audience becomes, as though responding to the new cultural 'pro-
fessionalism' of the poet, a specialized audience of connoisseurs.

The literary code, even more than serving to communicate, now
functions as a means of selecting and qualifying its users. The
audience is ecumenical, but it is selected and restricted; speaker
and listener are the peaks of a mountain range which is immensely
extended, but whose valleys are excluded from communication.
The awareness that not only a political epoch has ended, but also
a cultural one, leads to reconsideration of the whole complex of
'tradition' as a legacy to be recovered—by evaluating and selecting,
by taking this, refusing that. The philological meditation which
derives from this busies itself with erudite classifications and with
laborious textual systematizations, but it also generates both a
sophisticated rhetorical theorizing and a consciousness attentive to
the procedures of poetic creation. Literature is no longer something
obvious: whoever practises it must say what he is doing, because

everyone does it differently. The result is not merely marginal asseverations, but literary professions of faith, ambitious and all-embracing. *Programmgedichte* like Theocritus' *Thalysia*, Herodas' *Mimiamb* 8 (the Dream), Callimachus' *Epigram* 28, and especially the prologue to his *Aetia*, are manifestos of the new poetry, of the new way of conceiving and formulating the problematic relation between literature and reality. And the poet invents a new liturgy in the act of inaugurating his poetry, so that the public will know not only the object, the *quid*, of the incipient poem, but also and above all its individual artistic character—its *quale*. In this second aspect we can see the announcement of a new literary vocation (which polemically desires to renew itself even in its artistic materials) and the proposal of a new form of expression and of contents (comprising a liberty which refuses canonical measures and distinctions and which contaminates diverse modes of poetic discourse). At the same time, the restricted public of competent readers is practically required to adopt a role of jealous connivance. All this is the ambitious affirmation of the poet's ego, which far from hiding itself behind any sort of cover, now comes forward in the first person to proclaim everything which might serve to characterize him and to distinguish him from others.

The ancient structure of the proem is ready to welcome this new function, to turn itself on occasion into a declaration of poetics as well. Side by side with the thematic proem exists the programmatic proem. To be more precise, we often find a programmatic proem interwoven with and superimposed on the thematic proem: thus, alongside the *quid*, the *quale*.

Up to this point I have generalized, and a lot. But perhaps my doing so has made one thing clear: that these two forms of proem are functionally opposed in such a way that, even if both perform the ceremony of opening, one is concerned with what will be said, the other with how poetry will be made. This synchronic oppositional pair is, as often happens, the result of a diachronic evolution. On the one hand, that is, we find the persistence of an ancient feature, one virtually congenital with poetry (the expository proem), and, on the other hand, the insertion of a new proemial nature, in which a different culture comes to light (the programmatic proem).

I

This distinction will remain valid for the artistic consciousness of
poets to come—both a constraint and the sign of an artistic responsibility necessary for making poetry. At Rome such a consciousness is
fully revealed in the literary practice of Virgil. The architecture of the
Georgics is exemplary: four books, each one with a single subject that
is announced each time by a brief, precise proem, a specific *deigma*,
which takes up 'in variando' the plot-summary of contents prefixed
to the work as a whole in the first proem:

> Quid faciat laetas segetes, quo sidere terram
> vertere, Maecenas, ulmisque adiungere vitis
> conveniat, quae cura boum, qui cultus habendo
> sit pecori, apibus quanta experientia parcis
> hinc canere incipiam.   (1.1–5)

Each of these four lines proposes one of four themes. Then follows
the hymnic invocation to the divinities of the countryside and to
Caesar.

The proem of the second book has an analogous structure and
identical function. It is a naked *propositio* of the argument, cultiva-
tion of vines (followed by a dedication to Bacchus). Likewise the
proem to the fourth book is reduced to the exposition of its *summa
rerum*, the raising of bees.

On the other hand, the third book does not open with this type of
structure, a thematic proem; it has a programmatic proem which is a
genuine declaration of poetics:

> Cetera, quae vacuas tenuissent carmine mentes,
> omnia iam volgata: quis aut Eurysthea durum
> aut inlaudati nescit Busiridis aras?
> cui non dictus Hylas puer et Latonia Delos
> Hippodameque umeroque Pelops insignis eburno,
> acer equis? Temptanda via est, qua me quoque possim
> tollere humo victorque virum volitare per ora.
> Primus ego in patriam mecum, modo vita supersit,
> Aonio rediens deducam vertice Musas;
> primus Idumaeas referam tibi, Mantua, palmas
> et viridi in campo templum de marmore ponam
> propter aquam, tardis ingens ubi flexibus errat

Mincius et tenera praetexit harundine ripas.
In medio mihi Caesar erit templumque tenebit.
Illi victor ego et Tyrio conspectus in ostro
centum quadriiugos agitabo ad flumina currus.
Cuncta mihi Alpheum linquens lucosque Molorchi
cursibus et crudo decernet Graecia caestu.
Ipse caput tonsae foliis ornatus olivae
dona feram.   (3.3–22)

By now practically everything a poet can say has been said (*omnia iam vulgata*, 4). For the man who would rise to new regions of poetry, and to flattery on the mouths of men as a winner (*victorque virum volitare per ora*, 9), only a road which has never yet been tried can guarantee ascent to the mountain of the Muses; and it is Virgil, *primus*, who will know how to bring them to Italy.

This ambitious new poetry includes all the programmatic topics—in the proper order: the motifs of the *recusatio*, of *primus ego*, and of the Muses, once Greek, now finally Latin. And the path that leads to the temple dedicated to Caesar, the path of a great new epic poem, follows in the footsteps of the greatest of all Roman literary traditions, that of Ennius.[1] Precisely because he has chosen his own direction, the poet can reject a large part of what has already been said. The new song will arise, built along the the lines of that symbol in which Pindar had several times embodied the grandeur of poetry: an architectural monument, with the limpid proportions of a temple.

Here in Virgil the Pindaric metaphor takes on the form of a grandiose programmatic allegory: Caesar, the divinity of that temple, and Caesar's glorious deeds will be the object of the future poem; but the marble building will rise on the green banks of the Mincio River.[2] In this declaration, the poet Virgil is entirely present: he promises

---

[1] Besides the obvious presence of Ennius' epitaph (*volito* | *vivo' per ora virum*), the magnificent poetry of the *Annals* is also indirectly evoked by 10–11, *Primus ego in patriam mecum, modo vita supersit,* | *Aonio rediens deducam vertice Musas*, where there is an echo of Lucretius' praise of Ennius at 1.117 f., *qui primus amoeno* | *detulit ex Helicone perenni fronte coronam.*

[2] The water of the Mincio performs here the same symbolic function—it contributes to the poet's investiture—as the river Permessus performed in the landscape of Helicon, the Muses' mythical seat, just as Mantua will be the new Helicon of the Virgilian Muses. Cf. Wimmel (1960), 222–38; less useful is Kambylis (1965), *passim*, esp. 98 ff., 110 ff.

something completely new, but neither his memories nor his *Eclogues* have abandoned him. This emergence of the poet's own identity from his programmatic awareness is directly related to the Alexandrian and Neoteric experience, the cultural soil upon which the new edifice of Augustan literature was being constructed.

But there is another proem of Virgil's, or rather a proem in the middle, which shows much more immediate ties with that Alexandrian experience. I am referring to the beginning of the sixth *Eclogue*, almost as Alexandrian as the prologue to Callimachus' *Aetia* itself, to which it adheres quite closely.[3] The programmatic topics to which the poet has recourse in order to establish his declaration are, in this case too, the *primus ego*, the *recusatio* of what is extraneous to the new song (*cum canerem reges et proelia*), and the choice of what is appropriate for his new intentions. But the connection with that Alexandrian culture remains, so that, in contrast to his promise in the *Georgics*, this Virgil still rejects the grand themes so as to confine himself to small ones.

But I am not so much interested here in showing how contents that are related in substance become actualized in forms that are opposed. What I would like to point out instead is the persistence within different poetic genres—and distinct moments in the poet's career—of an identical function performed by the proem placed in the middle of the work: that of offering a specific declaration of poetics. In other words, the position within the compositional architecture (precisely at the beginning of the second half of the *Georgics* and of the bucolic collection) corresponds to a specific function, distinct from the one belonging to the proem placed normally at the beginning of the work. I shall explain its meaning in greater detail soon; now we must still consider, within in the Virgilian corpus, the proem placed at the beginning of the seventh book of the *Aeneid*, at the transition from the Odyssean part to the Iliadic one. Here the poet takes another, deeper breath, he invokes the Muse anew: in short, this is a new beginning, one which would seem to find its only rationale in the objective caesura which divides the material of the poem.

[3] Still fundamental is Reitzenstein (1931), 23–69; see also Pfeiffer (1928), 302 ff.; cf. Wimmel (1960), 132 ff., and finally Schmidt (1972), 19 ff., 239 ff.

Certainly, the empirical necessity of signalling in some way the passage from the adventures of Aeneas by sea to the harsh battles of Rome's destiny was easily solved by inserting a new proem.[4] But it would be a serious misunderstanding of the poetic architecture of Virgil to reduce it all to such mechanical requirements of composition; the poet says now what he will sing, and the proem declares the *quid* of the new narrative. So at least it seemed to Heyne who, commenting on the anaphoric lines *dicam horrida bella,* | *dicam acies actosque animis in funera reges,* explained *reges* with the annotation 'Latinum, Turnum, Mezentium'. I suspect that the commentator, anxious to give an objective denotation to every Virgilian word, misunderstood the meaning and the specifically literary function of the formula *bella et reges,* its implicit programmatic and declaratory connotation. It is the very formula which Horace employs in *Ars Poetica* 73 to designate the highest kind of heroic poetry: *res gestae regumque ducumque et tristia bella.* Heyne, in other words, misunderstood the *quale,* the qualities and characteristics of the Iliadic part which is about to begin, characteristics which Virgil, after a couple of lines, emphatically and explicitly announces with the words *maior mihi nascitur ordo,* | *maius opus moveo* (44–5). Here Virgil finally agrees to sing of *reges et bella,* he no longer refuses *tristia condere bella* (the formulae of *recusatio* prefixed to the sixth *Eclogue*), and he also satisfies the promise made in the proem in the middle of the *Georgics.* Thus the proem to the seventh book of the *Aeneid,* joined horizontally in a synoptic relationship to the thematic topics of the other two proems in the middle, not only refers to the contents of what the poet is about to sing, but is also enriched with a meaning which touches on the *qualitas* and the modes of poetry.

II

The regular recurrence in Virgil of the proem in the middle as the privileged locus of literary consciousness allows us to recognize in it a function of a systematic character, no different from those performed

[4] And of course we should not neglect the specific connection with the verses which open the proem to the third book of Apollonius Rhodius.

by other formal literary conventions. Now that the phenomenon has been identified, the philologist would be concerned at this point to discover its 'source'; and perhaps not wrongly, if it is true that—as one of the few Italian philosophers maintained—the nature of things often 'is in their birth'. One thinks immediately of Ennius, as is only natural, the true or presumptive *pater* of so great a part of Latin literature. Because of the fragmentary form in which his *Annals* have come down to us, no certainty can be attained; nevertheless, I believe that the hypothesis I shall formulate has a certain degree of plausibility.

Several books of the *Annals* opened with single thematic proems. But among these there is one which seems to have contained many of the same programmatic topics with which we have been concerned up to now: it is the celebrated proem to the seventh book. What remains is little but, perhaps, sufficient:

> scripsere alii rem
> versibus quos olim Fauni vatesque canebant,
> cum neque Musarum scopulos...
> ...nec dicti studiosus quisquam erat ante hunc.
> Nos ausi reserare...
> Nec quisquam *sophiam* sapientia quae perhibetur
> in somnis vidit prius quam sam discere coepit.
>
> (213–19 V²; 206–12 Skutsch)

Here is the poet's rejection of his predecessors and his separation of himself from them; here is his difficult ascent to the mountain of the Muses, a boast which inevitably precedes the motif of *primus ego* (connected with the symbolic theme of the fountain), and which proudly declares the new poetics of the *dicti studiosus*—the literary profession of the poet-philologist of the Alexandrian school.[5]

After the first six books (it matters little whether the publication proceeded by triads or hexads), Ennius was obliged to declare the

---

[5] That the verb *reserare* was completed by an object like *fontes* (the appropriate *Wassersymbol* of poetic imitation) has been proposed by Pascoli (1911), 34, on the basis of comparison with Virg. *Georg.* 2.175, *ingredior, sanctos ausus recludere fontes*, and has been supported by Klingner (1967), 241, who cites Stat. *Silv.* 2.2.38 f., *reseretque arcana pudicos | Phemonoe fontes*...The resulting image seems to me well suited to the context, *pace* Skutsch (1968), 124 f. For a good discussion of these verses, with full bibliography, see Suerbaum (1968), 249–95.

differences which separated him from his predecessor Naevius (since his own treatment of the Punic Wars began with the seventh book), and he was also obliged to respond to the attacks which inevitably came from the belated resistance of traditionalist schools. The circumstances required, in short, an open profession of literary faith, which found its most natural locus in a new proem, at the beginning of the new part which was now being published. And Ennius, now becoming polemical, in declaring his literary ideals again invoked his splendid allegory of the dream, the investiture (in the first proem) from which he had derived his own poetic *sophia*. Thus in Ennius too we find a proem which is inserted into the body of the poem with the specific function of declaring the author's programme—and which would have remained a genuine proem in the middle if the 'old Olympian racehorse' had in fact completely exhausted his forces, and had he not instead unexpectedly taken on new energy and a poetic second wind. Consider the close of the twelfth book:

> Sicut fortis equus, spatio qui saepe supremo
> vicit Olympia, nunc senio confectus quiescit.
>
> (374–5 V²; 522–3 Skutsch)

Upon finishing his work, at the point of farewell, the poet speaks about himself (the concluding *sphragides* of Callimachus' *Aetia* or of Virgil's *Georgics*, for example, are no different). Ennius compares himself to a strong but old horse, once victor at Olympia, but now obliged by age to take a well-earned rest. Even if it turned out that the old Olympian racehorse would after all find the energy for six more books, it is probable that at first he believed that the twelfth book would mark the end of his *Annals*.[6] This is, in short, the architectonic structure which the future reader of Ennius would have found in the

---

[6] Skutsch's edition of the *Annals*, Skutsch (1985), places the two lines that Vahlen put at the end of book 12 among the *sedis incertae fragmenta* (lines 522–3). Vahlen's reconstruction was based mainly on a reading (*duodecimum annalem* in Gellius 17. 21.43) which Skutsch has shown to be wrong (pp. 674–5). This now makes possible various collocations of these two lines: the end of book 15 (this seems to me to be the most attractive), the end of book 18, or even the beginning of book 16. I do not, however, believe that my line of argument is greatly affected by this. Two different problems must be distinguished. The first is that diachrony of composition, the ups and downs that accompanied the composition of the *Annals*, and the resulting collocation of those two lines at one or another stage in the process of composition; the second is the definitive form in which the *Annals* appear (or, rather, appeared to

Annals; and I suspect that, to make it even more perspicuous, there was probably a sort of *retractatio* at the beginning of the thirteenth book, designed to justify Ennius' renewed commitment to sing even the most recent history of Rome. This is just what Ovid does when he adds the third book of his *Ars Amatoria*, missing in the original plan; and in the same way Manilius justifies his fifth book.[7]

It is the lucid desire for proportion, typical of the new Roman classicism, which attaches an aesthetic value to this empirical and contingent opposition between two proemial functions and their respective collocations in the economy of the work, attributing to it a specific formal meaning. In other words, the empirical opposition will achieve pertinence: the circumstantial collocation will become a convention—a rhetorical institution—and win a place among the possible models of the literary system.

Roman classicism, and Virgil in particular, has a clear awareness of the difference in functionality between the two types of proem: the ancient proem of contents and the programmatic proem, Alexandrian and modern. These poets know the Alexandrian experience and have learned its lesson, but they seek a direct relation with that

its ancient readers) at the end of that process. It is possible to make out within this definitive form the great initial proem, one or more endings to sections of the text, and further proems in the course of the work. Of these, the proem to book 7 (which at least with respect to the whole plan of fifteen books had a collocation which can be called 'medial') must certainly have possessed—in length and in scope—a function comparable to that of the general proem, so that it appeared complementary to it. Thus the problem is not one of rigid geometry or numerical schemes (even if Ennius can hardly have been displeased that a formulation of his poetic ambitions found its place near the middle of his work); rather, the proem to the seventh book sprang from Ennius' practical need to compare himself with Naevius, his predecessor and rival, in treating a common subject. We are thus dealing with a fortuitous process and a contingent collocation which eventually served as a model in composition—which acquired, in other words, a paradigmatic function.

[7] Ovid justifies the addition to his original plan (cf. *Ars Am.* 1.36–40) on the clever grounds of fair play: 'Now that I have instructed the men, it is fair that the women too should know the weapons of amorous seduction, so that they can wage a fair battle' (cf. *Ars Am.* 3.1–6). Manilius justifies his fifth book thus: *Hic alius finisset iter... me properare... mundus iubet, Astron.* 5.1 ff.; he seem to have added to the plan of a work probably conceived of in four books, following the model of the didactic poem represented by the *Georgics*; cf. Romano (1979), esp. 64 ff. See further the way in which, according to Pliny (*Nat. Hist.* 7.101), Ennius himself motivated his decision to add book 16: *Q. Ennius T. Caecilium Teucrum fratremque eius praecipue miratus propter eos sextum decimum adiecit annalem* (cf. Vahlen[2] *Ann.* 16 fr. 1, p. 74).

ancient essentiality which at the beginning of the song simply said
'what' would be sung. Yet they also, in the fashion of the Alexandrians,
feel the need to say 'how'. Hence the need for a distinction—splitting
into two the proemial utterance—for which the architecture of
Ennius' gradually evolving proem opened up an opportunity
for a difference in location. To speak in the middle is also to assign
an appropriate place (a secondary position) to a function which must
remain secondary with respect to the effort to perform an unmediated
utterance, not a self-reflective discourse. It was necessary to create
a poetry which would again seem to be a 'naive' and, as it were, natural
utterance. This is the *tour de force* of the poets of Roman classicism
after the literary sophistication of the Neoterics.

But they could no longer ignore their self-reflective consciousness.
What they had to do was confine it to a position of lesser conspicuousness—of concealed conspicuousness. This seems to me the same
toned-down emphasis that we find in the figure of litotes, where an
idea is shrewd enough to express itself indirectly, where it is so sure of
re-emerging later in the ultimate meaning of the sentence that it
agrees to eclipse itself in an attenuating circumlocution.

The proem in the middle, in short, permits the poet to declare
himself, but with less conspicuousness. Horace too seems to have
profited from this possibility, when he located in the centre of the
fourth book of his *Odes* the eighth poem (the solemn motif of
dignum laude virum Musa vetat mori, 28), joining it immediately to
the ninth, the ode of the *vate sacro*; or when in the group of the six
Roman Odes he reserved the fourth place for the invocation of
Calliope and for a Pindarizing profession of a poetics of the sublime.
But often Horace's professions of his poetic vocation are placed
deliberately at the close of the books: a delayed and conclusive
presentation of himself and his own poetry rather than a problematic
declaration of poetic rationales, the author's seal in the Alexandrian
fashion but also a confident farewell to his readers.

III

The dossier of 'proems in the middle' could be enriched by other
examples, which all point, as has already been noted, towards the

Alexandrian character of this technique. Thus, examining the relations between the new Lille papyrus of Callimachus and Roman poetry, Thomas has shown how the central proem of the *Georgics* was influenced by the beginning of book 3 of the *Aetia* of Callimachus; and he has pointed out the notable 'Callimachean' continuity of the proems of *Eclogue* 6, *Georgics* 3, and *Aeneid* 7.[8] It should also be noted that the imitations of the 'medial proem' of the *Aetia* are all located, according to Thomas, in initial or functionally programmatic positions (besides *Georgics* 3, see Propertius 3.1 and Statius, *Silv.* 3.1). It is important to note that in all these Latin examples (Virgil, Propertius, Statius), the imitation of Callimachus, in a conspicuous position, takes on a precise character of metaliterary enunciation; Callimachus offered nothing more than a compositional framework, which the Latin poets transformed to create a new proemial institution.

Instead, I should like to conclude with a final hypothesis. It involved the famous proem to the fourth book of Lucretius—famous, unfortunately, not only for the grandiose beauty which makes it one of the most enthusiastic declarations of poetics in all of Latin literature, but also for the jungle of philological opinions and counter-opinions which has luxuriated around these verses. The problem, certainly, exists, and is of neither easy nor sure solution.[9] The problem, in a nutshell, is this. Verses 1–25, which constitute the proem to the fourth book, also figure, with two or three tiny changes, in 1.926–50, where they are preceded by verses 921–5, which are tightly connected to them. Was it the poet who wrote them in both

---

[8] Thomas (1983).

[9] But it is equally certain that the creation of a now suffocating *lukrezische Frage* has been fuelled by the scruples of some philologists (primarily German) who hesitate to rid themselves at the outset of baseless or arbitrary hypotheses, if only to make a show of a laborious 'scientific' apparatus. I agree in substance with the arguments of Gaiser (1961), 19 ff., who after an analysis of the context in which the disputed verses are found, and noting the evidence provided by study of the manuscript tradition, traces the difficulties presented by the text back to the very beginning of its transmission. Lucretius seems to have left his work by and large completed, but apparently without having been able to submit it to an organic revision; hence his manuscript was probably loaded with additions and corrections, second thoughts and improvements. The first editor of *De Rerum Natura* (perhaps Cicero), intervening in this text with an excessive conservatism, in a mechanical and not always critical manner, seems to have paved the way for many of the incongruities and errors of the tradition.

places? Or were they written in only one place and then transferred to the other by an editor or interpolator, surviving in their original location? In that case, which was their original location? Some scholars have found it in book 1; others have maintained that these verses, written as a proem to book 4, were later transferred to 1.926–50; and among these there are some who think it was Lucretius himself who transferred them, some who think it was an editor, and some a late interpolator.[10]

What has been outlined up to now, the specifically programmatic function which belongs to the proem in the middle, can perhaps contribute a new piece of evidence towards solving this question. In the fourth book, a declaration of poetics such as this is in exactly the right place. It is densely interwoven with programmatic *topoi*: among others, the new roads of Callimachus, the still untouched fountains of poetry and the coronation of the poet, and the motif of *primus ego*. It is Lucretius' solemn enunciation of his literary credo; it occupies the proemial position at the beginning of a book; and at the beginning of the fourth book it is conspicuously placed in the middle of the poem. This location, therefore, is typical; but one cannot say as much if the original location of these verses is sought in the first book. Will so much evidence of compositional care betray the intention of the poet (in that case Lucretius would have made those verses expressly for the fourth book, or at least it would have been he who transferred them there)? Or if that care does not betray the intention of Lucretius, does it not betray the critical intervention of the reviser?[11]

---

[10] For all the essential points of this problem, see the Oxford commentary of Bailey *ad* 1.925 ff. and Gale (1994). The complex procedure of proposals and discussion can easily be reconstructed with the help of the text and notes of Gaiser (1961).

[11] The present article is a slightly revised version of an essay earlier published in Conte (1980*a*). I should like to thank Professor Antonio La Penna for the gratifying fall-out initiated by his keen interest in this essay; curious readers may consult La Penna (1981) and (1983), and Conte (1982*c*) and (1983*b*).

Bibliography

THE abbreviations used are those for *L'Année Philologique*, listed online at http://www.library.uq.edu.au/endnote/ancient_hist_2001.txt.

ARDIZZONI, A. (1953), *POIHMA: Ricerche sulla teoria del linguaggio poetico nell'antichità* (Bari).

ARMSTRONG, D., FISH, J., JOHNSTON, P. A., and SKINNER, M. B. (2004) (eds.), *Vergil, Philodemus and the Augustans* (Austin).

ARRIGHETTI, G. (1987), *Poeti, eruditi e biografi: Momenti della riflessione dei Greci sulla letteratura* (Pisa).

—— (1991), 'Platone fra mito, poesia e storia', *SCO* 41: 1–22.

ASMIS, E. (1992), 'Crates on Poetic Criticism', *Phoenix*, 46: 128–69.

BANDERA, C. (1981), 'Sacrificial Levels in Virgil's *Aeneid*', *Arethusa*, 14: 217–39.

BARCHIESI, A. (1978), 'Il lamento di Giuturna', *MD* 1: 99–121.

—— (1980), *Virgilio: Georgiche* (Milan).

—— (1984), *La traccia del modello: Effetti omerici nella narrazione virgiliana* (Pisa).

BASSETT, S. E. (1938), *The Poetry of Homer* (Berkeley).

BEDNARA, E. (1908), 'Aus der Werkstatt der daktylischen Dichter', *Archiv für lateinische Lexicographie*, 15: 223–32.

BELL, A. J. (1923), *The Latin Dual & Poetic Diction: Studies in Numbers and Figures* (Toronto).

BERS, V. (1974), *Enallage and Greek Style* (Leiden).

BIANCHI BANDINELLI, R. (1979) (ed.), *Società e civiltà dei Greci* (Milan).

BIOTTI, A. (1994), *Virgilio: Georgiche libro IV* (Bologna).

BÖMER, F. (1965), 'Eine Stileigentümlichkeit Vergils: Vertauschen der Prädikate', *Hermes*, 93: 130–1.

BONFANTI, M. (1985), *Punto di vista e modi della narrazione nell'Eneide* (Pisa).

BREMER, J. M., DE JONG, I. J. F., and KALFF, J. (1987) (eds.), *Homer: Beyond Oral Poetry, Recent Trends in Homeric Interpretation* (Amsterdam).

BRIGGS, W. W. (1981), 'Virgil and the Hellenistic Epic', *ANRW* II. 31. 2: 948–84.

BRISSON, L. (1982), *Platon: Les mots et les mythes* (Paris).

BUCHHEIT, V. (1963), *Vergil über die Sendung Roms* (Heidelberg).

BURKERT, W. (1966), 'Greek Tragedy and Sacrificial Ritual', *GRBS* 7: 87–121.

Burkhardt, F. (1971), 'Zur doppelten Enallage', *Gymnasium*, 78: 407–21.

Cameron, A. (1995) *Callimachus and his Critics* (Princeton).

Canali, L. (1983), *Virgilio: Georgiche* (Milan).

Chuvin, P. (1976), *Nonnos de Panopolis: Les Dionysiaques, Chants III–V* (Paris).

Clarke, S. (1729–32), *Homeri Ilias*, 2 vols. (London).

Clausen, W. V. (1987), *Virgil's Aeneid and the Tradition of Hellenistic Poetry* (Berkeley and Los Angeles).

Coleman, R. (1962), 'Gallus, the *Bucolics*, and the Ending of the Fourth *Georgic*', *AJPh* 83: 55–71.

Conington, J., and Nettleship, H. (1858–71), *Virgili Opera*, 3 vols. (Oxford).

Conte, G. B.(1965), 'Il trionfo della morte e la galleria dei grandi trapassati in Lucrezio III, 1024–1053', *SIFC* 27: 114–32.

—— (1966*a*), '"Υψος e diatriba nello stile di Lucrezio (*De rer.nat.* II, 1–61)', *Maia*, 18: 338–68.

—— (1966*b*), 'Il proemio della Pharsalia', *Maia*, 18: 42–53 (repr. in Conte 1988).

—— (1966*c*), 'Uno studioso tedesco della letteratura latina: Friedrich Klingner', *Critica Storica*, 5: 481–503.

—— (1968), 'La guerra civile nella rievocazione del popolo: Lucano 2.67–233', *Maia*, 20: 224–53.

—— (1970*a*), 'Ennio e Lucano', *Maia*, 22: 132–8 (repr. in Conte 1988).

—— (1970*b*), 'Il balteo di Pallante', *RFIC* 98: 292–300 (repr. in Conte 1974*a* and 1985; tr. in Conte 1986*a*).

—— (1971), 'Memoria dei poeti e arte allusiva', *Strumenti critici*, 16: 325–32 (repr. in Conte 1974*a* and 1985; tr. in Conte 1986*a*).

—— (1974*a*), *Memoria dei poeti e sistema letterario* (Turin) (2nd edn. Turin, 1985; largely translated in Conte 1986*a*).

—— (1974*b*), *Saggio di commento a Lucano. Pharsalia 6.118–260. L'aristia di Sceva* (Pisa) (revised reprint in Conte 1988).

—— (1976), 'Proemi al mezzo', *RCCM* 18: 263–73 (repr. in Conte 1980*a* and 1984*a*; tr. in Conte 1992*a*).

—— (1978*a*), 'Saggio d'interpretazione dell'*Eneide*: ideologia e forma del contenuto', *MD* 1: 11–48 (repr. in Conte 1980*a* and 1984*a*; tr. in Conte 1986*a*).

—— (1978*b*), 'L'episodio di Elena bel secondo dell'*Eneide*: modelli strutturali e critica dell'autenticità', *RFIC* 106: 53–62 (repr. in Conte 1980*a* and 1984*a*; tr. in Conte 1986*a*).

—— (1979), 'Il genere e i suoi confini: interpretazione dell'egloga decima di Virgilio' in *Studi di poesia latina in onore di Antonio Traglia* (Rome), 377–404 (repr. in Conte 1980*a* and 1984*a*; tr. in Conte 1986a).

CONTE, G. B. (1980*a*), *Virgilio: il genere e i suoi confini* (Turin).

—— (1980*b*), 'Aristeo, Orfeo e le Georgiche: struttura narrativa e funzione didascalica di un mito'; introduction to A. Barchiesi, *Virgilio: Georgiche* (Milan) (repr. in Conte 1984*a*, tr. in Conte 1986*a*).

—— (1981), 'A proposito dei modelli in letteratura', *MD* 6: 147–74.

—— (1982*a*), 'Verso una nuova esegesi virgiliana: revisioni e propositi', in *Virgilio e noi. None giornate filologiche genovesi* (Genoa), 73–98 (repr. in Conte 1984*a*).

—— (1982*b*), 'L'inventario del mondo: ordine e linguaggio della natura nell'opera di Plinio il Vecchio', in *Plinio: Storia Naturale 1*, ed. A. Barchiesi *et al.* (Turin), xvii–xlvii (repr. in Conte 1991; tr. in Conte 1994*b*).

—— (1982*c*), 'Istituti letterari e stili di ricerca; una discussione', *MD* 8: 123–39.

—— (1983*a*), 'Fra stilistica e critica del testo: *Eneide* 10, 24', *RFIC* 111: 150–7 (repr. in Conte 2002).

—— (1983*b*), 'Una discussione impossibile', *MD* 9: 153–4.

—— (1984*a*), *Virgilio: il genere e i suoi confini* (2nd edn.; Milan).

—— (1984*b*), 'Aristeo', *Enciclopedia Virgiliana*, i (Rome), 319–22.

—— (1985), *Memoria dei poeti e sistema letterario* (2nd edn.; Turin).

—— (1986*a*), *The Rhetoric of Imitation: Genre and Poetic Memory in Virgil and Other Latin Poets* (Ithaca).

—— (1986*b*), introduction to *Ovidio: Rimedi contro l'amore*, tr. C. Lazzarini (Venice), 9–53 (repr. in Conte 1991; tr. in Conte 1994*b*).

—— (1987*a*), *La letteratura latina. Manuale storico dalle origini alla fine dell'impero romano* (Florence) (repr. several times; tr. Conte 1994*a*).

—— (1987*b*), 'Una correzione a Petronio (*Sat.* 89 v.31)', *RFIC* 115: 33–4.

—— (1988), *La 'Guerra Civile' di Lucano* (Urbino).

—— (1989), 'I giorni del giudizio: Lucano e l'antimodello', in *Mnemosynum: Studi in onore di Alfredo Ghiselli* (Bologna), 95–100 (also in Conte (1988), 33–9).

—— (1990), introduction to *Lucrezio: La natura delle cose*, tr. L. Canali (Milan), 7–47 (repr. in Conte 1991; tr. in Conte 1994*b*).

—— (1991), *Genere e lettori: Lucrezio, l'elegia d'amore, l'enciclopedia di Plinio* (Milan) (tr. in Conte 1994*b*).

—— (1992*a*), 'Proems in the Middle', in F. M. Dunn and T. Cole (eds.), *Beginnings in Classical Literature* (Yale Classical Studies, 29; Cambridge), 147–59.

—— (1992*b*), ' "La retorica dell'imitazione" come retorica della cultura', *Filologia Antica e Moderna* (Calabria), 41–2 (tr. in Conte 1992*c*).

—— (1992*c*), ' "Rhetoric of Imitation" as Rhetoric of Culture: Some New Thoughts', *Vergilius*, 38: 45–55 (repr. in Conte 1994*b*).

—— (1992*d*), 'Empirical and Theoretical Approaches to Literary Genre', in K. Galinsky (ed.), *The Interpretation of Roman Poetry* (Frankfurt), 103–24 (repr. as 'Genre between Empiricism and Theory', in Conte 1994*b*; earlier Italian version in Conte 1991).

—— (1992*e*), 'Petronio, Sat. 141', *RFIC* 120: 300–12.

—— (1994*a*), *Latin Literature: A History* (Baltimore).

—— (1994*b*), *Genres and Readers* (Baltimore and London).

—— (1996*a*), *The Hidden Author: An Interpretation of Petronius' Satyricon* (Berkeley and London).

—— (1996*b*), '*Defensor Vergilii*: la tecnica epica dell'*Eneide* secondo Richard Heinze', introduction to R. Heinze (tr. M. Martina), *La tecnica epica di Virgilio* (Bologna), 9–23 (repr. in Conte 2002).

—— (1998*a*), 'Aristeo, Orfeo e le *Georgiche*: una seconda volta', *SCO* 46: 103–36 (repr. in Conte 2002, tr. in Conte 2001).

—— (1998*b*), 'Il paradosso virgiliano: un'epica drammatica e sentimentale', introduction to M. Ramous (tr.), G. Baldo (comm.), *Virgilio: Eneide* (Venice), 9–55 (tr. as Conte 1999*a*).

—— (1999*a*), 'The Virgilian Paradox', *PCPhS* 45: 17–42.

—— (1999*b*), 'Tre congetture a Petronio', *MD* 43: 203–11.

—— (2001), 'Aristaeus, Orpheus and the *Georgics* again', in S. Spence (ed.), *Poets and Critics Read Virgil* (New Haven), 44–63.

—— (2002), *Virgilio: L'epica di sentimento* (Turin).

CONTINI, G. (1970), *Varianti e altra linguistica: Una raccolta di saggi (1938–1968)* (Turin).

COURTNEY, E. (1981), 'The Formation of the Text of Vergil', *BICS* 28: 13–29.

—— (1993), *The Fragmentary Latin Poets* (Oxford).

DE JONG, I. J. F. (1987), *Narrators and Focalizers. The Presentation of the Story in the Iliad* (Amsterdam).

DELRIEU, A., HILT, D., and LETOUBLON, F. (1984), 'Homère à plusieurs voix: les techniques narratives dans l'épopée grecque archaïque', in *Lalies: Actes des Sessions de linguistique et de littérature*, 4: 177–94.

DELVIGO, M. L. (1987), *Testo virgiliano e tradizione indiretta: Le varianti probiane* (Pisa).

—— (1995), 'Ambiguità dell'*emendatio*: edizioni, riedizioni, edizioni postume', in *Formative Stages of Classical Traditions: Latin Texts from Antiquity to the Renaissance. Conference held at Erice, 16–22 October 1993*, ed. O. Pecere and M. D. Reeve (Spoleto), 14–30.

DIGGLE. J. (1981), *Studies on the Text of Euripides* (Oxford).

—— (1994), *Euripidea* (Oxford).

DILTHEY, W. (1985), *Poetry and Experience* (Princeton).

DYSON, J. T. (2001), *King of the Wood: The Sacrificial Victor in Virgil's Aeneid* (Norman, Okla.).

EDWARDS, C. (1999) (ed.), *Roman Presences* (Cambridge).

EDWARDS, M. W. (1991), *The Iliad: A Commentary. Volume V: Books 17–20* (Cambridge).

EFFE, B. (1983), 'Epische Objectivität und Authoriales Erzählen', *Gymnasium*, 90: 171–86.

ELIOT, T. S. (1957), *On Poetry and Poets* (London).

ERBSE, H. (1974), *Scholia graeca in Homeri Iliadem*, II (Berlin).

FAEDO, L. (1970), 'L'inversione del rapporto poeta-Musa nella cultura ellenistica', *Annali Scuola Normale Sup. di Pisa*, 39: 377–86.

FANTUZZI, M. (1980), 'Oralità, scrittura, auralità. Gli studi sulle techniche della comunicazione nella Grecia antica 1960–1980', *Lingua e Stile*, 15: 593–612.

—— (1988), *Ricerche su Apollonio Rodio: Diacronie della dizione epica* (Rome).

FARRELL, J. (1997), 'Towards a Rhetoric of (Roman?) Epic', in W. J. Dominik (ed.), *Roman Eloquence* (London), 131–46.

FEENEY, D. C. (1984), 'The Reconciliations of Juno', *CQ* 34: 179–94 (repr. in Harrison (1990), 339–62).

FELSON-RUBIN, N. (1994), *Regarding Penelope: From Character to Poetics* (Princeton).

FELTENIUS, L. (1977), *Intransitivization in Latin* (Uppsala).

FORBIGER, A. (1852), *Virgili Opera*, 3 vols. (Leipzig).

FOWLER, A. (1971), *John Milton: Paradise Lost* (London).

FOWLER, D. P. (1990), 'Deviant Focalization in Virgil's *Aeneid*', *PCPhS* 36: 42–63 (repr. in Fowler (2000), 40–63).

—— (2000), *Roman Constructions* (Oxford).

FRAENKEL, E. (1960), *Elementi Plautini in Plauto* (Florence).

FRIIS JOHANSEN, H., and WHITTLE, E. W. (1980), *Aeschylus: The Suppliants*, 2 vols. (Copenhagen).

FUSILLO, M. (1985), *Il tempo delle Argonautiche: Un'analisi del racconto in Apollonio Rodio* (Rome).

GAISER, K. (1961), 'Das vierte Proömium des Lukrez und die lukrezische Frage', in Kroymann and Zinn, 19–41.

—— (1984), *Platone come scrittore filosofico: Saggi sull'ermeneutica dei dialoghi platonici* (Naples).

GALE, M. (1994), 'Lucretius 4.1–25 and the Proems of the *De rerum natura*', *PCPhS* 40: 1–17.

GEORGE, E. V. (1974), *Aeneid VIII and the Aitia of Callimachus* (Leiden).

GERMANUS VALENTIS GUELLIUS [Germain Vaillant de Guélis] (1575), *P. Virgilius Maro et in eum commentationes* (Antwerp).

GEYMONAT, M. (1973), *P. Vergili Maronis Opera* (Turin).

GIBSON, R. K., and KRAUS, C. S. (2002) (eds.), *The Classical Commentary: Histories, Practices, Theory* (Leiden).

GÖRLER, W. (1979), '*Ex verbis communibus KAKOZHLIA*', in *Le Classicisme à Rome* (Fondation Hardt Entretiens, XXV; Geneva), 175–211.

GRIFFIN, J. (1979), 'Virgil, the Fourth *Georgic* and Rome', *G&R* 26: 61–80 (repr. in Griffin (1985), 163–97).

—— (1980), *Homer on Life and Death* (Oxford).

—— (1985), *Latin Poets and Roman Life* (London).

GRIFFITHS, M. (1999), *Sophocles: Antigone* (Cambridge).

GRUPPO μ (1976), *Retorica generale* (Milan).

HARDIE, P. (1986), *Virgil's Aeneid: Cosmos and Imperium* (Oxford).

—— (1993), *The Epic Successors of Virgil* (Cambridge).

—— (1994), *Virgil: Aeneid IX* (Cambridge).

—— (1995), 'Vergil's Epic Techniques: Heinze Ninety Years On', *CPh* 90: 267–76.

—— (1997), 'Virgil and Tragedy', in Charles Martindale (ed.), *The Cambridge Companion to Virgil* (Cambridge), 312–26.

HARRISON, S. J. (1990) (ed.), *Oxford Readings in Vergil's Aeneid* (Oxford).

—— (1991), *Vergil: Aeneid 10* (Oxford).

—— (1998), 'The Sword-Belt of Pallas (*Aeneid* X.495–506) : Symbolism and Ideology', in H.-P. Stahl (ed.), *Vergil's Aeneid: Augustan Epic and Political Context* (London), 223–42.

HEADLAM, W. (1902), 'Metaphor, with a Note on Transference of Epithets', *CR* 16: 434–42.

HEINZE, R. (1902), *Virgils epische Technik* (1st edn.; Leipzig and Berlin).

—— (1915), *Virgils epische Technik* (3rd edn.; Leipzig and Berlin).

—— (1930), *Die Augusteische Kultur* (Leipzig and Berlin).

—— (1993), *Virgil's Epic Technique* (Bristol).

—— (1996), *La tecnica epica di Virgilio* (Bologna).

HENRY, J. (1889), *Aeneidea*, IV (Dublin).

HEYNE, C. G. (1803), *P. Virgilius Maro*, 3 vols. (Leipzig).

HOEKSTRA, A. (1976), 'Enallage and the Transferred Epithet: Some Remarks on Condensed Effects in Aeschylus', in J. Bremer, S. Radt, and C. J. Ruijgh (eds.), *Miscellanea Tragica in honorem J. C. Kamerbeck* (Amsterdam), 157–71.

HORSFALL, N. M. (1995) (ed.), *A Companion to the Study of Virgil* (Leiden).

—— (2003), *Virgil Aeneid 11: A Commentary* (Leiden).

HUNTER, R. L. (1993), *The Argonautica of Apollonius Rhodius: Literary Studies* (Cambridge).

JACOBSON, R. (1987), *Language in Literature* (Cambridge, Mass.).

JAEGER, W. (1944–6), *Paideia: The Ideals of Greek Culture*, 3 vols. (Oxford).

JAHN, P. (1904), 'Aus Vergils Dichterwerkstaette, *Georgica* IV 1–280', *Philologus*, 63: 66–93.

—— (1905), *Aus Vergils Dichterwerkstaette, Georgica IV 281–558* (Berlin).

JANKO, R. (2000), *Philodemus, On Poems, Book 1* (Oxford).

JOCELYN, H. D. (1979), '*Vergilius cacozelus* (Donatus *Vita Vergilii* 44)', *Proceedings of the Liverpool Latin Seminar*, 2: 67–142.

—— (1981), 'Servius and the "second edition" of the *Georgics*,' in *Atti del Convegno mondiale scientifico di studi su Virgilio (Napoli 19–24 settembre 1977)* (Milan), 431–48.

JOHNSON, W. R. (1976), *Darkness Visible* (Berkeley and Los Angeles).

KAMBYLIS, A. (1965), *Die Dichterweihe und ihre Symbolik* (Heidelberg).

KERÉNYI, K. (1951), *La religione antica* (Rome).

KIPARSKY, P. (1976), 'Oral Poetry; some linguistic and typological considerations', in Stolz and Shannon, 73–106.

KLINGNER, F. (1930), 'Richard Heinze', *Gnomon*, 6: 62.

—— (1942), 'Virgil. Wiederentdeckung eines Dichters', in H. Berve (ed.), *Das neue Bild der Antike*, 2 (Leipzig), 219–45 (repr. in Klingner (1961), 239–74).

—— (1961), *Römisches Geisteswelt* (Munich).

—— (1967), *Virgil: Bucolica Georgica Aeneis* (Zurich and Stuttgart).

KNAUER, G. N. (1964), *Die Aeneis und Homer* (Göttingen).

—— (1980), 'Virgil and Homer', *ANRW* II. 31. 2: 870–918.

KNIGHT, V. (1995), *The Renewal of Epic: Responses to Homer in the Argonautica of Apollonius* (Leiden).

KROLL, W. (1916), 'Das Historisches Epos', *Sokrates*, 4: 2–16.

—— (1924), *Studien zum Verständnis der römischen Literatur* (Stuttgart).

KROYMANN, J., and ZINN, E. (1961) (eds.), *Eranion: Festschrift H. Hommel* (Tübingen).

KÜHNER, R., and GERTH, B. (1898), *Ausführliche Grammatik der griechischen Sprache*, II. *Satzlehre, Erster Band* (Hanover and Leipzig).

KYRIAKIDIS, S., and DE MARTINO, F. (2004) (eds.), *Middles in Latin Poetry* (Bari).

LABATE, M. (1984), *L'arte di farsi amare: Modelli culturali e progetto didascalico nell'elegia ovidiana* (Pisa).

LA CERDA, J. L. (1612–19), *P. Virgili Maronis Opera Omnia*, 3 vols. (Lyon).

LADEWIG, C., SCHAFER, E., and DEUTICKE J. (1912), *Vergilii Opera*, 3 vols. (13th edn.; Berlin).

LAIRD, A. (2002), 'Juan Luis De La Cerda, Virgil and the Predicament of Commentary', in Gibson and Kraus, 171–203.

LA PENNA, A. (1980), 'Mesenzio. Una tragedia della tirannia e del titanismo antico', *Maia*, 32: 3–30.

—— (1981), 'I proemi del "come" e i proemi del "che cosa", ovvero i futili giochi della filologia strutturalistica', *Maia*, 33: 217–223.

—— (1983), 'A proposito di proemi poetici e di vaniloqui metodologici', *Maia*, 35: 115–21.

LEFÈVRE, E. (1978), 'Dido und Aias. Ein Beitrag zur römischen Tragödie', *Abhandlungen der Akad. der Wissensch. in Mainz*, 2.

LEO, F. (1895), *Plautinische Forschungen* (Berlin).

—— (1903), review of Heinze (1902; = Heinze 1915 in all details except date; first edition), *Deutsche Literaturzeitung*, 10: 594–6.

LOMBARDO, G. (1988), *Hypsegoria. Studi sulla retorica del sublime* (Modena).

LONG, A. A. (1968), *Language and Thought in Sophocles* (London).

LYNE, R. O. A. M. (1987), *Further Voices in Vergil's Aeneid* (Oxford).

—— (1989), *Words and the Poet* (Oxford).

MARCH, J. (1987), *The Creative Poet: Studies on the Treatment of Myths in Greek Poetry* (London).

MARTIN, R. P. (1994), *The Language of Heroes: Speech and Performance in the Iliad* (Ithaca, NY).

MILES, G. B. (1980), *Virgil's Georgics: A New Interpretation* (Berkeley, Los Angeles, London).

MILLER, J. F. (1982), 'Callimachus and the Augustan Aitiological Elegy', *ANRW* II. 30. 1: 371–417.

MOSKALEW, W. (1982), *Formular Language and Poetic Design in the Aeneid* (Leiden).

MOST, G. W. (1985), *The Measures of Praise: Structure and Function in Pindar's Second Pythian and Seventh Nemean Odes* (Göttingen).

—— (1999) (ed.), *Commentaries—Kommentare* (Göttingen).

NIEBUHR, B. G. (1842), *Nachgelassene Schriften nichtphilologischen Inhalts* (Hamburg).

NISBET, R. G. M. (1987), review of Griffin (1985), *JRS* 77: 184–90.

—— and HUBBARD, M. (1970), *A Commentary on the Odes of Horace: Book I* (Oxford).

—— —— (1978), *A Commentary on the Odes of Horace: Book II* (Oxford).

NORDEN, E. (1901), 'Vergils *Aeneis* im Lichte ihrer Zeit', *Neue Jahrbücher für das klassische Altertum*, 7: 249–82, 313–34 (repr. *Kleine Schriften* (Berlin, 1966), 358–421).

—— (1902), *P. Vergili Maronis Aeneis Buch VI* (Berlin).

NORDEN, E. (1930), 'Richard Heinze: ein Gedenkblatt', *Das Humanistische Gymnasium*, 41: 21–4.

—— (1934), 'Orpheus und Eurydike', *SB Berlin* 12: 626–83 (repr. *Kleine Schriften* (Berlin, 1966), 468–532).

—— (1954), *Die römische Literatur* (Leipzig; 1st ed. 1914).

ODERBRECHT, R. (1931), *Schleiermachers Aesthetik* (Berlin).

O'HARA, J. J. (1990), *Death and the Optimistic Prophecy in Vergil's Aeneid* (Princeton).

OTIS, B. (1964), *Virgil: A Study in Civilized Poetry* (Oxford).

PARRY, A. (1972), 'The Idea of Art in Virgil's *Georgics*', *Arethusa*, 5: 35–52.

PASCOLI, G. (1911), *Epos* (2nd edn.; Livorno).

PASQUALI, G. (1942), 'Arte allusiva', in his *Terze Pagine Stravaganti* (Florence), II. 275–83.

PERKELL, C. (1997), 'The Lament of Juturna: Pathos and Interpretation in the *Aeneid*', *TAPhA* 127: 257–86.

PERUTELLI, A. (1973), 'Genesi e significato della "Vergils epische Technik" di Richard Heinze', *Maia*, 25: 293–316.

—— (1980), 'L'episodio di Aristeo nelle *Georgiche*: struttura e tecnica narrativa', *MD* 4: 59–76.

PFEIFFER, R. (1928), 'Ein neues Altersgedicht des Kallimachos', *Hermes*, 63: 302–41.

PLÜSS, H. T. (1884), *Vergil und die epische Kunst* (Leipzig).

PÖSCHL, V. (1950), *Die Dichtkunst Virgils* (Innsbruck).

—— (1977), *Die Dichtkunst Virgils* (3rd edn.; Berlin and New York).

PRIDIK, K.-H. (1971), *Vergils Georgica: Strukturanalytische Interpretationen* (Diss. Tübingen).

PUTNAM, M. C. J. (1965), *The Poetry of the Aeneid* (Cambridge, Mass.).

—— (1979), *Virgil's Poem of the Earth: Studies in the Georgics* (Princeton).

QUINT, D. (1989), 'Repetition and Ideology in the *Aeneid*', *MD* 23: 9–54.

—— (1993), *Epic and Empire* (Princeton).

RADKE, G. (1964), 'Fachbericht über Augusteische Dichtung', *Gymnasium*, 71: 72–108.

REITZENSTEIN, E. (1931), 'Zur Stiltheorie des Kallimachos', in E. Fraenkel *et al.* (eds.), *Festschrift Richard Reitzenstein* (Leipzig and Berlin), 21–69.

RIBBECK, O. (1866), *Prolegomena ad P. Vergili Maronis opera maiora* (Leipzig).

ROMANO, E. (1979), *Struttura degli Astronomica di Manilio* (Palermo).

ROSATI, G. (1981), 'Il racconto dentro il racconto: Funzioni metaletterarie nelle *Metamorfosi* di Ovidio', in AA.VV., *Atti del Convegno Internazionale 'Letterature classiche e Narratologia'* (Perugia), 297–309.

—— (1996), 'Sabinus, the *Heroides* and the Poet-Nightingale: Some Observations on the Authenticity of the *Epistula Sapphus*', *CQ* 46: 214–15.

Rossi, L. E. (1971), 'Wesen und Werden der Homerischen Formeltechnik', *GGA* 223: 161–74.

—— (1978), 'Il mondo omerico: poemi epici come testimonianza di poesia orale', in Bianchi Bandinelli, 73–147.

Russo, J. A. (1976), 'Is "oral" or "aural" composition the cause of Homer's formulaic style?', in Stolz and Shannon, 31–71.

Sabbadini, R. (1887), *Virgilio: Eneide libro IX* (Turin).

—— (1888), *P. Vergili Maronis Aeneidos libro XII* (Turin).

Sainte-Beuve, C. A. (1857), *Étude sur Virgile* (Paris).

Scaglione, A. (1972), *The Classical Theory of Composition from its Origins to the Present: A Historical Survey* (Chapel Hill).

Scaliger, J. C. (1561), *Poetices libri septem* (Lyons).

Schenk, P. (1984), *Die Gestalt des Turnus in Vergils Aeneis* (Königstein).

Schleiermacher, F. (1935), *Reden und Abhandlungen* (Berlin).

Schlunk, R. R. (1974), *The Homeric Scholia and the Aeneid* (Ann Arbor).

Schmidt, E. A. (1972), *Poetische Reflexion* (Munich).

Schneidewin, F. W., and Nauck, A. (1899), *Sophokles: Achter Band* (Berlin).

Scully, S. (1986), 'Studies of Narrative and Speech in the *Iliad*', *Arethusa*, 19: 135–53.

Sedley, D. N. (1998), *Lucretius and the Transformation of Greek Wisdom* (Cambridge).

Segal, C. P. (1966), 'Orpheus and the Fourth *Georgic*: Vergil on Nature and Civilisation', *AJPh* 87: 307–25 (repr. in id., *Orpheus: The Myth of the Poet* (Baltimore and London, 1989), 36–53).

—— (1994), *Singers, Heroes and Gods in the Odyssey* (Ithaca and London).

Sellar, W. Y. (1876), *Virgil* (Oxford).

Serpa, F. (1987), *Il punto su Virgilio* (Bari and Rome).

Skutsch, O. (1968), *Studia Enniana* (London).

—— (1985), *The Annals of Quintus Ennius* (Oxford).

Sparrow, J. (1931), *Half-lines and Repetition in Virgil* (Oxford).

Stok, F. (1993), *Cicerone: Il sogno di Scipione* (Venice).

Stolz, B. A., and Shannon, R. S. (1976) (eds.), *Oral Literature and the Formula* (Ann Arbor).

Stone, M. (1999), 'A Flexible Rome: Fascism and the Cult of *Romanità*', in C. Edwards, 205–20.

Suerbaum, W. (1968), *Untersuchungen zur Selbstdarstellung älterer römischer Dichter* (Hildesheim).

Taplin, O. (1992), *Homeric Soundings: The Shaping of the Iliad* (Oxford).

Taubmann, F. (1618), *P. Virgili Maronis Opera Omnia: Bucolica, Georgica, Aeneis, Ciris et Culex* (Wittenberg).

TEUFFEL, W. S. (1870), *Geschichte der römischen Literatur*, I (Leipzig).

THILO, G. (1886), *P. Vergili Maronis carmina* (Leipzig).

THOMAS, R. F. (1983), 'Callimachus, the *Victoria Berenices*, and Roman Poetry', *CQ* 33: 92–113 (repr. in Thomas (1999), 68–101).

—— (1988a), *Virgil: Georgics I–II* (Cambridge).

—— (1988b), *Virgil: Georgics III–IV* (Cambridge).

—— (1999), *Reading Virgil and his Texts* (Ann Arbor).

TIMPANARO, S. (1986), *Per la storia della filologia virgiliana antica* (Rome).

—— (2001), *Virgilianisti antichi e tradizione indiretta* (Florence).

TORZI, I. (2000), *Ratio et usus: Dibattiti antichi sulla dottrina delle figure* (Milan).

TRAINA, A. (1977), *Forma e suono* (Rome).

—— (1988), entries 'Pietas', 'sibilus', *Enciclopedia Virgiliana*, IV (Rome), 93–101, 831.

—— (1997), *Virgilio: L'utopia e la storia* (Turin).

UNTERHARNSCHNEIDT, M. (1911), *De veterum in Aeneide coniecturis* (Diss. Münster).

URSINUS, F. [Fulvio Orsini] (1568), *Virgilius* (Antwerp).

VAHLEN, J. (1914), *Beiträge zu Aristoteles' Poetik* (2nd edn.; Berlin).

VON ALBRECHT, M. (1970), 'Zur Tragik von Virgils Turnusgestalt', in M. von Albrecht and E. Heck (eds.), *Silvae: Festschrift E. Zinn* (Tübingen), 1–5.

WAGNER, G. P. E. (1833), *P. Virgilii Maronis Opera III* (4th edn. of Heyne) (Leipzig).

WARDE FOWLER, W. (1917), *Aeneas at the Site of Rome: Observations on the Eighth Book of the Aeneid* (Oxford).

WEST, D. (1969), 'Multiple Correspondence Similes in the *Aeneid*', *JRS* 59 (1969), 40–9 (repr. in Harrison (1990), 429–44).

WILKINSON, L. P. (1969), *The Georgics of Virgil* (Cambridge).

WILLIAMS, G. (1983), *Technique and Ideas in the Aeneid* (New Haven and London).

WILLIAMS, R. D. (1967), 'The Purpose of the *Aeneid*', *Antichthon*, 1: 27–41 (repr. in Harrison (1990), 21–36).

WIMMEL, W. (1960), *Kallimachos in Rom* (Hermes Einz. 16; Wiesbaden).

WLOSOK, A. (1973), 'Vergil in der neueren Forschung', *Gymnasium*, 80: 129–51.

—— (1976), 'Vergils Dido-Tragödie. Ein Beitrag zum Problem des Tragischen in der *Aeneis*', in H. Görgemanns and E. A. Schmidt (eds.), *Studien zum Antiken Epos* (Meisenheim am Glan), 228–50.

WOLF, F. A. (1787), *Geschichte von Römischen Litteratur* [*sic*] (Halle).

WÖRRINGER, W. (1975), *Astrazione e empatia* (Turin).

ZEITLIN, F. I. (1965), 'The Motif of the Corrupted Sacrifice in Aeschylus' *Oresteia*', *TAPhA* 96: 463–508.

ZIEGLER, K. (1988), *L'Epos ellenistico: Un capitolo dimenticato della poesia greca* (Bari).

Index Locorum

General Index